GUIDE TO
SOUND SYSTEMS
FOR
WORSHIP

EDITED BY
JON F. EICHE

Hal Leonard Publishing Corporation

7777 West Bluemound Road P.O. Box 13819 Milwaukee, WI 53213

Library of Congress Cataloging-in-Publication Data

The Yamaha guide to sound systems for worship / edited by Jon F. Eiche.

   Includes bibliographical references and index.
   ISBN 0-7935-0029-X
    1. Public address systems. 2. Churches—Electronic sound control.
3. Church supplies. I. Eiche, Jon F.
TK7881.9.Y36   1990
621.389'2—dc20   90-6496
                                                     CIP

First Printing, August, 1990

Printed in the U.S.A.

PREFACE

Worship is an important activity. The ability to hear what is going on in a worship service is therefore important, too. It affects not only what the congregation "gets out of" the service, but also what it puts into it. In pursuit of the twin goals of communication and participation in worship, it often is desirable to augment the sound—to make it louder, to carry it farther, to distribute it more evenly and clearly. This task of *sound reinforcement* is the primary one of a sound system in a house of worship, and the primary subject of this book. The ancillary tasks of recording and broadcast, in which many worship facilities also engage, are also touched upon.

This book is written to assist in the design, purchase, and operation of a sound system. You may be a minister, a member of the Board of Trustees or the worship and music committee, a "sound man" or woman, an electronics repair person pressed into the service of your congregation, or even an employee of a musical instrument store that sells sound systems. Whatever your background, here you will find information that will assist you in better understanding the basics of acoustics, sound reinforcement, equipment performance and selection, system installation and operation, and minor troubleshooting.

You may want to underscore that word "basics." This book does not purport to turn amateurs into professional acoustical consultants or sound system designers. If your congregation is committed to designing and installing a sound system on its own, this book can help you do it successfully, and avoid some pitfalls along the way. At the same time, you will find repeated exhortations to defer to professionals whenever you're in over your head (the book also helps you identify *when* you're in over your head). This is especially important for large facilities, but also true in small- to medium-size ones. In any case, whether you "do it yourself" or rely on others—or combine the two approaches—the information contained herein will help you understand sound systems better.

Of course, design and installation are only the preliminaries. It is the operation of the system that ultimately determines its value.

And here, too, you will find practical information. What microphones should be used and how should they be placed? What are the best settings for the levels on the mixing console? Questions such as these find answers here.

Two comments are in order regarding the source and intended destination of this book:

1. This book is applicable to all brands of equipment. You have noticed, by now, the name "Yamaha" on the cover. Can a manufacturer of professional audio equipment (in addition to musical instruments and motorcycles) produce an impartial book about sound systems? A look through these pages should convince you that it can, and has; while this is a Yamaha product, it is not a promotion for other Yamaha products.

2. This book is applicable to all faiths. Sound is a nonsectarian phenomenon, and a sound system is a sound system regardless of the messages it is used to convey. Although different beliefs and traditions have engendered different styles of worship, the need to hear and be heard are universal.

References to religions and denominations have been avoided as much as possible—except in cases where it has been necessary to illustrate a situation specific to a certain group. As you have already seen in this Preface, it is necessary to employ a kind of shorthand in referring to offices and edifices—using "minister" as the most generic substitute for priest, pastor, rabbi, imam, etc., and "house of worship" or "facility" for church, synagogue, mosque, temple, etc. Please accept this as the necessity it is, with the sincere attestation that we mean no offense to any group. Our hope is that all who read this book will find it useful.

Jon F. Eiche

THE
YAMAHA
GUIDE TO
SOUND SYSTEMS
FOR WORSHIP
PAGE iii

ACKNOWLEDGMENTS

One of the real joys in assembling this book has been the privilege of working with the many people who contributed to the project in one way or another.

First of all, deepest thanks to the authors:

Gary Davis and Ralph Jones, of Gary Davis & Associates. A substantial portion of this book was excerpted from their earlier work, the *Yamaha Sound Reinforcement Handbook*. In addition, the staff at Gary Davis & Associates proofread the manuscript and supplied numerous corrections and improvements to the text.

Curt Taipale, of Taipale Media Systems, Inc. In addition to writing Chapters 1, 2, and 13, he provided valuable advice for just about all of the remaining chapters.

Paul Ingebrigtsen, Vice President of Marketing for Williams Sound Corp, who wrote Chapter 10 and produced all of the illustrations for it.

Chris Hinkle, Director of Technical Services at First Baptist Church in Orlando, Florida. His contributions to Chapter 14 are greatly appreciated.

Gerry Tschetter, of Yamaha Corporation of America, who provided additional material for Chapters 2, 13, and 14.

In addition to those who actually did the writing, there were several others who contributed to creation of the book:

Howard W. Sams & Company gave permission for the inclusion of two diagrams used in Chapter 14, originally published in *Handbook for Sound Engineers*, edited by Glen Ballou (© 1987).

Otari Corporation provided photographs of equipment for inclusion in Chapter 11.

Peter Chaikin and Michael MacDonald helped check the book for technical accuracy.

Bill Thrasher, of Thrasher & Company, contributed valuable advice on hanging loudspeakers.

Chris Albano and Jack Schechinger of Hal Leonard Publishing "got the ball rolling" on the project, and the staffs of the graphics arts and production departments made it a reality. Herman Knoll and Gary Meisner, my superiors, cleared enough time in my schedule to allow me to assemble the book.

Last and most importantly, thanks to Bob Davis, Gerry Tschetter (again), and John Gatts, from the Professional Audio Division of Yamaha Corporation of America, for seeing the need for a book such as this and for committing to the publication of it.

J.F.E.

THE
YAMAHA
GUIDE TO
SOUND SYSTEMS
FOR WORSHIP
PAGE iv

TABLE OF CONTENTS

TABLE OF CONTENTS

THE
YAMAHA
GUIDE TO
SOUND SYSTEMS
FOR WORSHIP
PAGE vi

CHAPTER 1.
WHAT A SOUND SYSTEM CAN DO FOR YOUR WORSHIP SERVICE

Imagine that you're sitting out in your house of worship, visiting with a friend. The distance between you is about eight feet. That should be a warm, intimate sound. Wouldn't it be nice if the minister could sound that intimate at every seat in the house when he addresses the congregation? Actually, that is entirely possible (room acoustics permitting). Surprised? The reality is that the information to design and install such a system has existed for a number of years. An intelligent, well-equipped sound system designer can use that information to aid him in the task of designing and installing a sound system.

So why are there so many poor-sounding public address (PA) systems in worship facilities all across the country and around the world? Personal observation leads to the conclusion that most of the sound systems in houses of worship were installed ten, fifteen, even twenty years ago. From the standpoint of technology alone, the quality of everything from microphones to mixing consoles to amplifiers to loudspeakers has seen a quantum leap in that period of time.

In addition, many people also fail to realize that the acoustical design of their facility can affect the performance of their sound system. If you decide to make the room acoustically "dead," it may simplify the job of the sound system designer, and it will probably be of great benefit in contemporary music settings, particularly when a rhythm section is used. But choirs often sound better when placed in a live, more reverberant setting. Your choice here will have a dramatic effect on the sound that your audio crew is able to create. To make matters worse, many structural designers don't really understand the art of sound system design, and place unrealistic constraints on the system designer.

Another more subtle point is that our ears have been "educated." Today we are exposed to high-quality sound on albums, tapes, and compact discs, on television and radio, and in concerts by well-known artists. You might come home from a concert, or from visiting another house of worship, and then compare what you heard there with what your own system sounds like—and you might not be impressed.

So is it perhaps time to replace or upgrade your tired old sound system? With the myriad of equipment choices and opinions in the audio industry, who is going to make those choices for you? Do you trust them? If they blow it, can you get your money back? What if you depend on the advice of someone in your congregation; does he really know what he's talking about?

DO YOU NEED A SOUND SYSTEM?

One sign of a seasoned, well-trained recording engineer is that before he starts placing microphones on the instruments or voices he is about to record, before he settles into his chair behind the mixing console in the control room, he walks about the studio listening to what those instruments and voices sound like. Then, and only then, can he make a proper and informed choice on what mics to use and where to place them.

From a similar standpoint, one of the best ways for a sound system designer to truly understand what kind of sound system is best for your facility is for him to spend a great deal of time listening to the sound of your room.

Have you ever tried that? Have you ever gone in the assembly room with a friend and just listened to the room and how it responds to your voice or hand claps? Have you tried turning off your sound system, and asked the minister to take the platform and talk to you while you sat in the room? If not, try it. It can be a revealing exercise.

What do you hear? Can you understand his words clearly, or does your room sound more like a racquetball court than an auditorium? What if you move about the seating areas, especially in the back rows—

can you still understand him? Here's a hard question: Do you need a sound system at all? Why? What will a sound system do for you? If you can understand the spoken word better in your room when the sound system is turned off, then either your system is not doing a good job or perhaps you don't even need a sound system in the first place. Oh, you want to have music, too? Well, that's a different story.

THE TASK AT HAND

The job of a sound reinforcement system is to distribute sound evenly to all listener areas, while at the same time to not distribute sound to any non-listener areas, such as the walls or the ceiling—an unassuming description of a complex task. Worship should be the noblest, most exalted activity in which man can engage. It should be engaged in with excellence. In pursuit of that excellence, is it appropriate to skimp on the sound system?

When you participate in the worship service, the musical instruments and voices on the platform contribute a certain amount of acoustic power to the room. Some instruments, such as an organ, are capable of being played quite loudly, and can be heard without further reinforcement. Others are inherently soft, such as a finger-picked acoustic guitar, and may need to be amplified so the congregation can hear them clearly. Voices come in all shapes and sizes. Achieving a musical blend of these diverse elements usually requires the use of a sound reinforcement system. Certainly, the larger the room, the greater this need becomes. A quality sound reinforcement system also gives the music director more flexibility, in the long run, to combine instruments and voices in musical styles that would not be possible any other way. You hear many examples of this on records and tapes today. Naturally, the music director will want to incorporate those kinds of sound combinations and textures in a live worship setting (though this is more easily accomplished in a recording studio than in an auditorium).

In most worship settings, a basic requirement of the sound reinforcement system is to reinforce the spoken word. The important frequency range for speech is 200 Hz to 6,000 Hz. (See Chapter 3 for more on frequencies and other aspects of sound.) Once

you add the requirement of reinforcing music, the frequency range requirement jumps to roughly 40 Hz to at least 16,000 Hz! This added requirement can increase the complexity, and therefore the cost, of the system.

The classic comparison in the life of every sound contractor is called the ear-to-rear ratio. Elders and administrators know how to sit. From experience, they know they like to sit on soft pews. Not only that, the congregation *really* likes to sit on soft pews, so spending a lot of money on soft, nice-looking pews is an acceptable expenditure.

But through the advice of many back-pew engineers and resident "experts," the administration is led to believe that they needn't spend a lot on a sound system. Stories of previous "successes" fill the room, and the administration soon becomes convinced that just maybe they're right. They certainly want to believe these storytellers, or anyone else who will tell them what they hope to hear—that a sound system needn't cost a lot of money. The reality is that the ear-to-rear ratio should probably be 1:1. If you just spent $20,000 on nice, comfortable pews, you should probably expect to spend another $20,000 on the design, purchase, and installation of a high-quality sound system for that facility. Not first-class—just reasonably high quality. If your music production needs are complex, and you want your worship service to sound like a professional recording, expect to invest more.

SPEECH INTELLIGIBILITY

And purchasing a high-quality, high-intelligibility sound system *is an investment*. The message being proclaimed is important. It deserves to be clearly heard and understood, but the intangible benefits make it difficult to determine a justifiable price. What are the considerations?

First off, the acoustical design of a room does play a role in speech intelligibility. Many congregations today want to simply build a steel shell—little more than a warehouse space. One argument for that choice is that it is good stewardship of the money—it costs less to build than a more traditional design. Secondly, if the young congregation doesn't "make it," the bank can

THE
YAMAHA
GUIDE TO
SOUND SYSTEMS
FOR WORSHIP
PAGE 2

sell a warehouse easier than it can a fancier building. That's fine, but you can't ignore the laws of physics. If you decide to build a warehouse for your worship facility, it will probably *sound* like a warehouse as well. The mistake is to then assume that the sound system designer can somehow solve the intelligibility and sound quality problems of the "warehouse" by brute force. A reasonable sound may indeed be obtained, but it will always be limited by the lack of acoustical design considerations.

The speech intelligibility achieved in an auditorium is a function of both the acoustic design of the room and the design and installation of the sound system. The acoustic designer attempts to achieve maximum speech intelligibility while maintaining a natural voice quality. To control intelligibility, he must balance how loudly the sound system will be run, how quiet the room can be (determined by everything from how loud the air handlers in the room are, how loud street noise and air traffic are heard inside the building, even how well isolated the cry room is), and the reverberation characteristics of the room. Natural voice quality in a room is largely determined by how sound reflects off of walls and other surfaces, how it is absorbed by furnishings such as pews and people's clothing, and by how strongly the minister speaks. The larger the room, the more of an effect the sound system will have on the quality and intelligibility of speech.[*]

The proper design and installation of the speaker cluster is critical, and here's one reason why: We've all heard the sound of a jet airplane passing high overhead. The sound of the jet engines travels directly to your ears, but also combines with the sound of the engines splashing off the ground around you and traveling back up to your ears. The path of the reflected sound is longer than the path of the direct sound. As those two sounds combine at your ears, certain frequencies will cancel—a phenomenon known as *acoustic phase cancellation*— while others will increase in strength. The relationship of those travel paths changes as

the jet flies overhead, which causes the overall "swooshing" character to change as well. If you kneel down to get your ears closer to the ground, the pitch of the overall phase-cancellation sound will rise. This same effect occurs with sound from the loudspeakers in an auditorium.

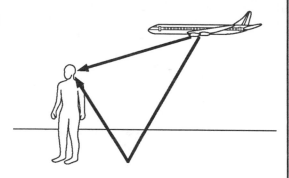

Figure 1-1. Acoustic phase cancellation, caused by the combination of sounds traveling different path lengths.

Acoustic phase cancellations result from the multiple arrival paths of sound at the listener's ears as sound comes directly from the talker, the loudspeakers, and from reflections off walls, ceiling, and other reflective surfaces. Keeping these cancellations from adversely affecting intelligibility and overall sound quality is a major task for both the sound system designer and the system operator. The system designer can have a direct and major impact on phase cancellations by virtue of the way he installs and aims the loudspeakers. This effect is most noticeable in speakers operating in the same frequency range, such as high-frequency horns covering adjacent seating areas. If these horns are simply pointed "that-a-way," it is quite likely that acoustic phase cancellations will degrade the sound quality in several seating locations. This is one of a few reasons why the sound at some seats may be too loud, while at others it is too quiet. If, instead, those speakers are precisely positioned and carefully aimed, the severity of those phase cancellations can be minimized. Quite literally, a misalignment of one inch can make the difference between a sound system with high speech intelligibility and high maximum levels without feedback, and one where the music sounds unfocused and the minister struggles for the congregation's attention.

---

[*] Rollins Brook and Ted Uzzle, "Rooms for Speech, Music, and Cinema," in *Handbook for Sound Engineers*, ed. Glen Ballou (Indianapolis: Howard W. Sams & Co., 1987), p. 157.

MUSIC PERFORMANCE

As a society, we are drawn to excellence. Given the choice between listening to a song recorded on the finest equipment in the best-sounding studio with first-rate musicians and singers, and listening to that same song performed by Aunt Betty and Cousin Zeke recorded in their living room ten years ago on a $30 mono cassette recorder—wouldn't you choose the higher-quality recording? Probably. So would most of the world. If you want to attract people into your services so that they can hear your message, then you have a little competition for their attention. Yet you can defeat that competition with proper attention to the basics.

The traditional worship setting of a choir, piano, and organ, and perhaps the music minister leading the worship, benefits just as much from an improved sound system as does the service with a full rhythm section and several background vocalists. Both styles of music employ similar instruments, and therefore have similar needs in regard to the range of frequencies that the sound system can faithfully reproduce.

Even in the simplest sound system, the sound of your voice or an instrument must be faithfully reproduced as it is amplified and distributed by a microphone, a mixing console, a power amplifier, and a loudspeaker. In purchasing and in operating that equipment, remember that a sound system is only as good as the weakest link in the chain. Just as it takes a skilled craftsman to build a great-sounding trumpet or violin, it takes skilled people to design and build high-quality audio gear. The sheer fact that designers can come up with a great-sounding product, that manufacturers can produce it in a quality fashion, and that a good engineer can use it as a creative tool to shape a great sound, is nothing short of staggering. That process is so common, however, that we tend to take it for granted. In reality, using quality gear is your only hope of ever achieving a "natural" sound. (Quality equipment alone does not assure "natural" sound—the equipment has to be properly installed and operated, too.)

On the surface, you wouldn't think that one loudspeaker could sound much different than another, or that a particular mixing console has a sound of its own. They all look a lot alike. They've all got woofers to woof and tweeters to tweet and lots of knobs to twiddle. You might be hard-pressed to tell the difference unless you can arrange an opportunity to hear them side by side, which is seldom an available opportunity. If you ever get that chance, boy are you in for a surprise—they don't all sound alike.

Your sound man (a *sound man* is a common term for an *audio mixing engineer*) also plays a significant role in determining the ultimate sound quality. The sound man performs a tremendously creative task that balances the gift of music and a complex technical craft. Nowhere can this audio engineer's knowledge and talents, or lack thereof, be heard more clearly than in the music mix for the worship service. The hard work in rehearsal of gifted musicians and singers can either be refined to a polished masterpiece or reduced to rubble by the sound man.

Ideally, the sound man should have a strong background in music. Some of the best professional audio engineers either have a degree in music or have performed with music groups for many years. (Some of the best-paid engineers are able to follow an orchestral score during the recording or performance, allowing them to foresee upcoming changes in their mix and so on.) The sound man's understanding of music will help him communicate insightfully with the music director and the worship team, allow him to create a better musical mix more quickly, and will be invaluable whenever large-scale musical productions are considered. But if you don't have a well-trained musician available to do your mixing, that's okay. The most important ingredients are a willing heart and an eagerness to learn.

Two additional points to consider: First, it's got to be coming off the stage before the sound man can do anything with it. That is to say, the music mix heard over the sound system or on tape will only be as good as the quality of sound produced by the musicians and vocalists on the platform. No one has yet invented a knob to fix the pitch of flat vocals during a live mix. Second, cooperation and mutual respect are necessary for both the worship team and the audio ministry to achieve their common goals. Always strive to keep the overall goals and the many details in proper perspective.

THE
YAMAHA
GUIDE TO
SOUND SYSTEMS
FOR WORSHIP
PAGE 4

TAPE AND BROADCAST MINISTRIES

As your ministry grows in size, a natural desire is to begin to reach out to more people in the community and beyond. Many people are out there who want to attend worship, but who may be physically unable to do so due to health, work, or other reasons. Others may attend local services hundreds of miles away, but also enjoy the opportunity to learn from select teachers across the country through their tape ministry or satellite broadcasts.

What does that mean in terms of your audio investment? For one thing, the mix requirements between the PA sound and the broadcast or tape sound can be radically different. The sound reinforcement mix is tailored for listeners who are physically in the same room as the musicians and singers.

When you listen to a cassette tape of the service, however, you are no longer benefiting from the acoustic power of those instruments or choir voices bouncing around the room. Instead, your entire perspective is determined by what is picked up by microphones in the room, and then what the mixing engineer does with those elements at his console. So it becomes a matter of sound *reproduction* rather than *reinforcement*.

Although many valiant efforts have been made from coast to coast, it is difficult to obtain a great sound reproduction mix by standing over the house engineer's shoulder, twiddling knobs on the PA (Public Address) console's auxiliary sends or matrix output mixing section. (The "house engineer" is the sound man controlling the reinforcement mix for the live service or other live event.) If you're serious about getting better sound for the broadcast and tape ministries, then having a separate mixing engineer operating a separate console in a controlled (spelled Q-U-I-E-T) environment is the only valid choice. Just as it is important for the house engineer to have his ears where the congregation's ears are, the tape or broadcast engineer needs to have his ears in a controlled environment, similar to the quiet environment in which someone will ultimately listen to that cassette tape or radio/TV broadcast. Headphones won't solve the listening problems, and besides, the house engineer is busy—he doesn't need the extra distraction of another pair of hands darting around the same console he's using for a house mix trying to adjust the recording or broadcast mix.

The miking requirements may change slightly as well. For example, the house mixing engineer has no need to mic the congregation. But the person sitting at home listening to the radio broadcast wants to have a sense of the involvement—to know that there really is a congregation present, that this is not taking place in some vacuum. For this reason, the broadcast mixing engineer does need to mic the congregation.

AUDIO AMBIENCE AS IT AFFECTS THE SPIRITUAL ENVIRONMENT

Do the acoustics of your room and the operation of the sound system work well together? Do they help create or enhance the sense of corporate worship, or can you barely hear the guy singing next to you?

Worshipping in a service along with a large congregation is a wonderful experience and an unforgettable sound. That sense of corporate worship can play a tremendous role in allowing people to forget their troubles for a time and enter into worship. In a sense, the sound system, lights, and overall environment of the room can help establish an initial focal point for entering into worship. Your attention is first drawn to the platform. But as the worship begins, the system should ideally "disappear." Its clean, focused sound should allow you to think only of worship itself.

Equally important is the ability of the operator to subtly adjust the "house mix" of the worship team to allow them to lead the congregation into worship. Certainly he needs to provide an excellent music mix for the house sound system. Part of that subtlety is refraining from any abrupt changes that may be heard in the house, and obviously avoiding all potential for feedback ("howling"). If he is also mixing monitors (separate loudspeakers) for the worship team, he must be certain that their needs are taken care of. If their monitor mix is not right, they cannot hear themselves and one another, and therefore cannot be expected to lead others into worship.

Not only must an audio minister understand music and the technical craft of audio, he must also have a sensitivity to worship that allows him to flow with the service. The creative side of mixing a worship service allows the engineer to enhance and emphasize certain moments. But it goes beyond that. Here, unlike any other mix, the congregation's singing is part of the overall "live" sound. The engineer must consider the congregation as *part of his mix*. To a degree, he must adjust his mix in response to the leading of the congregation.

The engineer and his crew must also be sensitive not to disturb the congregation. An abrupt fader (level control) move made at just the wrong time could distract a person just as he is about to make a life-changing decision. Inattention that leads to a moment of feedback can have similar disrupting results.

The "job" associated with serving in an audio ministry is a role that should not be taken lightly. It should not be entered into on a whim. If a person is not trained in audio, then he clearly has a lot to learn. The material exists, and it is up to the individual to study it. The administration must also see the need for training. Face it, you're probably not going to start your audio ministry with the finest sound engineer alive. You will start with someone in your congregation who has a willing heart, a responsible attitude, and some basic technical information under his belt. Then you're going to support him as he learns whatever he needs to learn by way of books and workshops in sound reinforcement. Later on, as his talents grow, and in order to keep him from burning out, you'll need to support him as he starts to build a volunteer ministry. This means that over time he will need to train others, teaching them how to mix and how to get the most out of the sound system. A young engineer cannot learn how to mix simply by watching over his teacher's shoulder—he has to do it. Your courage through this period of training will make or break your audio ministry. By this time you've become accustomed to smoothly running services; as these budding audio engineers start to learn the craft, mistakes will be made. Accept those mistakes graciously. Learn to applaud their efforts.

The goal is a smooth-running service. All of the technical support ministries, the audio ministry included, are "unseen" groups.

They support the work of the minister, of the music director and worship team, and of the staff. If there were no problems with feedback, if the appropriate mic was open every time someone started to speak, if the sermon did in fact get on tape, if the left front speaker cluster came back on (after secretly frying three power amps), if the "oh, by the way" offertory music sounded like an album mix—if, in short, the audio ministry went completely without recognition, then the audio engineer has done his job well.

Accomplishing that task takes a lot of work. The larger the congregation, the more people that will need to be brought into the ministry. The numbers ensure 1) that there are enough people on hand to get the job done, especially when big musicals and dramatic events are planned for the holidays; 2) that finding a replacement for someone who is unable to make it to the service at the last minute is not a major ordeal; and 3) that no one in the audio ministry gets burned out by having to work every single service without a break. Remember that they first came to your congregation to worship and learn. They joined your technical support ministry out of their desire to serve. While performing that task, they can't truly worship with the same freedom as those in the congregation can, or even those in the worship team, because the level of concentration demands attention to other details. It is a sacrifice that they make. They need time away from all the technical stuff, a time to worship, a time to remember the reason they're doing this in the first place.

Whenever the audio ministry is not taken seriously, by the minister, music director, or even by the ministry itself, the services can be a disaster waiting to happen. A lot can be said for finding the right personality for the job. But it starts at the top, doesn't it? If the minister and the music director are not excited about and supportive of the efforts of the audio ministry, if they don't promote the importance of that job, then the work of the ministry may be doomed from the start. The lazy sound engineer will find comfort in the lazy attitude; the inquisitive, talented engineer will be frustrated and eventually quit.

THE
YAMAHA
GUIDE TO
SOUND SYSTEMS
FOR WORSHIP
PAGE 6

PRESBYCUSIS AND OTHER HEARING IMPAIRMENT

Loss of hearing acuity simply due to age doesn't seem quite fair. But we all have to deal with it. *Presbycusis* is the technical term for this loss of hearing sensitivity, and it affects the perception of high frequencies especially. It degrades speech intelligibility and can reduce musical listening pleasure. Presbycusis comes with age, but hearing impairment is not limited to the more mature members of the congregation. Given the many current and former rock musicians with impaired hearing attending services, plus the countless others who work in loud, ear-damaging environments, you need to be sensitive to their needs, informed about the possible solutions, and prepared to invest in such a solution.

One of the first ways to address the problem is simply to be certain that your present sound system is doing its job. If it is a well-designed, -installed, and -operated high-intelligibility sound system, run at an appropriate volume, then it may well take care of most listeners who have this condition.

The next logical step in addressing this problem is to look into a special sound system for the hearing-impaired. (See Chapter 10.) They come in a variety of styles. Your audio ministry could install a simple audio system that would take an output from the sound reinforcement console and feed it, via an amplifier, to several small headphones. Perhaps arranged in a special seating area, they would provide an adjustable increase in volume for those who need it. A more flexible solution would be to purchase one of the wireless systems for the hearing-impaired, essentially a low-power "radio station" that feeds the output from your sound reinforcement console to a radio frequency or infrared light transmitter. The transmitter sends that signal to as many pocket-sized receivers as you wish; the receivers are loaned to those who need them. The receivers have small, discreet headphones that the listener wears. The fact that they are wireless allows the users to sit almost anywhere in the room that they choose. By comparison, the hard-wired system mentioned earlier would probably require a more restricted seating arrangement, if for no other reason than simplicity of installation.

LEVEL

Ministers have various styles of delivery. Some simply visit with the congregation as if it were a family get-together. Others scream at the top of their lungs throughout their sermon. The greatest "opportunity" for any engineer is to run sound for someone who is screaming one minute, and then the next moment drops to a whisper. A minister of that style does so for a reason, but he doesn't understand that our hearing often cannot receive such fast changes in level and still understand what he meant to convey.

So the engineer must "ride gain" on his mic, chasing his volume up and down. When the minister is screaming, the engineer must lower the volume to protect someone in the audience from having a sizzling loudspeaker drop in his or her lap. When the minister whispers, the engineer must bring up the volume so that people will be able to hear him loudly enough to understand. There is no human whose brain and finger that can chase a fader that well. But there is an electronic device that will chase the level quite nicely—it's called a *compressor* (see Chapter 7). Now, some may balk at the thought of an electronic device lowering their shrieks and raising their whispers. But people generally know when they're being yelled at by the *tone* of a person's voice, not by the ear-splitting volume. Why not use the sound system to keep the voice at a reasonable level that allows everyone to hear clearly but not be blasted?

This whole matter of level is a point of concern. The more traditional denominations don't necessarily experience this problem, but certainly those who perform contemporary music in their worship services do. Some services measure at around 105 dB SPL (sound pressure level), and some worship leaders' stage monitors at 110 dB SPL. Scientists have designated 114 dB SPL as the Threshold of Feeling, where 50% of the people feel discomfort in their ears. At 120 dB SPL, most people are uncomfortable. Do these levels belong in a worship service?

We all have a responsibility to protect our hearing. Is there a level beyond which we shouldn't go? Who is going to make that determination? Should babies or small children be allowed in a service where the volume often tops 105 dB SPL? Tough questions, but ones you should be considering.

KNOWLEDGE

An audio consultant visited a church once and noticed that the house loudspeakers were mounted to either side of the platform, about eight feet up the wall and actually angled *up* slightly. Upon questioning the fellow responsible, he learned that he had the mistaken idea that aiming a loudspeaker was similar in nature to artillery fire—so he aimed the speakers up slightly in order to "lob" the sound out into the proper location in the congregation. He knew where to aim the sound, but he had a mistaken idea of how to get it there. (Artillery shells have mass, and hence a curved trajectory due to gravity; sound waves do not have mass and travel in straight lines unless reflected or refracted by some object.)

The concern in using the resident expert is simply his level of knowledge of audio, or more importantly the gaps in that knowledge, and his ability to use that knowledge to design and install a quality sound system for you at a reasonable price. Maybe you know of congregations who have installed three, four, even five different sound systems in their quest for great sound. When you total up all the money spent in that search, wouldn't it have paid for hiring a first-rate consultant in the first place? Not to mention the aggravation and disruption of everyone's schedules along the way. (Ah, but you say you *did* hire a "first-rate" consultant in the first place? Chapter 2 will provide some counsel along those lines.)

A properly designed, installed, and operated sound system can make your services a delight. It can make tremendous improvements in the speech intelligibility, the music performance, the quality of sound from your tape and broadcast ministries, the audio ambience as it affects the spiritual environment, and in the ability of members who are experiencing a slight loss in their hearing to take part in the service.

An improperly designed, installed, and operated sound system can create problems in each of these areas. And since perhaps no one on staff understands how to correct those problems as they are recognized, the problems somehow combine to become greater than their individual parts. Correcting the situation then becomes an overwhelming task, and may settle into nothing more than a lively debate for years. It won't get resolved until someone is simply tired enough of the situation to finally deal with it.

But resolving an existing problem, or setting out on the right path in the first place, takes education. Quality audio gear costs a fair amount of money. And it's difficult to convince an "uneducated" sound committee about the realities of the professional audio world when they have a host of other poorly educated people offering poor advice. They become confused about who's right. It becomes especially difficult when the person responsible for presenting these ideas to the decision makers is not equipped with the words to express first the need, and second the ultimate benefit of a great system to the staff and the congregation. But there is hope. It can be done. This book can help.

Hopefully everything that has been said here will be taken in the positive manner it was intended. All you can do is all you can do, and sometimes the money simply isn't there to purchase the best-quality everything. What you should do, though, is try to understand the reason for investing in a high-quality sound system, accept the fact that it may cost a little more than you had planned for, and then aim for the best quality you can afford. And through it all, remember to take good care of your audio crew. They need your support.

THE
YAMAHA
GUIDE TO
SOUND SYSTEMS
FOR WORSHIP
PAGE 8

CHAPTER 2.
WHERE AND HOW TO BUY A SOUND SYSTEM

Okay, so you've decided that it's time to consider buying a sound system. Now what? If you're like most ministers or sound committees, you may distrust anyone who has anything to do with sound systems in the first place. Your needs are simple. All you want is a first-rate sound system that will perform a basic task at a price that fits your budget. But your specialty isn't audio. You're a minister, for goodness' sake. You know deep inside that you'll be at their mercy the moment you walk in the door.

A number of options lay before you. First, you could simply design the sound system yourself. If you or someone you know enjoys a technical challenge, perhaps you can come up with your own design. Or you might go to a music retail store—many of them sell road-worthy PA loudspeakers, amplifiers, and even complete, prepackaged systems. Your third choice would be to contact a pro audio dealer or sound contractor. A major part of their business involves designing and installing sound systems for many different needs. Some even specialize in houses of worship. A fourth choice would be to hire an independent sound system designer, a consultant who simply tells you what to buy and provides diagrams on how it should be installed.

OPTIONS

In discussing these four potential sources for a sound system, some observed generalities will be made. Please understand that the capabilities and level of knowledge varies widely among these groups, and even within the individual groups. The direction you choose will probably be based primarily on your budget, but don't overlook any of these avenues. Considering all available options will give you the perspective necessary to make an informed decision.

DESIGNING THE SYSTEM YOURSELF

It's okay to design and build a sound system yourself. No one says that only experienced system designers can have all the fun. The advantage of designing and installing your own sound system is that, if the system is installed right and works great, you may have saved a fair amount of money for the effort. One word of caution, though: designing a proper sound system can be a complex task, one that should not be attempted lightheartedly. Weigh the emotional and financial costs covered in this chapter before you cross that line.

The disadvantage of having an audio layman in your congregation design the system is the very real possibility that you could be wasting your money—that the system may not perform as you require and therefore that the work may need to be redone by someone else at additional expense. Every congregation has someone named Wilbur[*] who lurks behind the equipment rack or in the ceiling adjusting loudspeaker aiming, as resident experts will do from time to time. However good Wilbur's intentions are, the best you can hope for is a system installed with the LAR (Looks About Right) approach to system design. His limited knowledge does not provide him with the insight necessary to design a complex system.

Few congregations have a knowledgeable resident expert in their midst. So unless your audio needs are very simple, it is unlikely that you will find someone within your congregation equipped to do the job. If you do, then great! Sadly, there are some congregations that do have a talented, educated, experienced audio person in their midst, and know about them, and yet won't

---

[*] Our apologies, Wilbur, if you aren't the person we allude to here. Obviously, the name isn't important; it's the role that concerns us.

THE
YAMAHA
GUIDE TO
SOUND SYSTEMS
FOR WORSHIP
PAGE 9

heed their advice or even ask their counsel. There seems to be an unwritten rule that says to be an expert one must live more than 100 miles away from the job site.

Maybe you find yourself with a lay person in your congregation who really doesn't have much experience in audio, but who wants to take on the job of putting in a new sound system. Where's the dividing line between allowing him to proceed and seeking professional counsel instead? Well, once again it depends on many variables, but a reasonable guideline might be that if your facility seats fewer than 200 people and has no serious acoustic problems, and if the technical production demands of your service are not extraordinary, Wilbur's system will probably sound just fine. Chances are that by the time you finish reading this book, if you see him walking in on Saturday morning with forty-seven 6" x 9" car speakers, you'll already know he's in over his head.

Why such a cautious approach? Well, remember how Chapter 1 touched briefly on speech intelligibility? In a large array of speakers, quite literally even a one-inch misalignment of drivers can degrade the speech intelligibility of the speaker system. Are you really going to let Wilbur get up there with his circle saw and two-by-fours and your $20,000 investment in equipment?

Speaking of saws, the carpenter in all of us is going to convince some resident experts to try to build their own speaker boxes for their installation. While this may save a bit of money, the physical box isn't what makes a speaker expensive—the loudspeaker inside the box and the engineering that makes the box and speaker perform well together are what cost so much. If you must proceed with this plan, at least do the research. No matter how good the carpenter, the enclosure may be awful unless built with correct dimensions and materials to suit a given loudspeaker. There are books available on building a proper speaker enclosure (see "For Further Reading," on page 182), or you can purchase the plans for many common loudspeaker enclosures directly from the manufacturer.

One aside: For the Wilburs reading this book—and you know who you are—you are to be congratulated. You're making a positive step toward better sound reinforcement in your place of worship. Your heart is in the right place. Keep it

there, continue to learn more of the craft of audio, and you'll become a tremendous asset to your congregation.

MUSICAL INSTRUMENT STORE

Many sound systems for worship facilities have been purchased at musical instrument (MI) retail stores. This is the store where the music director goes to ogle all the neat synthesizers, where you walk in and do your level best to keep from tripping over keyboard stands and from hitting your shins on guitar amps and monitor speakers.

Get to know them, though. For all their loud sounds, strange hair, and colloquial terminology, those who run such a store are typically business-minded people engaged in a serious effort to make a difficult business succeed.

Much of their expertise in portable systems is also applicable to sound systems for worship—especially if your need is for musical reinforcement. From a technical point of view, the needs of a traveling contemporary religious musical group are quite similar to those of the secular entertainer. Packaged, portable systems are also widely used by new congregations that do not yet have a worship facility, but are renting school auditoriums in which to hold their services.

The MI retailer may not be familiar with the requirements for speech intelligibility, ease of operation, and even coverage that exist in the house of worship. In recent years, some MI retailers have branched into the installed sound market. They have trained or hired system designers and installers who are capable of building top-quality systems. Ask your local MI store if they offer such services. If so, they will be pleased to provide you with a list of installations.

SOUND CONTRACTOR OR PRO AUDIO DEALER

A sound contractor or pro audio dealer typically has a staff capable of designing, selling, and professionally installing the equipment he recommends. The largest dealers have certain people who simply sell equipment, others who do nothing but design systems, plus a crew of technicians who like to climb around in ceilings and squeeze behind equipment racks with

THE
YAMAHA
GUIDE TO
SOUND SYSTEMS
FOR WORSHIP
PAGE 10

screwdrivers in their teeth. In addition, some may even be able to help you with advice regarding acoustic control for your facility, either through a staff person or through a professional acquaintance.

In new construction, the sound contractor may work as a subcontractor to the electrical contractor.

Reputable contractors and pro audio dealers will typically service and repair systems they have designed and installed as part of the deal. The savings in peace of mind and potential repair costs should be part of your considerations when selecting a sound system supplier.

By the way, you won't find a major difference between a pro audio dealer and a sound contractor, except that the pro audio dealer will have a showroom floor to display lots of equipment and the sound contractor probably won't. The pro audio dealer also services recording studios and radio and TV broadcast facilities in your area, and may be involved in both selling home stereo (high-fidelity) equipment and designing systems for the lucrative "home media room" market. But in regard to your purchasing a sound system from either type of company, if they are equally knowledgeable in sound system design and installation, their services will be much the same.

But beware. A "hi-fi" (high-fidelity) store is not necessarily a pro audio store. Hi-fi stores typically offer only home stereos, car stereos, and home video equipment. Pro audio stores, on the other hand, offer a broader range of gear that may include both high-fidelity equipment and professional audio gear. The typical hi-fi store is not capable of designing or installing a high-quality sound reinforcement system. Terrifying tales have been told of hi-fi sound systems being passed off as professional sound reinforcement systems in houses of worship. Partly because of this, insiders to the sound contracting business often consider these high-fidelity systems as "high-futility" systems.

INDEPENDENT CONSULTANT

A consultant really works as a third party in the job, since the equipment will still need to be purchased from another source, and the installation may need to be performed by a professional crew. His basic task is to design your sound system, oversee its proper installation, and then perform the final adjustments to ensure its proper working order. Depending on who does the actual installation, he may or may not need to actually be on the job site very often. More than likely his input will be given during periodic visits to check on the progress of the job. Some have a set fee for their work, while others charge an hourly rate. An independent consultant acts as your advocate, protecting your interests and his reputation by assuring that equipment is properly selected and installed; his primary profit is from design and oversight, not equipment sales margins.

At the same time, using a contractor who designs and builds the system eliminates the possibility of controversy over who (contractor or consultant) is responsible for dealing with a problem.

It is also common practice for the audio or acoustic consultant to work as a subcontractor to the architect.

Although hiring a consultant is often the best choice you could make, as in most things, you get what you pay for. The design fee alone can range anywhere from $800 to $8,000, sometimes higher. It will depend on the size of your facility, the scope of the project, and how in-demand the consultant is. But don't let that scare you off. Some designers specialize in the 300- to 1,000-seat facility, and trim their design fee accordingly. You may even find a talented young designer trying to break into the market who is willing to work for less. Although there are many talented third-party designers, the problem is finding them. Your best method of research will probably be word of mouth.

THE
YAMAHA
GUIDE TO
SOUND SYSTEMS
FOR WORSHIP
PAGE 11

GENERAL PRECAUTIONS

Ask the contractor, consultant, or pro audio or music dealer for references. The reputable, competent firm will be pleased and proud to show you a portfolio of their installations and to put you in touch with previous clients. Contact these references. Once you determine that the firm you are considering is capable and consciencious, it may well be that it is worth the additional expense.

There is a growing number of legitimate, caring, hard-working audio dealers out there who will do their level best to deliver a great system at a fair price. They are equipped with the knowledge and the tools to do it right the first time, and will go out of their way to do a first-class job for you.

A special word to congregations who are building a new facility, or redesigning an existing one: If you plan on seeking the help of an outside expert, be it a sound contractor or an audio consultant or whatever, it can't be stressed enough that you involve him or her as early as possible in the design process—before ground is broken, if possible. Many consultants and contractors are experienced in acoustics as well as sound system design. It is much cheaper to build a structure with good acoustic design than it is to fix bad acoustics. There is a traditional rivalry between architects (who are frequently more concerned with visual aesthetics) and sound system designers (who always want to place those annoying loudspeakers where the sight lines to some breathtaking architectural vista are blocked). By considering the audio needs during the planning stages, such conflicts may be resolved in ways that maintain visual and audio integrity. (The same might also be said of an acoustical consultant.) By taking the needs of the sound system into account from the outset, you may save a big expense later from having to redo things. Consider a few examples:

- A conduit to take wires from the platform to the mixing console can easily be laid in a concrete floor if the need for it is known before the floor is poured.

- If the electrical requirements of the sound system are known in advance, it can save having to add AC circuits later.

- Unless the number and placement of audio jacks, AC outlets, and other connectors are well planned, you may find yourself faced with having to tear out perfectly good sheets of drywall to correct the situation.

THE LAR FACTOR

Even with a reasonable effort in planning for a system, there's still a potential for problems. Many people start out on the right track. They solicit and receive proper design and installation bids from first-rate companies, but later decide to buy the lower-priced, "it's-just-as-good, really," equipment from a competitor. What usually happens then is that the congregation or administration will fuss and complain about the inability of the system to do the job they expect of it for the next three to five years, at which time they, in desperation, return to the quality dealer for help. The reality is that a high-quality, great-sounding system could have been installed by the better dealer in the first place for just a slightly higher price...and in the long run, saving a great deal of money.

Despite the widespread availability of the critical information for designing proper sound systems, a disturbing number of people who call themselves sound system designers operate with the LAR (Looks About Right) approach to system design. They tend to solve design problems with poor research and inadequate systems, an approach that actually does a disservice to both the customer and the original equipment manufacturer. The music director is unhappy because the system doesn't do the job the congregation expected of it, and the manufacturer is unhappy because word will get around that his product is "obviously no good" since it didn't work in that situation. The product may be a perfectly good device that was used in the wrong situation or wrong placement.

The comments above are not at all meant to discredit low-priced equipment. One reason it exists is because there is a genuine need for it. Just don't make the mistake of expecting first-rate sound from a much less expensive piece of equipment. Also remember that sometimes long-term reliability and a low price don't go hand-in-hand. If the quality serves your purpose and if you're happy with the sound, then fine. The caveat is: Know what you're buying, and

THE
YAMAHA
GUIDE TO
SOUND SYSTEMS
FOR WORSHIP
PAGE 12

don't believe the salesman's "it's just as good" pitch. If there's a question, simply ask for an A/B (comparison) demonstration. By the time you read and apply the information in this book, your ears will become good instruments for evaluating systems; trust them. Such a demonstration will be most effective when conducted in your facility, and most firms will allow FREE "demo loans" for a couple of days at a time or over a weekend.

QUESTIONS TO ASK

In your initial discussions with any potential candidates to be involved with your new sound system, there are a number of questions you can ask to determine their ability to perform the task and how seriously they take their job. Ask these questions after the company has a rough idea of what your needs are and the overall scope of the project. Good ones to start with include:

1. What experience does your company have in designing or installing sound systems in houses of worship similar to ours? (You may be surprised to learn that some sound contractors, for example, do most of their work with shopping malls and hotels. A broad experience is a plus, but you will prefer working with a company that has experience designing and installing systems for houses of worship.)

2. Will you arrange a tour of a representative sample of those facilities for our committee? (They should be able to either arrange a guided tour or provide you with contact names so that you can make your own tour of other worship facilities with which they have been involved. Take that tour, and ask questions of staff members at those facilities regarding their impression of the company and of the finished job.)

3. What brands of equipment does your company carry, and are you an authorized dealer for all of those brands? (Most companies are authorized by the manufacturer to carry specific lines of equipment.)

4. Is your company adequately equipped to service what you sell, and are you authorized to provide warranty repair on items that require it? (Most companies

do offer warranty repair service on the gear they sell. Those same reputable companies may not be authorized dealers for other brands of gear, but if requested, may be able to obtain one or two pieces from legitimate sources. But beware, there are also companies that sell "grey market" equipment—that is, without the manufacturer's authorization—at which point you may be outside the limit of guaranteed warranty repair. Grey market equipment is frequently intended for overseas distribution and may be designed to operate on the electrical power standards of other countries. It also may not meet local safety code requirements.)

5. How quickly will your company respond during the warranty period to system failures that require the presence of your repair personnel at our facility? What if we have a major system failure during a service, for example? (Many companies will provide service of the system for a specified period. Examine the service agreement and negotiate those points that don't meet your needs. It is also a good idea to request that a company representative attend the first service with the new sound system to help with any glitches that may occur.)

6. If service takes longer than a couple of days, is your company prepared to lend or rent us temporary replacement gear? (This should not pose a problem for most companies, particularly for MI stores or pro audio dealers who keep a fair amount of gear around.)

7. What promises and guarantees does your company offer related to your sound system and its installation beyond the manufacturer's warranties? (An important feature, this is explained in more detail later in the chapter. Expect bigger promises and guarantees from larger companies.)

8. At some point before or during the initial design phase, will your design engineer attend one of our worship services to experience first-hand the type of worship service we hold? (As explained later, this is a vital link to a successful sound system.)

THE
YAMAHA
GUIDE TO
SOUND SYSTEMS
FOR WORSHIP
PAGE 13

9. If the cost of installation is quoted as a flat fee, will there be any additional costs if the installation goes beyond your original estimates? (Expect additional costs if delays to the installation are caused by you or your ministry volunteers.)

10. In the interest of controlling installation labor costs, may individuals from our audio ministry be allowed to assist in certain installation tasks? (If audio laymen from your congregation are available and interested in volunteering their time, negotiating this point may save you a bundle. More details later in this chapter.)

11. Does your company have a standard contract for this type of work, and what will the payment schedule be? (Contracts are common and should protect both sides. Expect to pay a certain percentage up front and the balance within 30 days after the system is completed to your mutual satisfaction. Leverage is good, but not at the expense of poor relations. You will get better work out of a company that enjoys working with you.)

Having looked over these questions, you are probably thinking of even more to add to the list. Your goal is not to "grill" your system candidates, and hopefully this won't brand you as being hard to work with. But their response to these types of questions will give you valuable insight into what it would be like working with each company.

HOW TO KNOW WHEN YOU NEED HELP

When are you in over your head? Some of us are brave, ready to take on any new challenge. Others are timid, and shrink from anything that even looks like it might be overwhelming. The smart ones do their research, hire the right team for the job, and go on about their own work.

WHEN TO CALL AN AUDIO PROFESSIONAL

Let's imagine that, rather than using the services of a professional sound company, you have embarked on the mission of designing and installing your own sound

system. You are halfway into the task and find yourself sitting on a box of equipment, wondering what in the world to do next. Maybe you lack one simple piece of information to make the rest of the puzzle fit. Or worse, maybe you originally felt confident in taking on your own installation, but now, looking at all that equipment, you feel overwhelmed at the thought. Why not seek guidance from an audio consultant, someone who can fill in those blanks in the puzzle, someone who has been through it before?

Don't be embarrassed in making that call. Take comfort in the fact that no one knows everything there is to know about acoustics and sound system design. Even talented sound system designers seek professional guidance from their peers or from someone in another discipline when they encounter an especially difficult problem. Every time even the best sound system design engineer does a new system, he learns something he didn't know before. That's the nature of the business.

Specifically what kinds of problems would warrant a call to an audio professional? Call for help when:

1. You hear any hum or buzz over the sound system that you can't seem to get rid of.

2. You hear radio interference from CB radios, nearby radio stations, and so on, and you're not sure how to get rid of it.

3. Certain areas of the congregation are getting blasted by the sound volume while other areas are straining to hear clearly.

4. You hear audible distortion over the sound system, especially distortion heard when the system is run at a relatively soft volume.

5. You can't get enough gain out of the microphones before the system goes into feedback. (Most lapel mics [wireless or not] are very susceptible to feedback.)

6. You are considering hanging speakers but lack knowledge or experience. This is a critical safety concern and should be handled by someone with structural engineering or theatrical rigging credentials. Even the smallest speaker

THE
YAMAHA
GUIDE TO
SOUND SYSTEMS
FOR WORSHIP
PAGE 14

enclosure can be a lethal projectile if it falls.

7. You find yourself about to use small-gauge wire for the speaker connections.

These are just a few of the common problems encountered in installing a sound system. If you have any of these problems, or others similar in nature, then go ahead and seek out professional help. Calling for help is not a sign of weakness, it's a sign of good management. The reality is that everything—from the size of the room to how the seats are arranged to the kinds of lights used to how clean the AC power that operates your audio equipment is—will affect the functional success of your sound system. Everything must be taken into account. It is all a part of the system. Ask yourself, "Do I have the knowledge necessary to answer those questions and solve the problems that will surface along the way?" Then look for help in the areas in which you don't feel confident.

Just don't sit there and let mistake after mistake be made. Make the call before it's too late. A professional's fee may turn out to be an insignificant expense compared to the cost of redoing the sound system a year or two from now.

WHEN TO CALL AN ACOUSTICIAN

A great sound system may sound mediocre at best if the acoustics of a room don't complement it. When this happens, the unfortunate tendency is to blame the sound system designer for his "poor work." Sound systems are such a hot issue, and there is so much written about them, that common knowledge seems to give us the right to criticize the work of any designer. By comparison, the complex nature of sound and how the acoustics of a room interact with it are not at all common knowledge, so they are generally left out of the conversation entirely.

This is where most lay people need help. The science of acoustics is in many ways an art form. The lay person's answer to acoustic control is to glue some carpet on the wall. Unfortunately, this old idea will help only in a handful of cases. And just because it helped in one facility doesn't necessarily mean it will work in yours. In fact, a current trend in acoustic control is to

purposely diffuse the sound—scatter it about the room in a controlled fashion—rather than absorbing it, or sometimes in conjunction with absorbing it. The roll-of-carpet philosophy of acoustic control won't help much there.

Another oversight is that, while many designers of houses of worship build great-looking buildings, many of those same designers have a serious lack of knowledge regarding current practices of sound system design. If you were left with an auditorium that sounds more like a racquetball court when you clap your hands in the room, then you were shortchanged on acoustic control. If you stand on the platform talking over a microphone and can hear a distinct "slapback" echo of your voice a fraction of a second later, then you *may* have been shortchanged on acoustic control. Although it is likely that an acoustic control problem exists, it's only a "maybe" in this case since it is possible that the house loudspeakers were improperly aimed. An acoustical consultant may prove helpful in ferreting out and solving these types of problems.

The best time to deal with the acoustics is before your facility is built. If you are currently in the design stage, make an effort to go and visit other similar buildings that your chosen worship facility designer has been involved with. Listen for problems with the room. Listen in enough buildings to convince yourself whether the problems are the result of poor acoustic control or a poor sound system. You would be surprised to know how much of the art of electro-acoustical design is just plain common sense. That shouldn't encourage you to go off and start designing everything yourself. But it should comfort you in the thought that, with a little practice, you can start to hear the problems and maybe even understand what is causing them. You might not know exactly what to do about it, in which case you will need the help of a consultant, but being aware of the problem is often half of the solution.

The bottom line is that much of the art of sound system design and acoustic control comes down to an educated guess. There are few absolutes. It would stand to reason, then, as you enter into your quest for a new or replacement sound system, to let the person with the most education about the subject make that "guess" for you. You alone are in the position to make that choice for your situation. When you don't feel comfortable with the knowledge within your organization about either the engineering or the acoustics of your planned facility, start asking questions. Seek out respected people in those fields and talk with them. If their services are within your financial means, then consider hiring them for your project.

But don't follow along blindly. One of the most frustrating situations occurs when an administration vests total faith in the knowledge and abilities of their chosen design companies, and stops listening to the advice of those in their own organization who have inside knowledge of your everyday technical needs. Besides, outside designers must be in touch with your objectives, and your help here is essential.

WHAT TO EXPECT

One comfort in going to a professional sound system designer or installer is that he may be in a position to offer you certain promises and guarantees regarding his work. Hopefully, the more serious those statements are, the more qualified and equipped he is to make good on them.

Whenever you start the process of choosing a company to design or install your sound system, you should make an effort to see and hear one or more sound systems that each of your candidates has done. There are certain things to look for and to listen for in a quality sound system. When you come to this point, you may already have bids from those candidates, and it will be interesting for you to compare the price they have quoted for your system with the quality of their typical installation. (To compare apples to apples, ask them what the audio budget was for each of the "sample facilities" they send you to.)

Despite the precision of certain design formulas, designing a sound system is still somewhat of a personal task. (Even the computer sound system design aids available are subject to human input. For example, those programs don't tell a designer which loudspeaker to use. They are primarily a "number-crunching" aid.) The bottom line is this: Without examining work of the person whom you want to design or install your system first-hand, you have no idea whether he can capably do the work or not.

A model of a quality installation and of reasonable written system guarantees and tolerances may help you understand what you are seeing, and analyze the comparative strengths and weaknesses of your design candidates.

What does a professional installation look like? One quick way to spot a professional installation is to look at the wiring job. Poke your head into the equipment racks. The wiring should be neat, almost to a fault. The solder connections and other terminations should be absolutely clean. Wires should run together, fanning out from the bundles at smooth 90° angles. Mic lines should not be mixed with line-level feeds (e.g., the output of your console feeding to the power amp). Neither mic "snakes" (snakes are multiconductor cables capable of carrying eight or more different mic signals) nor line-level feeds should be run adjacent to speaker lines. Power cables should be kept away from all low-level wiring (such as the lines running to and from the console), and should be run neatly to the AC power source. A good treatment is to cut the power cords to length, and run them directly to an AC outlet provided close to the unit inside the rack. Where AC cords must cross audio cables, they should cross at right angles.

The loudspeaker cluster should look clean and organized. If you make the request, it can be hidden behind a framework scrimmed with acoustically transparent material. All exposed panels, such as mic input plates, stage speaker outlets, intercom panels, and so on, should be clean and carefully marked. It is not difficult for the installer to have these custom-engraved to your specifications prior to installation.

You are likely to have an awful lot of wires running all over your facility. Tracing those wires by hand would be a nightmare, so all wires related to the installation should be marked with a number or a written flag to identify them, and adequate documentation of the system should be provided for use by a repair technician or for possible future system modifications. Remember, the people who installed the system may not be around to work on it years in the future; if you have detailed system block diagrams with wire IDs noted, any competent technician will be able to handle troubleshooting in a fraction of the time that might be required without such documentation.

THE
YAMAHA
GUIDE TO
SOUND SYSTEMS
FOR WORSHIP
PAGE 16

These principles apply to sophisticated and simple systems alike; good workmanship is always good workmanship.

What does a great installation sound like? First, a professionally installed sound system should be completely free of extraneous noises such as buzzes, hums, hisses, and so on. It should also reject all radio interference from CB radios, powerful radio stations nearby, and the like.

Second, a good sound system for worship should cover all seats in the room evenly. There should be no "hot spots" or dead spots. A good specification for smooth, even coverage might read "the SPL (sound pressure level) will be 90 dB, plus or minus 2 dB, from 500 Hz to 5,000 Hz, at every seat in the house." (See Chapter 3 for more about the meanings of these specifications.)

The frequency response should be reasonably smooth throughout the room. There should be no harshness to the sound. If the sound system will be used to reinforce contemporary worship music, it should sound full in the low frequencies and crisp in the high frequencies. A reasonable specification of frequency response for a sound system for music might call for a flat response "within plus or minus 3 dB from 500 Hz to 5,000 Hz at every seat in the house." (That won't make the system "full in the low frequencies and crisp in the high frequencies," but it may be the best quote you'll get.)

The frequency range capability, known as the *bandwidth* of the system, should be adequate for your requirements. Since a common practice nowadays is to use accompaniment soundtracks for vocal solos, the system should be a wide-bandwidth system capable of reproducing the full range of music on the soundtrack. Even if your congregation doesn't have an orchestra that includes bass viols or timpani, the accompaniment track probably will. A system capable of reproducing frequencies from 40 Hz or 50 Hz to as high as 16 kHz (16,000 Hz) may be needed here. However, since high energy levels at high frequencies can add a harsh edge to the sound, above 8 kHz you may not want the response to be "flat" within plus or minus 3 dB but rather you may prefer some attenuation (roll-off) at the higher frequencies. (The whole area of high frequency response is complex, however, because air attenuates high frequency sound

more than low frequency sound, so you may need a lot of high frequency energy at the loudspeakers in order to end up with a modest amount of highs at the pews.)

The sound system should also perform without any audible distortion. In your early meetings with your sound system designer, you should determine how loud the system needs to be capable of reaching. It should be able to reach that level easily and without any audible distortion.

Many installers will provide their customers with a list of guarantees summarizing the agreed-upon performance specifications of the system, similar to the comments above. (This is more customary for large facilities—1,000 seats and up—than for smaller ones.) The guarantee may even go as far as to say that if the sound system does not meet any or all of the written guarantees, the installer will provide whatever equipment and labor necessary at his company's expense to bring the system into agreement with those guarantees. Furthermore, if the system still does not meet those guarantees, that the company will remove the system and refund your money. Those are pretty bold statements. You'd better believe he's going to do everything in his power at the outset to ensure that his design and installation will meet those guarantees!

What services should a third-party design consultant provide? This depends partly on the level of involvement you want from him. You might simply want to check his opinion on points your chosen sound company has made. Or you may want him involved from start to finish. A model consultant hired by you to fully design and supervise the installation of your complete sound system will:

1. Perform the design work and issue a performance specification.

2. Prequalify available installation contractors, determining their:
   a. financial ability to handle the job;
   b. personnel available, skills, union affiliations, compliance with federal rules (race, etc.), experience in type of job, etc.;
   c. test equipment, shop tools;
   d. desire to do the job.

3. Supervise the installation by:
   a. inspecting all electronic racks, both at the installer's shop and then at the site;
   b. aligning the loudspeaker cluster(s) when installed (final alignment);
   c. certifying that all specified items have been provided;
   d. equalizing the system when installed, and setting all signal delays.

4. Work with the installer's and customer's personnel to ensure their understanding of the basic intent of the system and how to maintain the system at the desired level of performance.

5. Make sure that the contractor supplies a full set of written system specifications.*

The installer chosen by your consultant should also offer proof that he is an authorized dealer for the equipment he provides and therefore able to support the manufacturer's warranty program. When your system is completely installed, the consultant should hand you a system manual that will include the following items: a copy of the "as built" drawings containing block diagrams that describe the signal flow logic of the system and details of the equipment interconnections (including wire identification numbers); original equipment literature detailing the products you will be using; and data sheets verifying that the guaranteed performance criteria have been met. He should also turn over to you all manufacturers' equipment operations and owner's manuals.

WHO DEFINES "GOOD SOUND"?

Who decides what "good sound" is? Using standard formulas, and given an understanding of what the ministers and music directors expect the system to reinforce, a good sound system designer can design what he believes will serve your needs. But part of his job is to accurately interpret the sea of information that the sound committee gives him. He is going to take your complaints of past system performance, requirements of the proposed system, comparisons to so-and-so's worship sound, and personal embellishments of the committee members, and turn that into a big picture of what he thinks you want.

Your first big red warning flag should go up if he suggests to you that he doesn't need to sit in on one of your worship services. That's nonsense. How can he possibly know what your particular style of worship service is like, or the extremes to which it may vary over the year, if he won't bother to sit in on at least one of your services? There are no rules in his bag of tricks that say, "If you're designing sound for a Baptist church, use formula #27." There are no such rules because no two congregations are exactly alike.

Someone is going to come to you and tell you that he can take your building plans and design a proper sound system on paper. If he knows what he's doing, he can. Even if you haven't broken ground for your building yet, and if you give him an accurate set of plans, if the facility is actually built exactly according to those plans, if all the materials called out in the specifications are actually installed that way, he can design a system and guarantee its performance within a given set of tolerances before you ever break ground. (This also assumes that his system is installed the way he designed it!) But this does not free him from the need to experience one or more of your worship services first-hand.

THE
YAMAHA
GUIDE TO
SOUND SYSTEMS
FOR WORSHIP
PAGE 18

* Don and Carolyn Davis, *Sound System Engineering*, 2nd ed., (Indianapolis: Howard W. Sams & Co., 1987), pp. 539–540.

THE GREY AREA

The grey area is this: The designer can prove by simple measurement techniques that the performance of the system is within his guaranteed tolerances. But does it sound good to you?

It's important that you remember that this is a two-way process. The sound system designer's decisions rely on the accuracy of your comments to him. There is one case where a first-rate system designer went through the entire design process with a major house of worship. Their final word to him was that only the spoken word would need to be reinforced in their building. Given the extraordinary reverb time of the facility, his proper design choice was to install a quality pewback sound system. The problem came with their very first function held in the new facility—a concert of vocal music! Whom do you think that audience blamed for the "poor sound"?

You must also choose your words to him carefully when you compare your desires with the sound at so-and-so's place. There's nothing wrong with this idea. In fact, you should visit other facilities and develop a feel for what the possibilities are. But if one house of worship happens to use brand X speakers, you can't necessarily expect those same speakers to sound exactly the same in your facility. For one thing, the acoustics of your facility may be drastically different than the acoustics of the other room. If, however, you find in several settings that you always prefer the sound of those brand X speakers, then you may have sufficient reason to request that your chosen system designer try to use those devices in his design for your facility.

INSTALLATION BY VOLUNTEERS

In regard to installation, what should and shouldn't audio laymen attempt? This is a sticky problem. The thought of having your volunteers assist in all or certain parts of an audio installation is attractive for several reasons. The obvious one is that your group will likely save a fair amount of money by not having to pay the installation crew for the entire job. Another less obvious benefit is that the audio ministry volunteers who are used for this task will have a working knowledge of how the system was installed. Later on, should there be a problem with the system, this inside knowledge will prove invaluable in their ability to troubleshoot the system. As a result, the problem may be solved more quickly and may eliminate the need for an expensive service call.

Is it feasible? In many cases, particularly during the construction phase of a new building, labor unions may not allow your volunteers to perform any jobs whatsoever. Often these matters can be negotiated, but be sure to check it out before the work starts.

What jobs should audio laymen attempt? That's hard to say. What are your volunteers' qualifications? Have they worked with audio specifically, or are they rocket technicians by day and sound men by night? There are certain idiosyncrasies of audio, particularly regarding connections between equipment, that for some reason even the best electronic technicians do not appreciate unless they have audio training. Here are a few of the jobs volunteers may be able to handle:

Pulling Cables

The first job that is typically handed to volunteer labor is to run the audio cables. Mic lines will need to be pulled from the platform to the mixing console. Speaker lines will need to be run from the power amplifiers to both the house speakers and to the stage monitors. With proper supervision, these cable-pulling jobs are fine for volunteer labor to perform. They can take a fair amount of time, and so may save you a fair amount of money.

Placing Equipment

Lifting equipment into place, such as the mixing console or the amplifier and outboard equipment racks, is another practical task for your volunteers to handle. If the amplifier racks are going to be built up on site, volunteers could even set about the task of unboxing the equipment and bolting it into the racks according to the specifications of the contractor.

Connections

Here's where it gets sticky. Some will scoff at this cautious approach to volunteer help with audio connections. But every seasoned sound man out there has seen exactly what can happen here. The task is not at all difficult, but it must be performed a certain way. If it is not, problems will surface when you least expect them, perhaps in the middle of an important service. Every seasoned sound man out there also knows that even the experienced installers can get careless and make occasional mistakes. At times, it may be better to do the work with your own crew—they might take longer, but they also may take more care than the contractor's crew will. A perfectionist bent, an end-user's concern for the job being done right, and some basic technical knowledge are the ingredients of a good wiring job. Properly done, this could save you quite a bit of money.

Wire Numbering

Here's another area in which audio laymen can shorten the installation time. While some mic snakes are available in pre-numbered styles, others are not. To keep things straight, the wires must be numbered. When an old installation is being refurbished, new wiring may be pulled in for some items and not for other less critical applications. If documentation is sketchy or not available, then the existing audio cables should be identified as to their source and destination, and then numbered accordingly.

Hanging Speaker Boxes

As stated earlier in this chapter, the suspension of even small, light-weight enclosures over the heads of choirs, clergy, and congregation raises serious concerns about liability and safety. The design and installation of any rigging system should be supervised and inspected by qualified engineers or technicians. Assembling a cluster of many speakers in midair is a fairly complex task. Not only must the speakers be aimed properly, but the installer must also be certain that the structure will support the cluster's weight, and that the boxes won't pull apart when they are required to support the weight of still more boxes. Also, the boxes have to be hung so they aim in the proper direction. Oftentimes, well-equipped installers will actually build up the cluster in their own shop, and then bring the assembled cluster to your facility to be hoisted into place. Perhaps your volunteers could assist in the muscle-work needed to get those boxes into place, but if the cluster is complex, the final hanging, placement, and aiming should be left to the contractor's crew.

Testing the System

With the proper supervision of the installer or designer, this process can also use the aid of the audio laymen. For one thing, it may involve a lot of running back and forth, or climbing up in the rafters to confirm proper function or to resolve problems that are found. Likewise, while setting the gain structure of the equipment in a permanently installed system requires a certain amount of expertise, the process can involve several trips from behind the equipment rack to the front of the rack, over to the console, and back again. Having an assistant on hand to do the legwork may help speed up the process considerably.

Equalization

Depending on the sophistication of the test equipment the installer uses, he may or may not need assistance with this procedure. This process can take a fair amount of time to be done properly. Since time is money, the one thing you should ensure is that Wilbur will keep

THE
YAMAHA
GUIDE TO
SOUND SYSTEMS
FOR WORSHIP
PAGE 20

his hands off the settings of the room equalizers after this work has been completed. There is probably no other piece of audio equipment so intriguing to the Wilburs of the world than the room equalizer. The reputation of many a system installer has been tarnished by well-meaning volunteers who attempted to operate the sound system improperly, decided that the poor sound was the fault of the original installer, and set about trying to "fix it" themselves.

Many of these types of jobs can be performed more quickly with the assistance of a volunteer. One secret, though, is not to have too many people around. The job will go fast only if there aren't people getting in the way or asking idle questions that are better off left to another time. The caveat here is simply to be cautious. Audio laymen should absolutely be included in whatever phases of the installation of a new sound system that are possible. This is an individual matter, but one that can be a benefit to all sides.

The key is proper and adequate supervision. If you work with a sound contractor or even a third-party designer, and part of the arrangement specifies work for your audio volunteers to perform, then the designer or contractor should provide the necessary supervision of that volunteer work so that his own guarantees to you regarding system performance and reliability are met. In a very real sense, that company makes a statement about its abilities and reputation with every job it installs. Their guarantees to you are simply to state that the system will do everything they say it will. They can't afford for something to be messed up because they weren't looking.

THE OTHER SIDE

Sound committees and ministers as a whole do have somewhat of a learned distrust of audio dealers. Unfortunately, they are not alone in this feeling of distrust. A recent poll of several sound contractors, pro audio dealers, and musical instrument stores revealed a troubling problem. The following question was put forth to individuals representing each of those businesses: What are your pet peeves, your aggravations, about working with houses of worship? Their answer? Sound committees and ministers in general are ignorant about the technical equipment they are looking for, they are over-demanding and hard to work with, and they do not pay their bills on time. Wow! Especially considering the "business" that houses of worship are in, that is a serious indictment.

Before you cast that opinion aside, realize that probably half of those businessmen polled are religious people. They are trying their best to give you a good deal. Those who do not profess to be religious do consider themselves fair and honest businessmen. These aren't the folks who are out to get rich off your audio needs. Both groups of businessmen are often frustrated at their working relationships with sound committees and ministers in general.

Furthermore, the businessmen complained that houses of worship often want free advice. This is a far too common abuse of the business relationship. You must remember that any audio consultant or sound contractor has studied and worked long hours to learn what he knows. Just like you, he needs to make a living. To ask him to share his hard-won knowledge for free is a slap in the face. Many would consider it stealing.

The following story has been repeated countless times. One house of worship asked a consultant to design a sound system and to provide them with all the necessary design details for free. Their idea was that they would ask this of a handful of designers, and then choose the one they thought to be the best. The truth of the matter was that they did not know enough about audio gear to design a sound system themselves, but they reasoned that if they just knew what to buy, they could look around for the best deal, buy the gear, and then try their best to install the system themselves. This kind of maneuvering has little to do with being a shrewd businessman. This attitude hints of misrepresentation, and has no place in the business dealings of a house of worship. It hurts us all.

In spite of their indictment, however, some of those polled still prefer to work primarily with houses of worship, because of the intangible benefits they derive from helping the work toward a common goal.

CONCLUSION

So, are you still ready to jump in with both feet? You can install a high-quality new or replacement sound system on schedule at a reasonable cost. Do your homework—not only to become conversant regarding the technology, but so that you also know what you're getting into. Develop a relationship with an individual you can trust; this won't be the last time you'll need help with audio. Don't be over-demanding; we all want the job done right, but there is a line beyond which one shouldn't tread. Don't destroy the hard work and reputation of the designer by making unauthorized modifications to the system. (Learn how to operate the system properly instead.) Oh, and remember to pay your bill on time.

NOTE: Portions of this chapter are reprinted from "The LAR Factor," by Curt Taipale, originally published in *Creator* magazine (September/October 1989 issue). Used with permission.

THE
YAMAHA
GUIDE TO
SOUND SYSTEMS
FOR WORSHIP
PAGE 22

CHAPTER 3.
UNDERSTANDING THE PHYSICS OF SOUND

In order to gain a basic understanding of sound systems, it is helpful to know some fundamentals about sound itself. This chapter provides those fundamentals, as nontechnically as possible.

WHAT IS SOUND?

Sound is vibration. In order for something to produce a sound, it has to vibrate—to move back and forth rapidly. Our vocal cords vibrate when we speak. A guitar string vibrates when it is plucked. The cone of a loudspeaker vibrates when the radio is on.

These vibrations (back-and-forth motions) disturb the air, causing it to move back and forth as well. This motion takes the form of small fluctuations in the air pressure—*sound waves*. If unobstructed, these waves spread outward from the vibrating object, like ripples on the surface of a pond.

When they meet the ear, sound waves cause the eardrum to vibrate. The eardrum transmits the vibrations to the inner ear, or cochlea, via a chain of three tiny bones. The cochlea translates the vibrations into electrical impulses, which are carried to the brain by the the auditory nerve. The brain says, in effect, "I hear something."

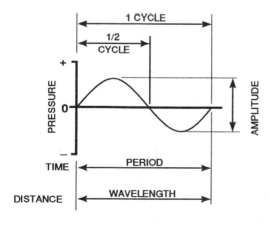

Figure 3-1. Representation of a sound wave (one cycle of a sine wave in air).

SOUND WAVES

A single complete motion of a sound wave, called a *cycle*, consists of one half-cycle of compression (higher pressure) of the air molecules, followed by one half-cycle of rarefaction (lower pressure) of the molecules. If graphed or converted to an electrical signal and displayed on an oscilloscope, the height of the wave from top to bottom is called the *amplitude*. Amplitude corresponds to the *volume* of the sound. The louder the sound, the greater the amplitude—the greater the extent of compression and rarefaction of the air.

The rate at which the air pressure fluctuates is called the *frequency* of the wave. In order to be classified as sound, waves of pressure in the air must fluctuate at a rate between 20 and 20,000 cycles per second (cps). Below this range, the waves are felt as discrete pulsations, rather than heard as sound; above this range, humans cannot perceive the waves at all (though animals such as dogs can).

Frequency corresponds to the musical attribute of *pitch*. Although pitch is a more complex attribute than frequency (it also involves amplitude), generally speaking, the higher the frequency, the higher the perceived pitch of the sound. The unit Hertz (abbreviated Hz; named for 19th-century physicist Heinrich Hertz) is used to indicate frequency in cycles per second:

20 Hz = 20 cps

Frequencies of 1,000 Hz or more are often expressed in thousands of Hertz, or *kiloHertz* (abbreviated kHz):

20 kHz = 20,000 Hz

The amount of time required for one complete cycle of a sound wave is called the *period* of the wave. The period of a wave is expressed in seconds per cycle, and is found by using the equation:

$$Period = \frac{1}{Frequency}$$

THE
YAMAHA
GUIDE TO
SOUND SYSTEMS
FOR WORSHIP
PAGE 23

For example, take a wave with a frequency of 20 Hz. The period is 1 ÷ 20; that is, one cycle of the wave lasts ¹⁄₂₀th of a second.

Sound waves travel through air at a speed of 1,130 ft/sec (344 m/sec)—at sea level, at a temperature of 59° F (15° C). The speed of sound is independent of frequency. The physical distance covered by one complete cycle of a given frequency as it passes through the air is called the *wavelength*. Wavelength is expressed by the equation:

$$\text{Wavelength} = \frac{\text{Speed of Sound}}{\text{Frequency}}$$

Taking the example of a sound wave with a frequency of 20 Hz, the wavelength is 1,130 ÷ 20, or 56.5 ft (17.2 m). The wavelength of a sound wave with a frequency of 20 kHz is 1,130 ÷ 20,000, or about ¹¹⁄₁₆" (17.2 mm).

FREQUENCIES

Figure 3-2 shows the frequency ranges of a number of common musical instruments and singing voices. Notice that, except for the synthesizer, none of these extends even as high as 10 kHz. You might conclude from this that a sound reinforcement system used for music might not need to reproduce the highest part of the audible frequency spectrum. But you would be wrong.

What about the spoken voice? The chart doesn't cover this explicitly, but let's use the soprano singing voice to make an extreme case. The highest note a soprano generally sings is a high C, which has a frequency of 1,046.5 Hz. Surely, you might say, the microphones, etc., used to pick up *speaking* voices need not respond to frequencies any higher than this. Wrong again.

What these figures fail to take into account is that a sound wave at a given frequency is usually a composite of many different frequencies, some of which can be quite a bit higher than the basic, or *fundamental*,

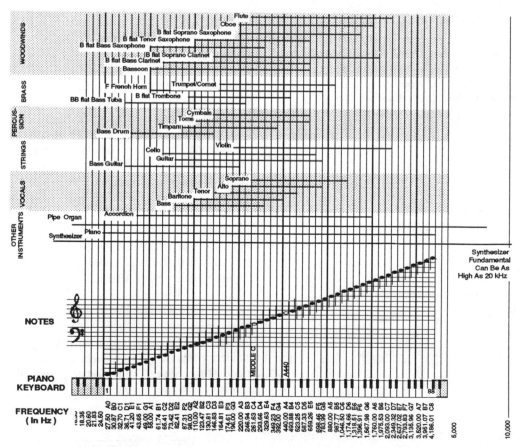

Figure 3-2. Frequency ranges of typical instruments and singing voices.

THE
YAMAHA
GUIDE TO
SOUND SYSTEMS
FOR WORSHIP
PAGE 24

frequency of the wave. These component frequencies are called *partials*, or *harmonics*.

Harmonics are what make a violin sound different from a saxophone, even when playing the same pitch at the same volume. In music this difference is called *timbre*, or *tone color*. Different harmonics are also responsible, in part, for the different vowel and consonant sounds that make speech intelligible.

The sound wave depicted in Figure 3-1 is described parenthetically as a *sine wave*. It is so called because its shape is an expression of the sine function in trigonometry. The sine wave is unique among waves in that it consists solely of one frequency—the fundamental—without any higher harmonics (overtones).

Since this is the case, more complex waves can be described as combinations of sine waves of different frequencies and amplitudes. Different combinations of sine waves result in different *waveforms*.

The precise amplitude relationships among the sine-wave components of sound determine the sound quality. For this reason, the *frequency response* of the components in a sound system—the range and accuracy with which they handle different frequencies—is of great importance. In particular, a lack of response to high frequencies can render the sound dull or muffled.

Some musical instruments produce partials with frequencies beyond the human limits of audibility (which range from 16 kHz to 20 kHz in young or sensitive ears), and it is not uncommon for speech to produce frequencies up to 8 kHz and higher

AUDIO SIGNALS

An *audio signal* is an electrical representation of a sound, in the form of a fluctuating voltage or current. In a sound reinforcement system, sound (acoustical energy) is converted into audio signals (electrical energy) so it can be amplified and/or distributed elsewhere, and then it is converted back into sound.

Within the limits of audio equipment, the signal voltage or current fluctuates at exactly the same rate as the acoustical energy that it represents, and then the amplitudes of the acoustical sound wave and the electrical audio signal are scaled proportionately.

The amplitude, or strength, of an audio signal is called the *signal level*. Many different signal levels exist in audio systems. Acoustical level is often expressed in terms of *sound pressure level* (SPL); electrical level is sometimes expressed in volts or watts, but more often in dBm or dBu (more about which shortly).

PHASE

The time relationship of a sound wave (or an audio signal) to a known time reference is called the *phase* of the signal. Phase is expressed in degrees. One complete cycle of a wave equals 360°. (The reason for this lies with the mathematics that describe the sine wave and relates to the 360° of a circle.)

The time reference may be an arbitrarily chosen, fixed instant in time. For example, Figure 3-3 shows a sine wave. The phase of this wave is expressed on the graph in relationship to a time reference called T_0. This happens to be the start time of the wave, although it could be designated at any time within the wave's period.

The time reference may also be another signal. If it is, the reference signal must resemble the signal whose phase is being measured; you can meaningfully compare only objects that are alike, or at least related.

Phase is extremely important in sound systems. The main reason that phase must be controlled is that it affects how sounds add together.

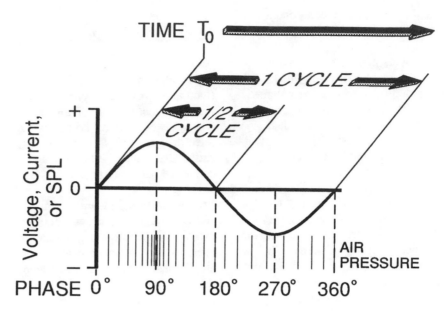

Figure 3-3. Representation of an audio signal (one cycle of a sine wave).

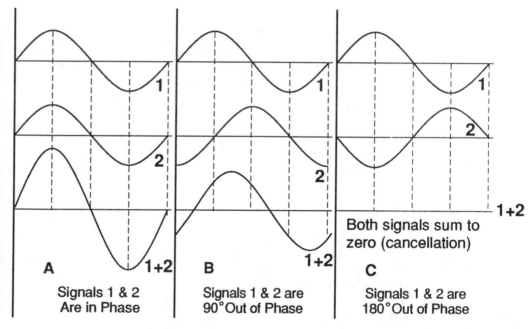

Figure 3-4. Phase affects the way two waves add together.

When audio signals are mixed in a console, or when sound waves mix in the air, they add algebraically. Figure 3-4 shows the effect of phase on the addition of two sine waves of equal level and frequency, but at different phase relationships.

In Figure 3-4A, the sine waves are *in phase* (both cross zero at the same time, going in the same direction); they add to form a sine wave of twice the level of either one. In 3-4B, the sine waves are 90° *out of phase*; they add to form a sine wave that is 1.414 ($\sqrt{2}$) times higher in level than either one. In 3-4C, the sine waves are 180° out of phase; they totally cancel one another.

Phase-related reinforcement or cancellation can be troublesome. It can occur among audio signals, as when two microphones pick up the same sound source from different distances, and the audio signals are combined in the mixing console. It can also occur acoustically, such as when two loudspeakers send sound to the same seating area from different distances, or when direct and reflected sound combine (see Figure 1-1, page 3).

Polarity is sometimes confused with phase. But phase involves time, while polarity does not. Polarity refers to the positive-and-negative relationship between the audio

THE
YAMAHA
GUIDE TO
SOUND SYSTEMS
FOR WORSHIP
PAGE 26

signal and the sound that it represents. Normally, the electrical signal will be positive when the air in front of the loudspeaker or mic is compressed and negative when it is rarefied (see Figure 3-3). But it is possible for this polarity to be reversed, so that a negative voltage or current represents high air pressure, and a positive voltage or current represents low air pressure. This might occur purposely within some audio equipment, or unintentionally, as when the wires to a loudspeaker are accidentally reversed.

Reversed polarity of one stereo speaker will result in bad imaging and degraded low-frequency response.

Although polarity is different than phase, they have this in common: *For symmetrical waveforms* (ones in which the top and bottom are mirror images of one another), *a reversal of polarity is equivalent to a 180° shift in phase*. Thus, combining a signal of correct polarity with one of inverted polarity can result in signal cancellation (see Figure 3-4C).

DECIBELS

Frequency is measured in cycles per second; wavelength in feet, inches, or meters. What is the measurement of the amplitude of a sound wave? Although there is such a measurement (dynes/cm^2), it is cumbersome to use in ordinary discussions of sound. More practical is a means of comparing the strength of one sound to another. The basic unit for this is called a *Bel* (named after Alexander Graham Bell, inventor of the telephone). It represents a ratio—a comparison—between two power levels, rather than an absolute value. The Bel is defined as the logarithm of the ratio of two powers. One Bel happens to correspond to a *perceived* difference of about two times (or one half) the sound level.

Since the measurement of ordinary levels of sound calls for finer divisions than "twice as loud," the Bel is usually divided into tenths—units called *decibels* (abbreviated dB).

When measuring sound pressure level (SPL), the reference point for decibels is usually

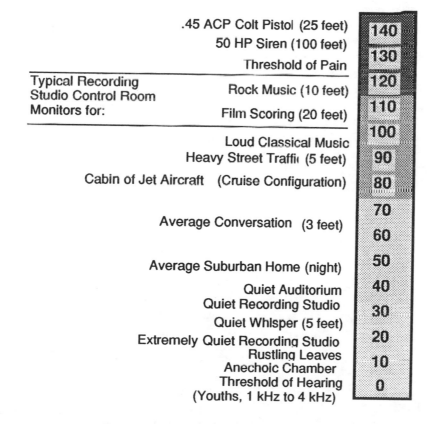

Figure 3-5. Typical sound pressure levels of various sources (at indicated distances from the ear, where appropriate).

the "threshold of hearing"—theoretically, the softest sound that can be heard by very sensitive ears. This is called 0 dB SPL, and all other levels are measured in relation to it. While 10 dB is "twice as loud," one dB is the smallest difference between two sounds that most people can detect. Figure 3-5 shows typical values of dB SPL for different sounds.

Like phase angle, the decibel does not express an absolute value if applied to an isolated signal; there must be something against which to compare. Since this is the case, the decibel can be (and is) used to measure electrical signal levels, as long as the 0 dB point is set in relation to a specific level. This has led to a number of different standards of measurement: dBm, dBV, dBv (not the same as dBV), and dBu (the same as dBv). It is beyond the scope of this book to define these units; suffice it to say that a value of 0 dBm is only the same as 0 dBu (the two most common systems in pro audio equipment) when the actual circuit impedance is 600 ohms. In all of these standards, the zero point does not mean "nothing;" rather, it means "no difference from the reference wattage (or voltage)."

When you double the power of a signal, you increase the level by 3 dB. When you double the voltage, you increase the power by four times, which corresponds to a 6 dB increase. Observe that doubling the power and doubling the voltage produce different dB changes. Notice that "dB" is the unit of measurement here, not dBm, etc. This is because the ratio in these cases is between the two signals, irrespective of their absolute values.

INVERSE SQUARE LAW

The farther you are from a sound source, the lower the sound pressure level that reaches your ears. This is because the greater the distance, the larger the area over which the sound is "spread out." The *inverse square law* describes the mathematical relationship between level and distance. The law assumes a point source of sound (omnidirectional radiator) and free-field conditions (no reflective boundaries).

The inverse square law states that the intensity of the sound varies inversely according to the square of the distance. For example, twice the distance means one fourth the intensity (power). In the discussion of decibels it was revealed that doubling the power increases the level by 3 dB. By extension, halving the power *decreases* the level by 3 dB; and cutting the power to one fourth decreases the level by 6 dB. Therefore:

For each doubling of the distance from the source, the measured sound pressure will drop by 6 dB.

For example, if the continuous output of a loudspeaker measures 100 dB SPL at 10 feet, then at 20 feet the sound pressure level will be 94 dB (100 – 6 = 94).

A 6 dB difference in SPL corresponds to a sound pressure ratio of 2:1. (Notice, the power ratio is $\frac{1}{4}$th, or 4:1, while the sound pressure ratio is 2:1; this is analogous to the relationship between wattage [power] and voltage [pressure] described at left.) But this is not a 2:1 loudness ratio; a 10 dB (1 Bel) difference represents a 2:1 change in loudness. Therefore, if you are twice as far from a point source as another observer, the sound will be a little more than half as loud for you as it is for that observer.

The inverse square law helps to explain why loudspeakers in many worship facilities are elevated, rather than being placed near the floor (and the front row of the congregation): If you call the distance from the loudspeaker to the nearest listener D1, and the distance from the loudspeaker to the farthest listener D2, the smaller the ratio between D1 and D2, the less the difference in loudness of the sound. One way to minimize the ratio is to move the loudspeaker up, thus increasing D1 considerably and D2 only slightly.

THE
YAMAHA
GUIDE TO
SOUND SYSTEMS
FOR WORSHIP
PAGE 28

BOUNDARIES

The walls, ceiling, and floor of a room are, to some extent, both flexible and porous to sound. Figure 3-6 shows what happens when a sound wave strikes such a boundary surface.

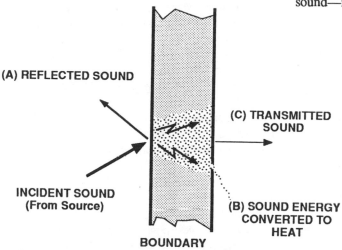

(A) REFLECTED SOUND

(C) TRANSMITTED SOUND

**INCIDENT SOUND
(From Source)**

(B) SOUND ENERGY CONVERTED TO HEAT

BOUNDARY

Part of the wave energy is *reflected* (A). The percentage of the energy that is reflected is related to the stiffness of the surface.

Wave energy that is not reflected enters the boundary. Part of this energy is *absorbed* (B) by the boundary through conversion into heat. The remainder (C) is *transmitted* through the boundary. Effects A and B are both related to the flexibility and porosity of the boundary.

When sound strikes a smaller obstacle (not a wall or ceiling, but perhaps a pulpit or podium), it bends around the object. This is known as *refraction*, and is shown in Figure 3-7.

Refraction, reflection, transmission, and absorption are all dependent on the frequency of the sound wave and the angle at which it strikes the boundary. (For example, low-frequency sounds, which have long wavelengths, are more likely to "bend around" the edge of an obstacle than are midrange or high-frequency sounds.) The effect is not generally dependent on the intensity of the sound.

Figure 3-7. Effect of boundary surfaces on sound refraction.

THE ABSORPTION COEFFICIENT

In architectural acoustics, a measure of the energy lost when a sound wave strikes a given material is specified by the *absorption coefficient* of the material. An open window—which does not reflect any sound—is defined as the perfect absorber, with a coefficient of 1 (100%). Similarly, the perfect reflective surface has a coefficient of 0.

The unit of measurement for acoustic absorption is the *sabin*, so named to honor the work of Professor W.C. Sabine, who did much early work on the relationship between acoustic absorption, reverberation time,

Figure 3-6. Effect of boundary surfaces on sound reflection and transmission.

and speech intelligibility. One sabin is equal to one square foot of 100% absorptive surface, such as an open window. The absorption coefficient of any material is thus a number between 0 and 1, and is readily converted into a percentage.

The relationship between the absorption coefficient of a boundary material and the intensity of the reflected sound wave is simple to calculate. Say, for example, that a given boundary material has an absorption coefficient of 0.15. This means that 15% of the sound is absorbed by the material. Therefore, 85% (100% − 15%) of the sound is reflected. The drop in level is calculated by applying a logarithmic function (10 log) to the figure of 85%: 10 log 0.85 = −0.7 dB. The reflected sound pressure is 0.7 dB lower than the incident sound pressure.

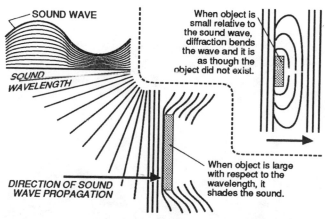

SOUND WAVE

SOUND WAVELENGTH

When object is small relative to the sound wave, diffraction bends the wave and it is as though the object did not exist.

DIRECTION OF SOUND WAVE PROPAGATION

When object is large with respect to the wavelength, it shades the sound.

THE
YAMAHA
GUIDE TO
SOUND SYSTEMS
FOR WORSHIP
PAGE 29

Figure 3-8 gives the absorption coefficients for a number of different typical boundaries. The coefficients for each material are given at different frequencies, since the effect varies with frequency.

MATERIAL	Frequency (Hz)		
	125	1k	4k
Brick Wall (18" Thick, unpainted)	.02	.04	.07
Brick Wall (18" Thick, painted)	.01	.02	.02
Interior Plaster (On metal lath)	.02	.06	.03
Poured Concrete	.01	.02	.03
Pine Flooring	.09	.08	.10
Carpeting (With pad)	.10	.30	.70
Drapes (Cotton, 2x fullness)	.07	.80	.50
Drapes (Velour, 2x fullness)	.15	.75	.65
Acoustic Tile (5/8", #1 Mount*)	.15	.70	.65
Acoustic Tile (5/8", #2 Mount*)	.25	.70	.65
Acoustic Tile (5/8", #7 Mount*)	.50	.75	.65
Tectum Panels (1", #2 Mount*)	.08	.55	.65
Tectum Panels (1", #7 Mount*)	.35	.35	.65
Plywood Panel (1/8", 2" Air space)	.30	.10	.07
Plywood Cylinders (2 Layers, 1/8")	.35	.20	.18
Perforated Transite (w/Pad, #7 Mount*)	.90	.95	.45
Occupied Audience Seating Area	.50	.95	.85
Upholstered Theatre Seats (Hard Floor)	.45	.90	.70

* #1 Mount is cemented directly to plaster or concrete,
#2 Mount is fastened to nominal 1" thick furring strips,
#7 Mount is suspended ceiling w/ 16" air space above.

Figure 3-8. Approximate absorption coefficients of common materials.

Note that for midrange and high frequencies, an occupied audience area has an absorption coefficient close to 1 (complete absorption). This is why the presence of an audience can have an enormous effect on the acoustics of a room, and will provide a significant contrast with unupholstered seats on a hard floor. This fact can be very important to the design and setup of sound systems.

Also note that drapes, which are sometimes used to control the amount of reflection of the sound, are ineffective in absorbing low frequencies.

STANDING WAVES

One significant effect of hard boundaries is the formation of what are called *standing waves*.

When a sound at a given frequency strikes a reflective boundary in such a way that the waves of the direct sound line up with the waves of the reflected sound, a standing wave is formed. The wave crests (maximum pressure) combine and reinforce one another. The troughs (minimum pressure) also combine. The result is a stationary pattern in the air, consisting of zones of low pressure (called nodes), alternating with zones of high pressure (called antinodes).

Walking through such a standing wave zone, you can easily identify physical places where the sound is very loud, and others where it is very soft. Their position in space is related to the wavelength, and therefore the frequency, of the sound.

Good acoustical design takes into account the *resonances*, or *modes*, of a room, which emphasize certain frequencies and can generate standing waves, and strives to minimize them through the use of nonparallel walls and various types of absorptive treatments. One of the most effective and simple treatments is to hang drapes. Absorptive material hung at a point ¼ wavelength from the reflective surface will have far greater effect on the standing wave than its absorption coefficient would indicate.

THE
YAMAHA
GUIDE TO
SOUND SYSTEMS
FOR WORSHIP
PAGE 30

REVERBERATION

Another substantial effect of boundary reflection is *reverberation*. Reverberation is a "wash" of sound that is created by multiple reflections, and is distinguished from discrete echoes.

Ignoring for the moment any standing-wave resonances or focused reflections, the reverberant field of sound in a room can generally be said to be of the same intensity at all points in the room, regardless of the distance from the sound source. When the sound source stops producing sound, this ambient sound takes time to die out. This decaying of the sound is what we perceive as reverberation. The amount of time that it takes for the acoustical energy to drop by 60 dB is called the decay time, or reverberation time, and is expressed as RT_{60}.

The length and spectral characteristics of the decay (that is, whether certain frequencies take longer to decay than others)—together with any resonances—form the acoustic signature, or characteristic sound, of a room. These factors are determined by the absorptive qualities of the room boundaries, and by the volume and shape of the room.

Relatively short to moderate reverberation with a smooth spectral characteristic is perceived as pleasant, natural, and musical. Moderate reverberation can enhance some types of music, though it will degrade speech clarity (or intelligibility). Excessive reverberation not only makes it difficult to understand speech, it can destroy the texture and impact of music. Most of us have strained to understand an announcement in a large, hard-surfaced gymnasium, arena, or transportation terminal—not because it wasn't loud enough, but because there was too much reverberation. Turning up the volume in such cases does not help at all.

CRITICAL DISTANCE

It was noted at left that a sufficiently excited reverberant field has uniform intensity throughout the space. Then what relevance does the inverse square law have?

To answer this question, you must distinguish between the direct sound (the initial sound emitted by the source) and the reverberant sound. The inverse square law applies to the direct sound; that is, the farther away you are from the sound, the less intense the sound will be. But it does not apply to the reverberant sound.

Therefore, close to the source, the direct sound will predominate. But at a certain distance from the loudspeaker (after the sound has existed long enough to reverberate), the intensity of the direct sound falls off to the point where it equals that of the reverberant sound. Ultimately, at a sufficient distance from the loudspeaker, the reverberant sound is predominant and swamps out the direct sound.

The distance from the sound source to the point at which the intensity of its direct sound equals that of the reverberant sound is called the *critical distance*.

You can increase the critical distance by using a directional loudspeaker instead of an omnidirectional one. If you concentrate the power of the system along a given axis that corresponds to an absorptive area (such as a seating area), the direct sound will predominate over a longer distance along that axis. Sound energy is concentrated more in a forward direction, with less energy radiated toward the sides, and hence less energy to reflect from walls, ceiling, floor, etc., so that the reverberant field does not receive as much of the loudspeaker's energy.

Since a directional loudspeaker's power decreases the farther you move off-axis, you will gain critical distance on-axis at the expense of the off-axis critical distance. The real benefit of the directional loudspeaker is that it increases the direct level in a portion of the environment.

This is a fundamental reason why directional loudspeakers are the norm in sound reinforcement. If you can maximize the system's critical distance, you have the best chance of maintaining intelligibility over the greatest distances.

THE
YAMAHA
GUIDE TO
SOUND SYSTEMS
FOR WORSHIP
PAGE 31

PREFERRED ACOUSTICAL ENVIRONMENTS FOR SPEECH AND MUSIC

Acousticians have developed methods for calculating the behavior of speech reinforcement systems in relation to critical distance, direct-to-reverberant ratios, and other aspects of hall acoustics. These methods are used routinely by consultants and contractors to design such systems. But once you enter the realm of music reinforcement, individual taste and subjective impressions often take precedence over such quantitative judgments.

A few general statements can nevertheless be made regarding reverberation time. First, there is no single ideal reverberation time; different types of program material call for different lengths of reverberation in order to sound best. Organ music may require a relatively long reverberation time—2.5 seconds or more—while speech is most intelligible with a much shorter time—less than 1 second. In between these extremes fall choral music, congregational singing, and music played on a piano or by a small ensemble, in order from longer to shorter.*

Second, worship is a participatory activity and not a "spectator sport." Some degree of reverberation not only benefits the sound of congregational singing (aiding in the blending of voices), it also encourages participation by helping the participants to hear each other.

A "compromise" reverberation time may be the most realistic solution, where possible—somewhere in the area of 1.5–2 seconds. (Keep in mind that, in order to obtain this reverberation time with a roomful of people, the reverberation time of the empty room will have to be longer.) The sound reinforcement system could then aid in making speech intelligible by directing the sound primarily at the congregation, not at any reflective surfaces. Furthermore, it could augment the acoustical reverberation

---

* Rollins Brook and Ted Uzzle, "Rooms for Speech, Music, and Cinema," in *Handbook for Sound Engineers*, ed. Glen Ballou (Indianapolis: Howard W. Sams & Co., 1987), pp. 182-183.

with electronic reverberation, in those situations where longer times would be appropriate. In one elaborate auditorium, acoustically porous walls and ceilings hide acoustic draperies that are electrically drawn, on command, to alter the reverberation time of the space to best suit speech or music.

ACOUSTICAL FOCUSING AND SCATTERING

The reflections generated in a room can be divided into two broad categories: *focused* and *diffuse*. Focused (or *specular*) reflections are discrete, separate echoes, and usually bounce back from flat surfaces, such as walls or ceilings. Diffuse reflections are tightly packed and random in direction. They can result from either multiple reflections off of boundaries or reflections from irregular surfaces. They are the basis of reverberant sound.

Focused reflections are problematic for both speech and music; they compromise the intelligibility of the former and the clarity of the latter, making listening fatiguing. The exception to this rule is when focused reflections occur within 30 to 40 milliseconds or so of the direct sound. Within this time, called the *fusion zone*, the listener perceives the direct and reflected sound as one event, rather than two; the sounds are "fused" together. This can actually enhance the sound, especially by making it seem louder.

Diffuse reflections are more beneficial to music than to speech (indeed, they can interfere with the intelligibility of speech), for they add to the impression of "warmth" and "space." As mentioned in Chapter 2, there is a trend in acoustic design that uses diffusing surfaces where once absorptive ones would have been used. Convex surfaces can help here, depending on the material and shape of the surface, but the greatest attention recently has been focused (or rather, scattered!) on surfaces specially designed with "grooves" or "wells" of different depths, based on complex mathematical equations.

THE
YAMAHA
GUIDE TO
SOUND SYSTEMS
FOR WORSHIP
PAGE 32

ELECTRO-ACOUSTICAL "TREATMENT" FOR ACOUSTICAL PROBLEMS

The best way to avoid acoustical problems is to have a capable acoustician involved in the design of the building. For existing buildings, the advice of an acoustician should be sought before the responsible committee decides that a more powerful sound system is needed; such a system might exacerbate problems that are best remedied acoustically—especially by the knowledgeable use of the right materials for boundary surfaces.

Once the acoustic solutions have been exhausted, however, a well-designed sound system can be called upon to control some of the inadequacies in the acoustics of the room. What follows is a brief collection of typical problems and possible solutions.

CERTAIN FREQUENCIES ARE LOUDER THAN OTHERS

In the discussion of standing waves earlier in this chapter, the idea of resonances, or room modes, was mentioned. Simply put, every room has certain frequencies that it tends to emphasize above others. Before taking any electro-acoustical action to correct such a problem, the first step is to try changing the placement or direction of the loudspeakers; this may solve the problem. Sometimes "holes" in the sound may require physical reinforcement of room walls that are diaphragmatically radiating sound out of the room.

If moving the loudspeakers fails, or if it is impractical to move them or rebuild the room, *equalization* can be used to compensate for the acoustics of the room. See Chapter 7 for more on this subject.

WEAK OR UNINTELLIGIBLE SPEECH

Perhaps the most basic task of sound systems for worship is reinforcement of the spoken word. A microphone placed on the lectern or pulpit, or a lavalier on the speaker's person, captures the sound so that it can be amplified and directed at the listeners via loudspeakers.

TOO MUCH REVERBERATION

Large buildings can have lengthy reverberation times—which may be fine for organ or choral music, but too long for clear speech. Placing the loudspeakers closer to the ears of the hearers can help in such cases. Loudspeakers placed at intervals down the sides of the room are the most common (not necessarily the most desirable) solution, though in extreme cases, speakers can be placed in the backs of the pews themselves. The level of the sound need not be high, since the speakers are close to the listeners; consequently, not much acoustic energy "spills" onto walls and ceiling to excite a reverberant field.

NOT ENOUGH REVERBERATION

The lack of reverberation is perhaps more common these days than the excess of it, especially as the number of small suburban congregations has risen. Electronic reverb can serve to augment the acoustic reverberation in such cases. It must be kept in mind, however, that in order for a sound to be affected by electronic reverb, it must first find its way into the sound system. This means that the organ and the choir, for example, may need to be miked (an electronic organ can be fed directly into the system, without need of a microphone).

A more elaborate (and expensive) version of this is referred to as *electronic architecture*, or *enhanced resonance*. By utilizing strategically placed microphones and loudspeakers, along with quality signal delays and reverberation devices, the apparent reverb time and size of the room can be electronically altered. Such a system is installed in addition to the house sound reinforcement system.

SLAPBACK ECHOES

Focused reflections can be more obtrusive to listening than excessive reverberation. Installing absorptive or diffusing surfaces is naturally the first course of action, though there can be cases—perhaps the most common is the rear wall made of glass—where this is not an option. The primary electro-acoustic solution lies in aiming the loudspeakers so that as much of the sound as possible reaches the congregation, and as little as possible reaches reflective boundaries.

POOR SOUND UNDER THE BALCONY

Sound under a balcony can be markedly lower in volume than elsewhere. Furthermore, depending on the placement of the main loudspeakers, midrange and high frequencies may be reduced more than low frequencies (the long low-frequency waves tend to refract around the edge of the balcony, rather than be blocked by it), resulting in a muffled sound. A "fill" system of loudspeakers aimed under the balcony is the solution here. Because of the distance from the main cluster and the different frequency response necessary, such a system should incorporate electronic delays and separate equalization. Chapter 7 discusses this in more detail.

THE CHOIR CAN'T BE HEARD CLEARLY

Why can't the choir be heard clearly? Is there too much reverberation? The reinforcement system can direct the sound to the listeners, rather than to the walls and ceiling (some acoustic treatment of the choir area may be used in conjunction with this). Is the choir overpowered by the organ? Amplification can help.

The same ideas can be applied to piano, small ensembles, or whatever musical forces might be employed.

FEEDBACK

Sometimes the sound system itself causes problems—beyond the elusive hums, buzzes, and crackles that seem to plague all audio equipment. One example of this is *feedback*. Feedback occurs when the sound picked up by a microphone is reproduced by a loudspeaker at a level that causes the sound to find its way back to the microphone, where it is *fed back* into the sound system, and the whole cycle repeats itself indefinitely. The result is a howling or squealing sound that can quickly reach overpowering levels if let go. Feedback usually occurs at frequencies that correspond to resonances of the room.

One of the goals in the operation of a sound reinforcement system is to produce the *maximum gain before feedback*—that is, to obtain as much usable power out of the system as possible, without causing feedback. To this end, three guidelines govern the placement and choice of equipment:

• Keep the distance between the microphone and the loudspeaker as large as is practical.

• Keep the distance between the microphone and the sound source as small as is practical.

• Use directional microphones and loudspeakers, placed so that their interaction is minimized.

The first two of these are self-explanatory. The directionality of microphones and loudspeakers will be discussed in the chapters devoted to those components.

Other means of controlling feedback are discussed in Chapters 5, 6, and 7.

THE
YAMAHA
GUIDE TO
SOUND SYSTEMS
FOR WORSHIP
PAGE 34

CHAPTER 4.
THE BLOCK DIAGRAM

GENERAL DISCUSSION

In order to take full advantage of the properties of any piece of equipment, you must understand how that equipment works—both in and of itself, and also in relation to any components to which it is connected. One important tool for gaining that understanding is the *block diagram.*

A block diagram is a graphic description of the signal path through a device. The block diagram treats the device as a system constructed of individual functional entities that are connected in a specific way. It employs simplified notation, representing the various functions of the device as single blocks.

The purpose of this method of notation is to present the logical structure of the equipment in a simple, readily accessible form.

Most manufacturers of active signal processing equipment (mixing consoles, delay lines, equalizers, and so on) provide block diagrams of their products. A block diagram may be found in the product data sheet (this is usually the case with complex equipment such as consoles), or it may be published in the instruction manual.

The block diagram is different, both in appearance and function, from another type of diagram called the schematic. Schematics present the component-level details of the actual circuitry of a device. The needs of the end user are generally best served by the block diagram, rather than the schematic. After all, he or she needs first to know how the equipment works, and how it can be used—not how it is constructed at the component level.

SYMBOLIC CONVENTIONS

The figures in this chapter show the symbols that are commonly used in block diagrams. Some of these symbols also appear in schematics.

In some block diagrams, you may see symbols other than those shown here. This may be because there is no convention for indicating what is shown in the diagram, or simply because the draftsman was feeling creative. Generally speaking, a responsible technical draftsman will label his drawings clearly, and provide a key to any nonstandard symbols.

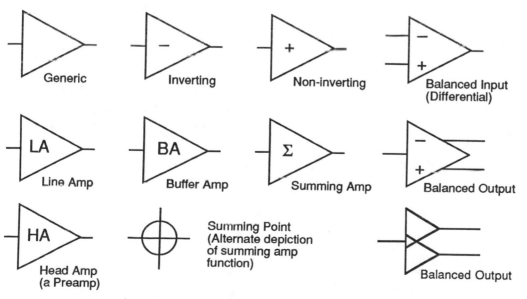

Figure 4-1. Block diagram symbols: amplifiers.

THE
YAMAHA
GUIDE TO
SOUND SYSTEMS
FOR WORSHIP
PAGE 35

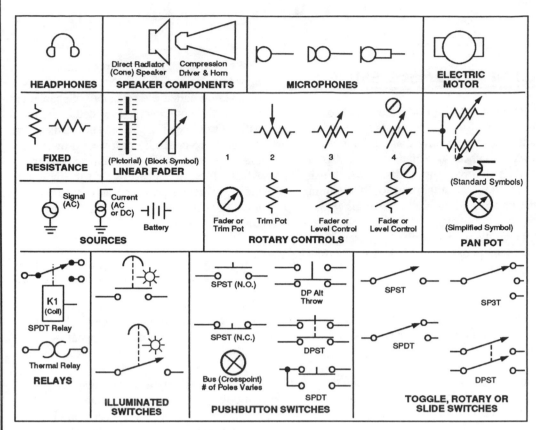

Figure 4-2. Block diagram symbols: miscellaneous components.

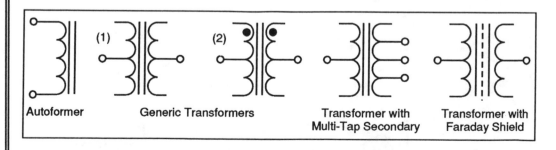

Figure 4-3. Block diagram symbols: transformers.

THE
YAMAHA
GUIDE TO
SOUND SYSTEMS
FOR WORSHIP
PAGE 36

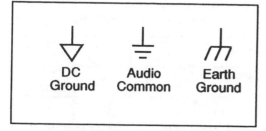

Figure 4-4. Block diagram symbols: grounds.

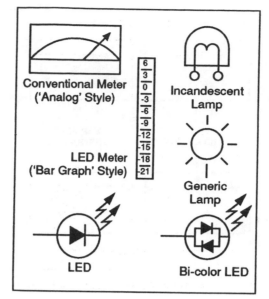

Figure 4-5. Block diagram symbols: indicators.

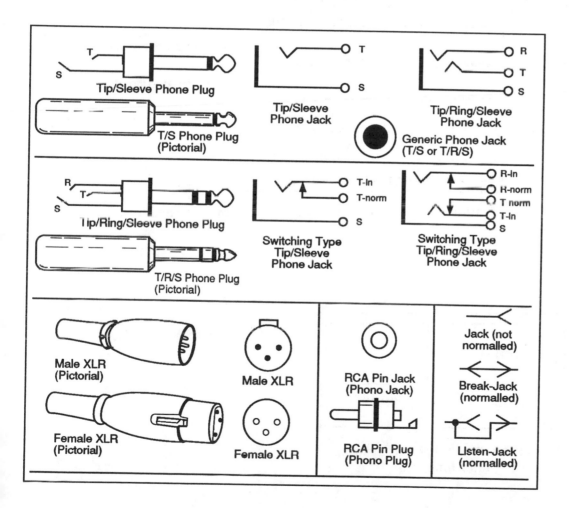

Figure 4-6. Block diagram symbols: connectors.

THE
YAMAHA
GUIDE TO
SOUND SYSTEMS
FOR WORSHIP
PAGE 37

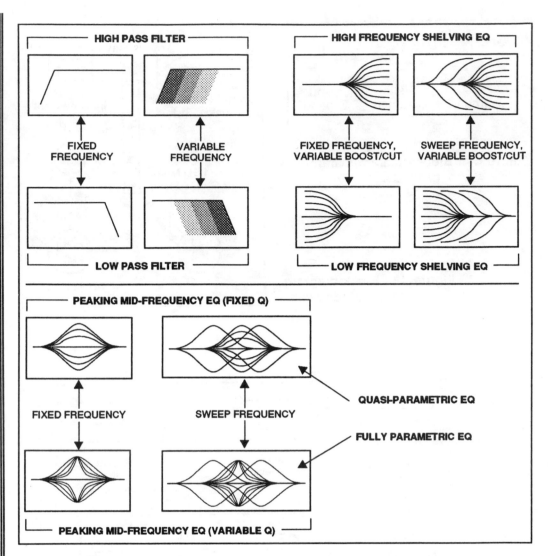

Figure 4-7. Block diagram symbols: filters and equalizers.

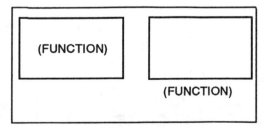

Figure 4-8. Block diagram symbols:
other functions.

THE
YAMAHA
GUIDE TO
SOUND SYSTEMS
FOR WORSHIP
PAGE 38

NOTATIONAL CONVENTIONS

Block diagrams are drawn to conform to the way Western languages are written: the signal flow is normally left to right and, as necessary, top to bottom. This practice is only violated in rare instances, and generally only for reasons of clarity, aesthetics, or economy of space.

Functional blocks, however they may be drawn, are connected with lines representing the signal path. Arrows may or may not be used to indicate the direction of signal flow; if the left-to-right rule is followed, they are not necessary.

Figure 4-9 presents some standard notational conventions. (Dotted lines indicate a mechanical connection—for example, a ganged level control.)

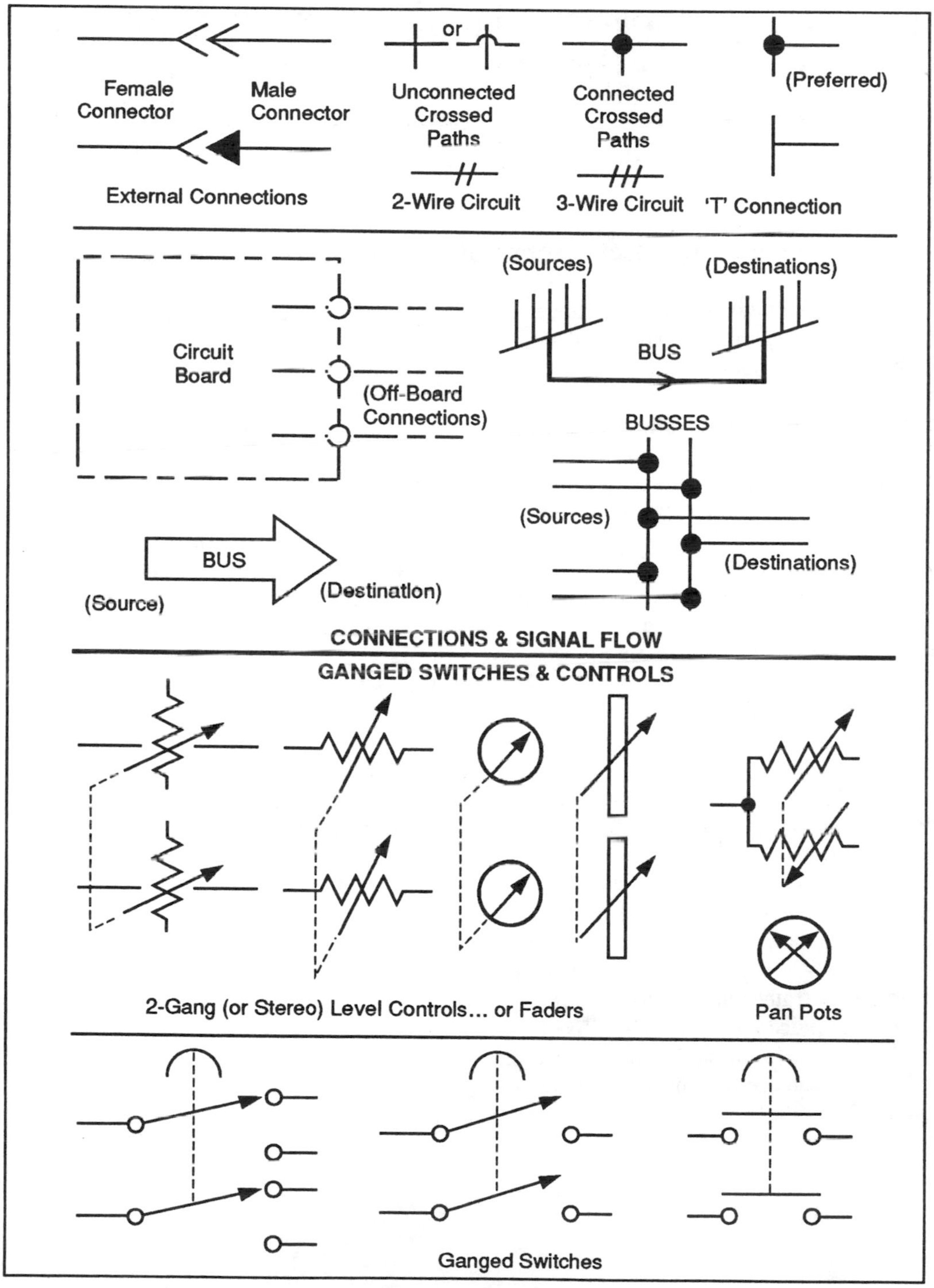

Figure 4-9. Block diagram notation.

ANALYSIS OF SIMPLE BLOCK DIAGRAMS

A MICROPHONE PREAMPLIFIER

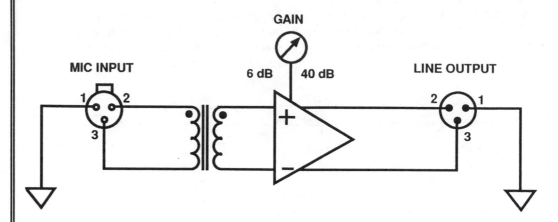

Figure 4-10. Block diagram of a microphone preamplifier.

From the block diagram of a microphone preamplifier in Figure 4-10, you can deduce a number of things about the unit.

Beginning from the left (following the convention for signal flow), you see first that the unit has an XLR-type input connector. Pin 1 is the ground connection.

Pins 2 and 3 of the input connector are both signal pins, and are connected to the primary winding of a transformer. The input is therefore transformer-isolated.

The secondary winding of the transformer is connected to a differential input amplifier (as indicated by the "+" and "–" amplifier connections; single-ended amplifiers are normally shown with just a single line going in and a single line going out, though differential input amps may be shown this way, too). A rotary gain control is shown, and from the way that it is drawn you can surmise that it directly controls the gain of the amplifier (rather than being a level control that precedes or follows a fixed-gain amplifier). From the labeling beside the control, you can see that the gain is variable from 6 dB to 40 dB.

The amplifier stage has a balanced output, and is not transformer-coupled, but rather drives the output connector directly.

This diagram gives you sufficient information to determine the input/output polarity of the preamp. Tracing from pin 2 of the input, note that it is connected to the "+" side of the transformer primary. The "+" side of the secondary is connected to the "+" input of the amplifier, and the "+" output of the amplifier is connected to pin 2 of the output connector. Likewise, pin 3 follows the "–" connections from input to output.

For this preamplifier, therefore, pin 2 of the XLR-type connectors is the "+", or noninverting, pin.

THE
YAMAHA
GUIDE TO
SOUND SYSTEMS
FOR WORSHIP
PAGE 40

A Graphic Equalizer

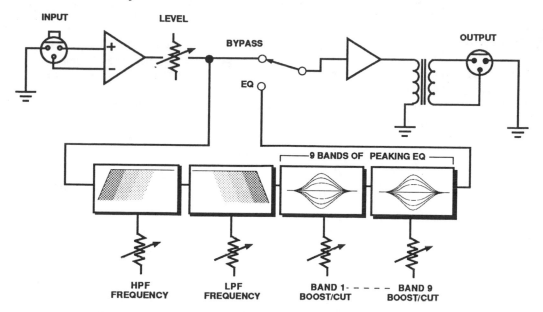

Figure 4-11. Block diagram of a graphic equalizer.

The graphic equalizer depicted in Figure 4-11 also uses XLR-type connectors, but the pins have not been labeled. Knowing the pin arrangement of such connectors, however, and knowing that pin 1 is always ground, you can deduce what the connections are.

Pins 2 and 3 are connected as the inputs to a differential amplifier, and no transformer is shown, so you know that this is an electronically balanced input. You do not know for certain that pin 2 is "high" and pin 3 is "low," but it appears so from the layout of the XLR. The input amplifier appears to have a fixed gain (although there is no indication of what that gain is), and is followed by a level control.

At this point the signal path splits, and one branch goes to the output amplifier, while the other goes to a side chain of filter stages. These are obviously the equalization stages, and they are shown connected in series.

The first is a high-pass filter with a variable cutoff frequency. While its frequency range is not shown, it seems reasonable to conclude that this stage is a variable low-cut acting on the lowest frequencies. (This you can check by looking at the data sheet.)

The high-pass filter is followed by a variable-frequency low-pass filter. This undoubtedly acts on the highest frequencies, functioning as a high-cut filter. Again, the

data sheet should give its frequency range.

The succeeding stages are the familiar bandpass stages of the graphic equalizer. Two are shown, with the dotted connecting line and accompanying bracket and label indicating that these are representative of nine stages, all presumably identical except for the range of frequencies in which they operate. Each is shown to have a single boost/cut control. While the block diagram does not indicate this, you might assume that the design uses sliders for these controls; this is another question that the data sheet or the front panel of the equipment will resolve.

The output of the last filter stage connects to the other pole of the switch that feeds the output amplifier. This is labeled "EQ/BYPASS." You can see the logic of its operation. The wiper of the switch connects to the output amplifier. In the BYPASS position (wiper up), the output amplifier sees only the signal coming from the input; it is assumed that signals do not "back up" in the signal path, so nothing from the filter stages moves into the circuit immediately after the level control. With the EQ/BYPASS switch in the EQ position (wiper down), the output amplifier sees the input signal after it has passed through the filter and EQ stages.

The output amplifier is shown using the simple, general symbol for an amplifier

THE
YAMAHA
GUIDE TO
SOUND SYSTEMS
FOR WORSHIP
PAGE 41

stage. You can make the assumption that it is noninverting, since there is no indication to the contrary. (This can be checked in the data sheet or instruction manual to verify signal polarity.)

The output amplifier drives a transformer, which is connected across pins 2 and 3 of the output connector (again, an XLR type), indicating that the output is balanced and transformer-coupled.

To trace the polarity of this device, you might make certain assumptions:

1. The output amplifier is noninverting.

2. The transformer is wired in phase (polarity is not indicated).

3. The EQ path is noninverting.

Given that these three assumptions are correct, you could conclude that the unit is noninverting and that pin 2 of the XLR-type connectors is taken to be the "+" pin.

But any one of the three assumptions above could be wrong. The fact is that this block diagram gives little information regarding polarity. For instance, many output amplifiers are inverting (the polarity is reversed as the signal passes through the amp), and sometimes pin 3 is the "+", or "high," connection in an XLR. Therefore, making assumptions can be misleading, and you should consult the data sheet or manual in order to learn what the input/output polarity of this device really is.

A DIGITAL DELAY UNIT

Figure 4-12 is the most simplified (but not the most simple) of the diagrams presented here. Neither the input connector nor the output connector is shown, and some of the blocks represent fairly complex functions. This block diagram, therefore, clearly concerns itself only with the logical structure of the device. Details such as connectors, input or output coupling, and input/output polarity and gain must (in most cases) be obtained from the specifications section of the data sheet or instruction manual.

Nonetheless, you can learn a great deal about the device from the block diagram.

The input is buffered by an amplifier whose gain is determined by a control marked "INPUT LEVEL." The buffer is followed by a low-pass filter, whose function presumably is to reject frequencies too high for the digital circuitry to deal with accurately.

After the low-pass stage, the signal path splits. One branch bypasses the bulk of the circuitry, and is connected to a control labeled "MIX." The other end of this control connects to the output of the main signal-processing chain, and the wiper of the control connects to the output block. You can therefore deduce that the control is used to vary the mix between the "dry" (unprocessed) signal derived just after the input high-pass filter and the "wet" (delayed) signal.

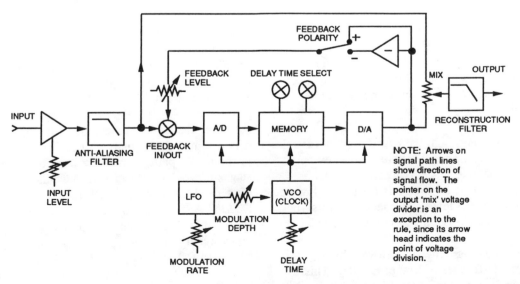

Figure 4-12. Block diagram of a digital delay unit.

THE
YAMAHA
GUIDE TO
SOUND SYSTEMS
FOR WORSHIP
PAGE 42

The other branch from the output of the low-pass filter connects to a switch that accepts a second input coming from farther down the line. The switch is labeled "FEEDBACK IN/OUT." You can see that the second input to the switch is a feedback path, then, and the switch allows you to select feedback if you want it.

The next block you encounter is a rectangle labeled "A/D." You know that this is a digital delay, so this must be the analog-to-digital converter. Hereafter, the audio signal is no longer analog (variations in voltage), but instead in the digital domain (a succession of numbers).

The output of the A/D converter (sometimes labeled "ADC") connects to a block labeled "MEMORY." This is where the actual delaying of the data occurs. (For more about digital delays, see Chapter 7.) Two switches connect to the block at the top, and are labeled "DELAY TIME SELECT." From this you can deduce that delay times are switched in ranges, by two front-panel switches.

The output of the MEMORY block connects to a block labeled "D/A." This is the digital-to-analog converter (sometimes labeled "DAC"). From here on, the signal is once again in the analog domain.

At the output of the D/A converter, the signal path splits again. One branch connects to the MIX control, analyzed earlier. The wiper of the MIX control connects to another low-pass filter, whose function you can assume to be to remove the digital clock frequency used by the memory so that it does not appear at the output. At this point, you have completed the main signal paths, but some branches remain to be analyzed.

The second branch from the D/A output splits once again, with one sub-branch connected to an inverting amplifier, which connects to a switch; the other sub-branch is a "feed forward" path around the inverter to the other pole of the switch. The switch is labeled "FEEDBACK POLARITY," and the two positions are labeled "+" and "−". You're following the feedback path, and the switch allows you to select between "in-phase" and "out-of-phase" (reversed-polarity) feedback. The feedback is used to generate multiple echoes, reverberation effects, or flanging, depending on the delay time.

The wiper of the switch connects to a control labeled "FEEDBACK LEVEL," which connects back to the "FEEDBACK IN/OUT" switch. You know, therefore, that you can control the amount of feedback, as well as defeat the feedback function, if you so desire. You also know that the signal flows right-to-left, due to the arrow on the line exiting the FEEDBACK LEVEL control.

All that remains to analyze is a side chain at the bottom of the diagram. This side chain provides the clock signal for the digital processing section of the device. It is not, therefore, an audio signal path: it is a control signal path.

The clock signal for all three digital blocks comes from a block labeled "VCO." The letters stand for voltage-controlled oscillator. You know, then, that the clock rate of this device, which controls delay time, is voltage-controllable.

You also see that there is a panel control associated with the VCO, labeled "DELAY TIME." Within ranges determined by the range switches, then, you have continuous control of the delay time.

Another signal path enters the VCO at the side. Tracing this path back, you see that it originates with a block labeled "LFO." The letters stand for low-frequency oscillator. This designation is normally reserved for oscillators designed to work at sub-audio frequencies (from as low as .001 Hz up to 20 Hz, or possibly as high as 100 Hz). This section is labeled "MODULATION." The LFO therefore provides a modulating signal for the clock VCO, varying the basic clock rate in a periodic pattern (from experience, you can assume the modulation wave to be a triangle waveform unless otherwise noted).

The LFO is connected to the clock VCO through a control labeled "DEPTH." This controls the amplitude of the modulating signal, and thus the extent to which it affects the clock rate. Lastly, you can see that the LFO frequency is varied with a panel control labeled "MODULATION RATE." (The presence of the VCO, LFO, and FEEDBACK LEVEL functions indicates that this is an effects delay [echo], as distinguished from the type of delay used to delay signal to, for example, an under-balcony speaker system.)

SUMMATION

Techniques similar to those used in the preceding examples can be used to analyze far more complicated block diagrams. The basic principles remain the same in all cases: read the signal flow left-to-right unless explicitly notated otherwise, and proceed logically through one path at a time.

Occasionally, some detective work will be necessary to ferret out the meaning of a symbol or a method of notation. This is the mark of a poorly made block diagram. But a little logical thought almost always is rewarded.

Some examples of mixer and console block diagrams can be found in Chapter 6.

The technique of block diagrams is easily extended to the diagramming of whole sound systems. Doing so often reveals potential problems. Furthermore, a good system diagram can be a handy aid in operating the system. An example of such a diagram is shown at the beginning of Chapter 13.

It may help you to trace the signal path using colored pencils or "highlighter" pens on a photocopy (not the original) of a function block diagram.

THE
YAMAHA
GUIDE TO
SOUND SYSTEMS
FOR WORSHIP
PAGE 44

CHAPTER 5.
MICROPHONES

Microphone is a generic term that is used to refer to any element that transforms acoustic energy (sound) into electrical energy (the audio signal). A microphone is therefore one type from a larger class of elements called *transducers*—devices that translate energy of one form into energy of another form.

Microphones can be categorized in different ways:

- By method of transduction;

- By functional design;

- By acoustical or electrical characteristics.

METHODS OF TRANSDUCTION

The fidelity with which a microphone generates an electrical representation of a sound depends, in part, on the method by which it performs the energy conversion. Historically, a number of different methods have been developed for varying purposes, and today a wide variety of microphone types may be found in everyday use.

DYNAMIC

By far the most common type of microphone in contemporary sound systems is the *dynamic*. The dynamic microphone is like a miniature loudspeaker, only it operates in reverse. A flexibly mounted diaphragm is coupled to a coil of fine wire; the coil is mounted in the air gap of a magnet so that it is free to move back and forth within the gap (see Figure 5-1).

When sound strikes the diaphragm, the diaphragm vibrates in response. This causes the coil to move back and forth in the field of the magnet. As the coil cuts through the lines of magnetic force in the gap, a small electrical current is induced in the wire. The magnitude and direction of that current are directly related to the motion of the coil, so that the current is an electrical representation of the original sound wave.

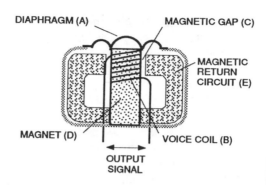

Figure 5-1. Construction of a dynamic microphone.

Dynamic microphones are highly dependable, rugged, and reliable. They are also reasonably insensitive to environmental factors, and so find use outdoors. Finally, moving-coil technology is refined to the point where dynamic microphones are capable of very good sonic characteristics.

CONDENSER

Next to the dynamic, the most common type of microphone is the *condenser*. Figure 5-2 illustrates the construction of a condenser element.

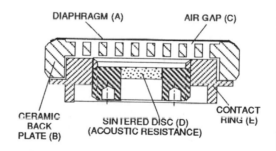

Figure 5-2. Construction of a condenser microphone.

A gold-coated plastic diaphragm is mounted above a conductive back plate, which is often made of gold plated ceramic. The diaphragm and back plate, separated by a small volume of air, form an electrical component called a capacitor, or condenser.

A polarizing voltage of between 9 and 48 volts is applied to the diaphragm by an external power supply, charging it with a fixed, static voltage. When the diaphragm vibrates in response to a sound, it moves closer to and farther from the back plate. As

THE
YAMAHA
GUIDE TO
SOUND SYSTEMS
FOR WORSHIP
PAGE 45

it does so, the electrical charge that it induces in the back plate changes proportionately. The fluctuating voltage on the back plate is therefore an electrical representation of the original sound wave.

Condenser microphone elements produce a signal voltage with almost no power. Thus they present a very high impedance. (For more on impedance, see page 51.) For these reasons, all condenser microphones incorporate an amplifier to drive the microphone line. Its function is both to boost the level of the signal and to isolate the condenser element from the lower impedance of the input to which the microphone is connected.

Because the diaphragm of a condenser is not loaded down with the mass of a coil, it can respond very quickly and accurately to sound. Condensers therefore generally have excellent sonic characteristics, and are widely used in recording. Being somewhat more sensitive to physical shocks and environmental factors such as humidity, however, classic condensers are less often used in live sound systems.

ELECTRET CONDENSER

The *electret* is a special class of condenser microphone. Electrets incorporate diaphragms made of a plastic material that retains a static charge indefinitely. The manufacturer charges the diaphragm when the element is made, so no external polarizing voltage is required.

Electrets still require a built-in amplifier, however, which is often powered by a battery—between 1.5 and 9 volts—housed in the microphone case. In some designs, the amplifier and battery are housed in a small case that is connected to the microphone proper by a cable. And increasingly, electret condenser microphones are being designed to use phantom power (see pages 55–56) rather than a built-in battery.

Electrets are increasingly common in both live sound systems and recording. Because they can be made very small, electrets make possible some unique close-miking techniques. The technology is also relatively inexpensive. Electrets can also be of high quality.

RIBBON

Ribbon microphones employ a method of transduction similar to that used in dynamic microphones. A very light, thin, corrugated metal ribbon is stretched within the air gap of a powerful magnet. The ribbon vibrates in response to a sound, inducing a voltage.

The voltage is very small and the ribbon impedance very low, so all ribbon microphones incorporate a built-in transformer. The transformer serves the two functions of boosting the signal voltage and isolating the ribbon impedance from the load presented by the input to which the microphone is connected.

Ribbon microphones tend to be more fragile than dynamic or condenser units, so they are used primarily in recording studios. Ribbon microphones usually have excellent sonic characteristics.

CARBON

The *carbon* type is among the oldest microphone elements. The movement of the diaphragm varies the density of some pulverized carbon in a small container. This results in varying resistance to a voltage.

Carbon microphones are not known for excellent sonic characteristics, but they are rugged and quite inexpensive. (The standard telephone microphone element has long been a carbon type, though dynamic and electret mics are used in many newer phones.)

PIEZOELECTRIC

Another early microphone type is the *piezoelectric*. Here the diaphragm is connected to a crystal element. The crystal is of a material that exhibits the *piezoelectric* (pressure-electric) effect: When it is physically deformed by pressure or torsion, it generates a voltage.

Piezoelectric microphones (sometimes called *crystal*, or *ceramic*, types), like carbon types, are not generally known for their sound quality, but are quite inexpensive. Properly implemented, a crystal element can perform very well, and the principle is often used for contact-type pickups (see pages 47–48).

Piezo elements are high-impedance devices, and they produce substantial output levels. They can be damaged irreparably by physical abuse, and are susceptible to both heat and humidity.

THE
YAMAHA
GUIDE TO
SOUND SYSTEMS
FOR WORSHIP
PAGE 46

FUNCTIONAL DESIGN

In addition to the method of transduction and pickup pattern, microphones are further classified according to their functional design. Many designs are available, each optimized for a specific range of uses.

HAND-HELD

By far the most prominent microphone design is the *hand-held* type. As the name implies, this microphone is designed so that it can be held in hand by a speaker or a singer. Of course, such microphones are also very often mounted on a stand or "gooseneck" using a threaded mounting clip.

The most common pickup pattern (see pages 49–50) in hand-held microphones is the cardioid, although other patterns are available. Whatever the pickup pattern or type of capsule (sound generating element), if it's in a hand-held mic, it must be well isolated from physical vibration to prevent handling noise, and the capsule must be protected from being dropped. Rubber shock mounts and protective screens are standard features of most hand-held mics.

STAND-MOUNTING

Some microphones are designed specifically for stand (or boom) mounting. Microphones like this are most commonly made for recording, because elaborate isolation from shock and external vibration is then possible. Small, unobtrusive modern stand-mounting microphones are usually electret types, and are designed specifically for use in live and broadcast applications where appearance is a primary consideration.

LAVALIER

Lavalier microphones are small elements that are designed to pin directly to clothing (also called lapel microphones) or to be hung on a lanyard around the neck. They find wide application in houses of worship (often coupled with a wireless transmission system), because they are unobtrusive and give the speaker the freedom both to move around and to use his or her hands.

It used to be that lavaliers were nearly always dynamics, since they were inexpensive to build in the required small package. Modern lavaliers are almost always

electret types, since electret elements now can be made very small, offering excellent top-end (high-frequency) response and sensitivity for a reasonable cost.

The most common pattern for lavaliers is omnidirectional, although recently some cardioid and hypercardioid types have been introduced. The omni pattern has several advantages in this application. It does not emphasize the already resonant chest cavity because it does not have proximity effect (see page 51), and it can be clipped in different orientations without its sound quality changing. This is crucial if the sound is to remain consistent.

A major advantage of lavalier elements is that, since they are affixed to the speaker's person, the distance between source and microphone is constant and the sound quality therefore is more consistent. Lavaliers must be mounted with care to avoid extraneous noise from clothing.

CONTACT PICKUP

Contact pickups are microphone elements designed to detect sound waves in a solid medium, rather than in air. Contact pickups are usually piezoelectric devices, although the dynamic principle has also been used for this application. A recent type of contact transducer that has garnered considerable interest, especially for the amplification of pianos, uses the condenser principle, and comes in the form of a flexible strip.

Contact pickups are used almost exclusively for instruments. Their placement is critical. The complex resonances of instrument bodies result in radically different sound qualities in different locations, and considerable experimentation is necessary to achieve satisfactory results. The means by which they are affixed to the instrument can affect the sound quality and the instrument. A sticky wax is often used, since it can be removed without damaging the instrument.

Because contact microphones rarely yield a true sound quality, they are not often used in recording, except for special effects. In live sound systems, however, they offer exceptional resistance to feedback, though they can be susceptible to handling noise. When using a contact pickup on an instrument, try miking the instrument, as well. The pickup can provide gain before feedback while the microphone will give you a more natural, open sound.

THE
YAMAHA
GUIDE TO
SOUND SYSTEMS
FOR WORSHIP
PAGE 47

PRESSURE RESPONSE

The so-called *pressure response*, or "boundary," microphone is a fairly recent development, and is subject to patent and trademark restrictions. The commercial implementation of the principle is commonly called the PZM™, and is manufactured under a licensing agreement by Crown International, of Elkhart, Indiana. Figure 5-3 shows one of the Crown PZM™ units.

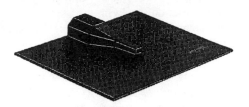

Figure 5-3. A Crown Pressure Zone Microphone (courtesy of Crown International Corp.).

The microphone is placed extremely close to and facing a flat plate. In theory, the microphone samples pressure variations in the tiny air gap between the element and the plate, rather than responding to air velocity.

Originally developed for recording and implemented using condenser elements, the pressure zone principle offers some benefits. Among these are good imaging qualities and, if the element is mounted on a floor or a wall, freedom from cancellations of certain frequencies stemming from different path lengths between sources and microphones. Low-frequency response is directly related to the size of the boundary plate—the larger the plate, the better the pickup of lows.

Pressure-zone microphones are sometimes used in live sound systems, but since their pickup pattern is inherently omnidirectional (or, more precisely, hemispherical; see "Pickup Patterns"), they offer little help with feedback. Recently, directional units have been developed to deal with this problem.

SHOTGUN

The *shotgun* microphone is a highly directional unit. Shotgun microphones are most often used in broadcasting and film work. Successful use of shotgun microphones in live sound reinforcement is rare.

PARABOLIC

The *parabolic* microphone is actually a conventional mic element coupled with a parabolic reflector that concentrates sound on the element. The microphone is thus both highly directional and highly sensitive. Parabolic microphones are widely used in nature recording and for broadcast of some sporting events. They are never used in sound reinforcement.

MULTI-ELEMENT ARRAYS

A few special microphones have been constructed using two or more transducer elements. Such units normally require auxiliary networks to control the combining of signals from the elements. The most widely used multi-element system is the *stereo recording microphone*, which incorporates two identical elements in one body.

NOISE-CANCELLING MICROPHONES

Noise-cancelling (or *differential*) microphones employ either two mic capsules wired in reverse polarity or a single diaphragm that is open on both sides to sound pickup. In such mics, distant sounds tend to produce equal pressures on both sides of the diaphragm (or both capsules) and thus are cancelled. This allows someone speaking into the microphone from a close distance to be heard, while any background noise is not. Such microphones are used primarily in noisy environments such as factories and airplane cockpits.

ACOUSTICAL AND ELECTRICAL CHARACTERISTICS

The acoustical and electrical characteristics of a microphone determine both the quality of its performance and its suitability for a particular application or system. No single factor predominates; all work together, and it is important to understand the range of qualities that may be expected in typical professional and semi-professional equipment.

THE
YAMAHA
GUIDE TO
SOUND SYSTEMS
FOR WORSHIP
PAGE 48

PICKUP PATTERNS

Microphones are classified not only by the method of transduction but also by the *pickup pattern*. The pickup pattern is the way in which the element responds to sounds coming in from different directions, and there are several different standard patterns. (This is akin to the polar response of a loudspeaker... in reverse. See Chapter 9.)

NOTE: Pickup patterns are shown as two-dimensional graphs on paper, but it is understood that they are actually three-dimensional. An omnidirectional pattern, for example, would be graphed as a circle, but actually is a sphere.

OMNIDIRECTIONAL

Omnidirectional elements, as their name implies, pick up sound more-or-less equally from all directions. (Typically, polar response will differ slightly in different ranges of the frequency spectrum.)

You might think that omnidirectional microphones are never used in live sound reinforcement systems, since they offer no protection from feedback (see Chapter 3, page 34). This is generally the case, but not entirely so. There is a myth that cardioids are better, but omnis have better low-frequency response and less susceptibility to breath and wind noise. Because omnidirectional mics tend to have much smoother frequency response than directional mics, there are fewer peaks to trigger feedback, so sometimes a good omni is as useful as (or more useful than) a mediocre directional mic. Lavalier mics are often omnidirectional.

CARDIOID

The *cardioid* is unreservedly the most popular of all microphone pickup patterns. Figure 5-4 shows a typical cardioid polar response pattern.

Note that the pattern is heart-shaped—hence the name "cardioid." As the figure clearly shows, the cardioid microphone is most sensitive to sounds coming in on the primary axis, and rejects sounds from the sides and rear of the microphone.

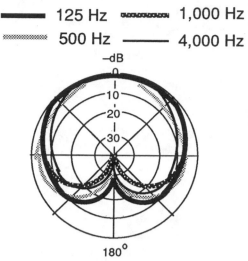

| —— 125 Hz | ····· 1,000 Hz |
| ······ 500 Hz | —— 4,000 Hz |

Figure 5-4. Polar pattern of a cardioid microphone.

The directional qualities of the cardioid make it a natural choice for use in worship, since they help in reducing feedback and increasing system gain (see "Feedback," page 34). This effect is overrated, and omnidirectional mics are often a better choice for close miking than cardioids. Cardioids tend to have more *coloration* when the sound does not arrive on axis, because their directional qualities vary with frequency. The choice is sometimes a subjective one, because often such coloration will benefit the sound, while at other times it will harm it.

Cardioids are common in recording, since they can be used to diminish unwanted sounds arriving off axis. Their frequency response is usually rougher than that of omnidirectional mics, and they are somewhat more sensitive to wind noise and breath popping.

BIDIRECTIONAL (FIGURE-8)

A somewhat more unusual but very useful pickup pattern is the so-called *figure-8*, or *bidirectional*. Figure 5-5 shows a typical polar response plot of a bidirectional element.

THE
YAMAHA
GUIDE TO
SOUND SYSTEMS
FOR WORSHIP
PAGE 49

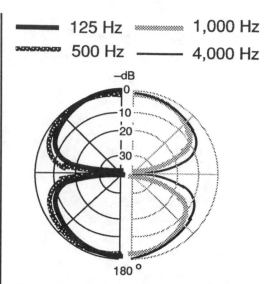

Figure 5-5. Polar pattern of a figure-8 microphone.

The derivation of the name for this pattern is obvious from Figure 5-5. Bidirectional elements are most sensitive to sounds coming in from the front or rear of the microphone, and reject sounds from the sides. Figure-8 microphones are useful in circumstances where pickup of two separate voices or instruments is desired.

SUPERCARDIOID, HYPERCARDIOID

The *supercardioid* is a highly directional microphone element. Figure 5-6 shows a polar response plot of a typical supercardioid microphone.

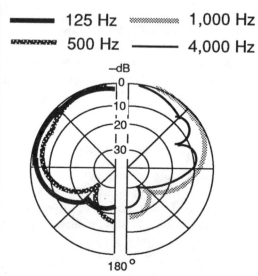

Figure 5-6. Polar pattern of a supercardioid microphone.

Note that, in contrast to the cardioid, the supercardioid does exhibit more of a rear pickup lobe, though small. It thus supplies far less rejection of sounds coming in

directly from the rear than does the cardioid. The forward pickup lobe is far more concentrated, and the supercardioid offers superior rejection of sounds coming in from the sides.

Supercardioids are used in special situations where greater side rejection is desired, but some rear pickup may be tolerated. Because of the concentrated forward lobe, they may also "reach" farther than a typical cardioid, and are sometimes used for pickup of distant sources.

Another highly directional microphone, called the *hypercardioid*, is similar to the supercardioid. It offers an even more concentrated forward lobe (and thus greater rejection of sounds coming in from the sides), at the expense of a larger rear lobe. This can be considered as being somewhere between a cardioid and a figure-8 response.

HEMISPHERICAL

The pickup pattern of a typical pressure response microphone is *hemispherical*, especially when such a microphone is placed on a boundary surface of some kind. Sound is picked up from all directions in front of ("above") the surface, while none is picked up behind ("below") the surface.

FREQUENCY RESPONSE

The *frequency response* of a microphone is a measure of the consistency with which it translates a given sound pressure level into a given audio signal level at different frequencies.

You could say that an ideal microphone would translate a given pressure level to the same signal level no matter what the frequency (within the limits of the audio band, or 20 Hz to 20 kHz). Such a microphone would be said to have flat frequency response.

While some microphones approach this ideal, most deviate from flat response. But this is not necessarily bad. With vocal microphones, it is not uncommon for response to fall off below about 100 Hz. Since the human voice is generally incapable of producing energy that low in frequency, the effect of this limitation is both to discriminate for voice frequencies and to help eliminate extraneous noise.

THE
YAMAHA
GUIDE TO
SOUND SYSTEMS
FOR WORSHIP
PAGE 50

Many microphones, especially vocal ones, exhibit a response peak in the upper frequencies, called a *presence peak*. This can help to increase the intelligibility of words, so it may be a desirable characteristic. But it can also increase the possibility of feedback.

It is most important, in the case of directional microphones, that the frequency response remain reasonably flat off-axis, although the sensitivity drops. Otherwise there will be a change in tone color if the person or instrument being picked up by the mic shifts off axis; this is known as *off-axis coloration*.

Variations in frequency response are a major factor governing the characteristic sound of a microphone. It is important that the sound of a mic be matched to the application and the sound source. You can get a clue from the spec sheet, but the ear is the best judge.

PROXIMITY EFFECT

Proximity effect is an increase in low-frequency response when a microphone is very close to the sound source, and is an inherent characteristic of directional microphones (omnis do not exhibit the effect). This can sometimes cause preamplifier overload, resulting in distortion. It can also destroy intelligibility, if the person speaking into the microphone is ignorant of it (a low-cut filter is usually an effective cure in this case). But exploited judiciously, it can add fullness to the sound of the voice.

TRANSIENT RESPONSE

Transient response is a measure of a microphone's ability to render very sharp, fast musical attacks and signal peaks. The main limitation on transient response is diaphragm mass, so condensers generally exhibit better transient response than even the best dynamics. For the same reason, the smaller the microphone, the better its transient response generally will be. As a rule, modern electret units (which have been getting smaller in recent years) have excellent transient response.

Transient response is not very important in vocal reproduction, but it attains great importance with percussive sources such as drums, piano, and plucked string instruments.

IMPEDANCE

Microphones are usually divided into two basic classes: *high-impedance* and *low-impedance*. These terms have to do with the output (source) impedance of the microphone, which is measured in ohms (symbolized by the Greek letter omega: Ω). Without going into the technical meaning of impedance, it can be said that most professional microphones are low-impedance devices (source impedance of 150 Ω or less). Piezoelectric contact pickups, guitar pickups, and inexpensive microphones usually are high-impedance (source impedance of 25 kΩ or more). The abbreviation Z, or Ƶ, is often used to indicate impedance.

Low-impedance microphones are preferred in live sound reinforcement and recording since, properly connected, they are far less susceptible to extraneous noise pickup in the cable. More important, low-impedance microphones can drive cables hundreds of feet long, whereas high-impedance mics are limited to cables about 20 feet long.

The source impedance of a microphone must be appropriate for the input of the device (such as a mixing console) to which the microphone is connected. Ideally, a microphone should be connected to a load whose input impedance is roughly ten times the source impedance of the microphone. (Thus a low input impedance would be 1,000-1,500 Ω, while a high input impedance would be 50-250 kΩ.) Where this is not the case (i.e., a high-impedance microphone or pickup connected to a low-impedance input, or vice versa), a *matching transformer* can be used to mate the two.

BALANCED AND UNBALANCED CONNECTIONS

An *unbalanced* connection is a two-wire system. One wire carries the audio signal, and the other (called the shield) is connected to ground, or the electrical reference point.

Unbalanced connections are used for high-impedance microphones and pickups, and sometimes for low-impedance mics in consumer equipment. The most common unbalanced microphone connector is the ¼" phone connector.

A *balanced* connection is a three-wire system. Two separate wires carry the signal—one inverted in polarity with respect to the other—and the third is the shield, which again is connected to ground.

Balanced connections are almost always used for low-impedance microphones. The balanced system is far more immune to noise, and is by far the preferred method in professional audio. The most common balanced connector is the three-pin XLR-type (or "Cannon plug," after the company that developed it).

SENSITIVITY, OVERLOAD

Microphones generate small signal levels when compared with line-level devices such as mixing consoles or tape machines. For this reason, a microphone requires a preamplifier to bring its output level up to line level. This function is normally included in the input section of the mixing console or recorder to which the microphone is connected. (This is not to be confused with the separate preamplifier found in condenser mics, which is really an impedance converter.)

The sensitivity of a microphone is defined by its output level for a given input sound pressure level. The more sensitive the microphone, the higher the output level at a given SPL. Generally speaking, the farther away the microphone is from the sound source, the greater the sensitivity of the microphone should be in order to pick up the sound adequately.

Distortion in a sound system is often blamed on microphone overload. In fact, it is rarely the mic that is overloading, but usually the preamplifier to which it is connected. This can be corrected by using an input "pad," or attenuator, to lower the signal to the preamplifier. Most quality mixers provide such a pad, either switch-activated or in the form of a continuous rotary control.

A good quality professional microphone should be able to withstand sound pressure levels of 140 dB SPL or more without overloading. This is sufficient for most applications. With condenser mics, the overload point will be reduced if a lower battery (or phantom power) voltage is applied. So microphone distortion in these cases might be cured by replacing the battery, or using a higher phantom power voltage, if permitted by the mic manufacturer.

MIKING TECHNIQUES

There are nearly as many techniques for using microphones as there are audio engineers to think them up. In the simplest situations, simple techniques suffice: to amplify or record the voice of a single speaker or singer, place a single microphone in front of his or her mouth. But beyond this, things become more complex, and call for a willingness on the part of the sound crew and the clergy, speakers, or performers to experiment with the choice and placement of microphones.

This section discusses some of the special cases that are often encountered in worship. In each of these—piano, choir, bell choir, and organ—monophonic recording or reproduction is assumed. Stereo techniques are handled in a separate section following these individual cases.

PIANO

There are many, many ways to mike a piano. Starting with the grand piano, the simplest is to use two mics, on booms extended into the piano. Place one over the bass strings and one over the treble. In spacing the microphones, remember the *three-to-one rule*: The distance from one microphone to the next should be at least three times the distance from the microphone to the sound source. This helps minimize phase cancellations due to different path lengths between the sound source and the microphones.

On a small grand, one mic might work. Omnidirectional mics can provide the best coverage, but cardioid mics, aimed at the sounding board, can help eliminate phase cancellations from reflections off the lid of the instrument.

Alternatives include pressure response microphones taped to the underside of the lid, or a strip-type contact pickup, often in combination with one of the above. Inductive pickups with the pickup coils suspended over the strings are also available. While somewhat cumbersome to install, these pickups probably offer the greatest gain before feedback possible from an acoustic piano.

An upright piano might be miked by opening the top and using a boom, as with the grand.

THE
YAMAHA
GUIDE TO
SOUND SYSTEMS
FOR WORSHIP
PAGE 52

But a visually less intrusive setup would be to place a mic on a short stand behind the piano, aimed at the sounding board.

CHOIR

The following suggestions constitute a realistic approach to the sometimes contradictory factors involved in miking a choir.

- Use unidirectional microphones. Cardioids work best for the distances suggested below.

- Use as few microphones as you can. A rule of thumb is to use one microphone for every 20–30 feet that the choir is wide, centering each microphone horizontally within the span that it is to cover. More mics than this can result in much double coverage of singers, with a resulting hollowness of sound due to phase cancellation.

- Place the microphone(s) at a height 1–2 feet above the heads of the singers in the last row, at a distance 2–3 feet in front of the singers in the front row. Aim them at the singers in the back row. (See Figure 5-7.)

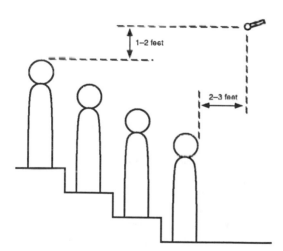

Figure 5-7. Miking a choir (side view).

BELL CHOIR

Bell choir differs from vocal choir in that the latter tends to be deployed in several rows once there are more than half a dozen or so participants, whereas the former is almost invariably stretched out in a single long line. Furthermore, while in vocal choirs several voices sing each part, in

handbell choirs no two performers play the same notes.

For these reasons, and because handbells are capable of producing some quite loud sounds, microphones should be placed farther away from a handbell choir than from a vocal choir — 4–5 feet at least.

The number and spacing of microphones can be figured using the same rule of thumb as for vocal choir (one for every 20–30 feet). This means that one microphone can be used for most bell choirs. With large groups, however, you may wish to try two widely spaced mics to see which setup produces the better results.

PIPE ORGAN

The pipe organ, like the handbells, is not miked for amplification, but rather for recording or to be piped into the cry room and other remote parts of the building. It should be miked from a greater distance than a choir — 10–20 feet — both to preserve the balance of the sound and to capture some of the reverberance of the room. Either directional or omnidirectional mics may be used, depending on how much reverberation you wish to pick up. The microphone(s) generally are suspended from the ceiling, and must be high enough to obtain a good balance of all the pipes.

If all of the pipes are located in one place, use one microphone; if they are separated into divisions that are physically removed from one another—for example, on opposite sides of the room—use one microphone for each such division.

Electronic organs can be treated similarly.

STEREO

Among the various techniques for stereo recording or reinforcement, three have emerged as the most common: the spaced pair, X-Y, and M-S methods.

The *spaced pair* is an extremely simple and successful technique. Two microphones are used, and these are placed on stands spaced 6–8 feet apart and 6 feet or so above the floor. Either omnidirectional or cardioid units may be used.

While the spaced pair can yield acceptable results, it is susceptible to problems

THE
YAMAHA
GUIDE TO
SOUND SYSTEMS
FOR WORSHIP
PAGE 53

associated with the different path lengths from sources to the two microphones. The *X-Y* technique represents an attempt to improve the stereo imaging.

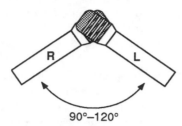

Figure 5-8. Stereo microphones in an X-Y configuration.

The technique requires two cardioid units, preferably with matched characteristics. The two are mounted on the same stand with a special mounting bar and angled at about 90°–120° from one another, with their diaphragms as close together as possible. Figure 5-8 illustrates this technique.

A variant to this so-called coincident technique is the *near-coincident* pair (see Figure 5-9). As developed by the French Office of Radio and Television (ORTF), the microphones are moved to about 6–7 inches apart. This arguably offers some improvement in the stereo image.

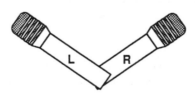

Figure 5-9. Near-coincident placement of microphones.

A third technique that is often used for recording for broadcast is the *M-S* method (an abbreviation for Mid-Side Stereophony). M-S recording requires one cardioid and one figure-8 element, placed with their patterns oriented as shown in Figure 5-10.

Stereo information is extracted from the mic signals by a matrix that produces a sum channel (the two added together) and a difference channel (the figure-8 signal subtracted from the cardioid signal). The technique is valued for broadcast because it retains mono capability: The sum of the two signals cancels the figure-8 signal, leaving only the cardioid signal.

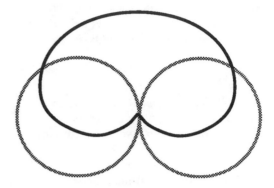

Figure 5-10. Sensitivity patterns of cardioid and figure-8 mics in an M-S stereo configuration.

APPLICATION INFORMATION

CHOOSING A MICROPHONE

There is no such thing as the perfect all-purpose microphone, simply because different applications call for different characteristics. Dynamic or condenser? Hand-held or lavalier? Unidirectional or omni? It depends on the use(s) you have in mind. The preceding sections have outlined the choices for you, as well as presented the basic considerations involved in making those choices.

WINDSCREENS AND POP FILTERS

Every microphone is, to some extent, susceptible to extraneous noise from breath pops (produced by P's and T's, for example) or, outdoors, from wind. For the most part, the effect of air noise is most pronounced with directional microphones.

Every microphone manufacturer provides some sort of windscreen, to protect the diaphragm of the microphone from noise. The most common modern type is made of acoustical foam. When these are built into the microphone, they often are covered by metal mesh for physical protection. Additional foam windscreens, which can be slipped onto the microphone, are often available as well.

THE
YAMAHA
GUIDE TO
SOUND SYSTEMS
FOR WORSHIP
PAGE 54

STANDS AND BOOMS

Microphone *stands* are available in a variety of heights. The most common allows the microphone to be mounted at mouth-height for a person who is standing and speaking or singing. The height can be adjusted easily.

Taller stands are useful for recording, especially when the microphones are on the main floor of the building and the choir and organ are in a balcony. There are also shorter "table-top" stands, ranging in height from 6 inches to 2 feet; these can be used for miking upright pianos at the sounding board, among other things.

A *boom* is a cross-pole that generally attaches to the top of a stand. It allows a microphone to be extended to the side of the stand. In addition to allowing the horizontal position of the microphone to be changed, booms can also be adjusted to different angles—so they can provide additional height when a taller stand is not available.

Booms are indispensable for miking inside grand pianos, and are also used for vocalists seated at the keyboard, as well as for miking drums and other instruments where a microphone on a simple stand would not reach far enough.

Many pulpits and lecterns employ a *gooseneck* to hold the microphone. This flexible metal conduit allows the position of the microphone to be changed easily to accommodate speakers of differing heights.

MOUNTS AND CLAMPS

Most hand-held microphones are provided with a holder, or *clip*, which screws on the end of the stand, boom, or gooseneck. The microphone can be slipped or snapped easily and securely into this holder for stationary use, or removed as easily to be held by hand.

Some holders are available in the form of a *clamp*, which attaches onto the side of a stand, rather than being screwed onto the end. This is typically used by an acoustic guitarist, so that a second microphone can be placed to pick up the guitar, in addition to the one that captures the voice.

Stand-mounted microphones are sometimes provided with elaborate *shock mounts*, which isolate the microphone from physical vibrations of the stand. These mounts suspend the microphone within a frame by a kind of cat's cradle of elastic bands. They are used more in studio recording than in live sound reinforcement.

When miking sound in stereo for reinforcement or recording, a *stereo mic bar* can be used to hold a pair of microphones on a single stand or boom.

In dramatic presentations, it is sometimes desirable to place microphones at the front of the stage area. But the use of even a short stand in such cases can result in phase cancellations, due to sound reflected from the floor into the microphone. The solution is to place the microphone as close to the floor as possible. For this purpose the *mic "mouse"* has been developed. It is simply a foam "cradle" that isolates the microphone from the vibrations of the floor while keeping it as low as possible.

PHANTOM POWER

Condenser microphones require a polarizing voltage and power for their built-in amplifiers. Sometimes provision is made to supply this voltage directly through the microphone cable. This procedure is called *phantom powering*. Phantom power supplies are commonly 48 volts DC, or sometimes 24 volts. Most phantom-powered mics can operate on a wide variety of supply voltages, from as little as 1.5 or 9 volts up to 50 volts.

Unless otherwise stated by the manufacturer, a microphone designed to operate on a lower phantom voltage (24 volts) will function perfectly well with a higher-voltage phantom power supply. Microphones intended for use with 48-volt supplies may work with lower-voltage supplies, but their ability to handle higher-level dynamic peaks will suffer.

In a phantom power system, the polarizing voltage is placed on both of the signal lines in a balanced connection, with the same polarity on each line. Dynamic microphones connected in a balanced system with a phantom power input are then protected from damage, theoretically, since the system results in a net zero DC potential across the coil. But a dynamic mic connected unbalanced to a phantom power input may be destroyed!

THE
YAMAHA
GUIDE TO
SOUND SYSTEMS
FOR WORSHIP
PAGE 55

It is therefore imperative to be aware of whether a mixing console input is wired for phantom power. (When making or breaking any connection to a mixing console channel with phantom power on, always mute the channel. An extremely high-level transient may occur at the moment the connector makes or breaks contact. These transients are at least annoying and at worst may actually damage speakers.) Large consoles provide a switch for each input channel to disable the phantom power when it is not needed; always be sure that this switch is set to OFF when a dynamic mic, or an electret condenser with internal battery, is connected to the input. On smaller consoles, however, phantom power is turned on or off for all channels by a single switch; in this case, if you are using phantom power, don't plug any unbalanced equipment (mics or electronic instruments) into the console without benefit of an intervening *direct box* (see Chapter 12). The transformer in the direct box will prevent the phantom DC voltage from reaching the unbalanced equipment.

EFFECT OF THE NUMBER OF OPEN MICROPHONES (NOM)

As mentioned in Chapter 3, a primary concern in sound reinforcement is maximizing the system's acoustic gain before feedback. As you add mics to a system, the potential acoustic gain decreases and feedback potential rises. In fact, every time you double the number of open mics (mics that are turned on or whose level is brought up on the mixing console), the system gain must be reduced by 3 dB to maintain stability and avoid possible feedback.

In operating a sound system, then, it is best to turn on only those mics that are required at any given time. When a mic is not being used, it should be muted, or its fader on the mixer should be brought down. (Muting is accomplished by switching it off, not by shielding with a hand, which actually exacerbates feedback.) By extension, there is something to be said for using the smallest number of microphones that you can.

WIRELESS MICROPHONES

WHAT IS A WIRELESS MICROPHONE?

A wireless microphone system is a small-scale version of a typical commercial FM broadcasting system. In a commercial broadcasting system, a radio announcer speaks into a microphone that is connected to a high-power transmitter in a fixed location. The transmitted voice is picked up by an FM receiver and heard through a speaker or headset.

In a wireless microphone system, the components are miniaturized but the same principles apply. The transmitter is small enough to fit into the microphone handle or into a small pocket-sized case. Since the microphone and transmitter are battery powered, the user is free to move around while speaking or singing into the mic, or playing an electric guitar connected to the wireless mic transmitter. The transmitted sound is picked up by a receiver that is wired to amplification and loudspeakers.

Two types of microphones are available with wireless mic systems: the hand-held mic, with a transmitter in its handle, and the lavalier mic, which is small enough to be concealed as a lapel pin or hung around the neck. Lavalier mics are wired to miniature body-pack transmitters, which fit into a pocket or clip onto a belt.

RADIO FREQUENCIES USED

In order for a wireless microphone to work properly, the transmitter and the receiver must be tuned to the same frequency. It is possible for more than one wireless mic to be used at the same time in the same location if each system (wireless mic transmitter and its corresponding receiver) operates on a different frequency. Interference will occur if two transmitters operate on the same frequency. This includes signals from outside the building (such as commercial TV transmission) as well as those from inside the building (some wireless systems come with one receiver and two transmitters: a hand-held mic and a lavalier with a body pack; if both transmitters are on at the same time, they will interfere).

Interference can also occur if the frequencies of two systems are too close, although a

THE
YAMAHA
GUIDE TO
SOUND SYSTEMS
FOR WORSHIP
PAGE 56

more common problem is when different frequencies mix in such a way that spurious frequencies result—a phenomenon known as *RF* (radio-frequency) *intermodulation.*

The frequencies available for use by wireless microphones are restricted by the Federal Communications Commission (FCC). Some inexpensive wireless systems use frequencies in the range of 49.81–49.90 MHz (MHz is an abbreviation for "MegaHertz," which designates a million cycles per second). These "VHF low-band" devices, as they are known, are limited in the amount of power they may generate, and in transmission bandwidth (the range of audio frequencies that may be transmitted). Furthermore, this segment of the RF spectrum is susceptible to noise from auto ignition, fluorescent lights, dimmers, and other devices. Only three wireless mics can operate simultaneously in this spectrum without interference.

Another range of frequencies, known as "VHF high-band," operates at 150–216 MHz. This range is also used by TV channels 7–13. In this range, man-made noise decreases significantly. UHF systems use frequencies in the ranges of 400–470 MHz (UHF low-band) and 900–950 MHz (UHF high-band).

With the higher power and larger transmission bandwidth allowed by the FCC, along with many more available frequencies and the shorter antenna requirement, operation on the VHF high band and higher is desirable.

In the VHF and UHF bands, an operating station license is required and the transmitter must be type-accepted under FCC regulations.

EVALUATING WIRELESS MICROPHONE SYSTEMS

BRANDS, SPECIFICATIONS, AND COST

As with other kinds of audio equipment, there are many respected companies producing wireless systems. But unlike other kinds of audio equipment, wireless systems of roughly equal cost, performance specifications, and brand-name recognition can yield widely different results in a given auditorium. This is just the nature of the beast. Therefore the first and most important guideline in evaluating a wireless system is "Try before you buy." Audition it *in your house of worship.* This is crucial. Your location, the structure of the building, and many other variables require on-site use as the only way to be certain that the system will work for you.

At the very least, you should arrange to have a salesperson or manufacturer's representative give you a demonstration. It may be wise to go beyond this and actually rent the system for a week or two, to see how well it works. If you do so, be aware that wireless mics are not necessarily "plug and play" equipment. They may require some fiddling with settings and placement before they operate at their best.

Different manufacturers measure specifications differently, so take them with a grain of salt. Specs are not as important as how well the microphone works—that is, how good it sounds, and how free the sound is from noise, distortion, interference, and dropouts (loss of signal).

The range of a system (how far the transmitter can be from the receiver) is a function of the power of the system, which is limited by FCC regulations, and of the selectivity and sensitivity of the receiver, which are related to the quality of the engineering and construction of the unit. Consequently, systems in the same frequency band will probably have similar ranges, at least on paper, though more costly systems may perform better if their receivers are better made. The actual limit can only be determined in your auditorium.

Different brands and models have different tone quality. This can be especially important if the microphone is to be used for singing. The difference here often lies in the capsule—the microphone element itself. Some tend to emphasize high frequencies, and thus produce a thin, strident sound.

With lavalier microphones it is generally possible to substitute a different capsule for the one that the factory provides with the system. Reasons for doing so include to obtain a better sound and to have a smaller, less obtrusive mic. As far as sound, the ideal (not always realizable) is for the wireless to be as good as a wired mic; when trying out a system, compare the mic wired and wireless.

If you add wireless systems after your original purchase, either permanently or by rental for a large production, you may not be able to avoid mixing systems from different manufacturers. This does not necessarily pose any problems. But don't mix one manufacturer's transmitter with another's receiver—the likelihood of incompatibilities is great. The same may be true for different models from the same manufacturer.

Good wireless systems are not inexpensive. At this writing, a good wireless system can easily cost $1,000 or more. The best systems cost two or three times that. How much should you spend? Enough to buy a system that will do a good job for you. Needless extravagance is unwise, but so is false economy.

DIVERSITY

One of the items that can affect the cost of a wireless system is whether or not it employs *diversity* reception. A diversity system uses two or more antennas on the receiver (some actually incorporate two receivers).

A diversity system can help minimize dropouts. In the simplest terms, when a signal is weak at one antenna, it is likely to be stronger at the other. The diversity system either switches between the antennas or combines the signals. Different manufacturers employ different means of achieving diversity reception.

Not everyone needs a diversity system. But they can be essential in some locations—especially buildings with metal frameworks. The signals from the transmitter reflect off of metal objects, which can result in dropouts from *multipath cancellations*—the

RF counterpart of acoustic phase cancellation. Diversity reception can help overcome this.

In evaluating a diversity system, listen for audible effects as reception shifts from one antenna to another. This should ideally be noiseless.

FREQUENCIES

A reputable dealer or manufacturer of wireless microphones should be able to determine what frequency or frequencies you can use without interference from RF intermodulation or local radio and TV transmissions. Some have charts of frequencies used in your area, and computer programs exist to calculate what frequencies are best for you. Such a source can also provide you with the necessary information regarding FCC licensing.

For your part, you should plan ahead: How many wireless systems will you use? Will you add more in the future? The frequencies must be coordinated. If you rent additional systems for large productions, allow plenty of time (weeks to months) so that frequencies can be planned to avoid conflicts.

TV frequencies can only be used on open (unused) channels. Which channels are open varies from city to city, so the manufacturer must set the frequencies for your geographical area. Touring groups may run into problems because an unused frequency in one area may be used in another. The FCC has assigned eight channels in the range of 169–172 MHz for such uses. Only about four of these channels can operate simultaneously without interference.

COMPANDING

There is some noise inherent in all radio transmission. In an effort to minimize the audibility of this noise, most professional-level wireless systems employ *companding*. The word "compand" is a contraction of "compress" and "expand," and this describes its operation on the signal.

The transmitter contains a compression circuit to narrow the dynamic range of the audio signal before sending it. The softs become louder, and the louds become softer. When this compressed signal is transmitted, the noise that accompanies such transmission

THE
YAMAHA
GUIDE TO
SOUND SYSTEMS
FOR WORSHIP
PAGE 58

is thus ideally below the level of the audio signal itself.

The receiver uses an expansion circuit to restore the original dynamic range. This also has the effect of pushing the level of the noise lower still.

While companding is essential for high-quality wireless operation, not all companders are created equal. Listen for "pumping" or "breathing" sounds—unnatural changes in level, especially when starting or stopping speech into the mic—when you evaluate a wireless system. Some of this is unavoidable, perhaps, but it should not be so noticeable as to be distracting.

USING WIRELESS MICROPHONE SYSTEMS

Wireless microphones can be highly desirable for providing mobility and lack of visual distractions, but they are not without their shortcomings. Much of the use of wireless systems involves troubleshooting.

ESSENTIALS

Check the essentials of operation every time you use a wireless system. This should also be the first step in troubleshooting the system. Use common sense—check all of the "dumb things," such as making sure the receiver is plugged into power and its output is connected to the mixing console.

Keep the antennas vertical, as a rule. (Some ministers feed the transmitting antenna through their belt loops, so it is horizontal. In these cases, the receiving antennas should be horizontal as well.) The receiving antenna(s) should be as close to the transmitter as possible. This can be done by using a cable between the antenna and the receiver, but is better accomplished by moving the receiver itself. Placing the transmitter and receiver in a line-of-sight path is ideal. If the person using the mic is on an elevated platform, the receiver may best be placed directly beneath him or her. The basement is another possibility, as long as there are no pipes or other metal objects in the transmission path. With a diversity receiver, moving the antennas apart can help prevent dropouts.

Watch out for metal objects, such as file cabinets; a receiver placed on top of a file cabinet may not cause any problems, but

placement next to one invites dropouts from multipath reflections.

Adjust the *squelch control* on the receiver to reject signals other than the one it is supposed to receive. Try changing this level in the event of interference.

Check all connections. Special connectors are available for lavalier mics so they can't be unplugged from the transmitter accidentally. Where the receiver offers a choice between mic and line output, set it to line; the mic output inserts a pad (attenuator) in the signal path to lower the level, and then the console input uses a preamp to raise it—both of which add noise to the signal.

Check that receiver is turned on. Check that the right transmitter is being used with the receiver.

Put a fresh battery in the transmitter every time you use it. Some people prefer rechargeable nickel-cadmium batteries as a way of saving money; but these must be maintained, and will not stay charged for as long as a non-rechargeable if they are not "deep-cycled" (fully discharged before recharging). Non-rechargeable batteries (preferably alkaline) represent a greater expense, but are more convenient. Furthermore, many "9-volt" rechargeable batteries typically put out only around 7.6 V at their best; this voltage is insufficient to operate most transmitters properly; consequently, the use of such batteries is not recommended.

The persons using wireless microphones should avoid wearing a lot of metal jewelry or sequins, as these can cause multipath reflections. They should avoid placing obstructions between the transmitter and receiver—including, if possible, the human body. Similarly, they should stay reasonably close to the receiver, and in a direct line of sight, if possible.

With a lavalier mic, they should make sure the antenna is fully extended, not crumpled up in a pocket; on some mics, the mic cable is the antenna. They should avoid the risk of acoustic feedback caused by moving into the "line of fire" of the loudspeakers.

Finally, when a speaker or singer is done using a wireless mic, he or she should turn it off. Don't be like the priest who

THE
YAMAHA
GUIDE TO
SOUND SYSTEMS
FOR WORSHIP
PAGE 59

accidentally left his on when he went to hear confessions, or the performer who went to the restroom with his wireless mic still turned on!

DISTORTION AND INTERFERENCE

Distortion and interference can result from several different causes. Check the essentials first: Make sure the mic has a fresh, fully charged battery. If you have a lavalier and a hand-held mic for the same receiver, be certain only one of them is turned on.

If you use more than one wireless system and they interfere with one another, relocating the receivers may help.

Some external RF interference may be beyond your control, especially in an urban area. If this is the case, try to determine which wireless system is being affected. You may have to send the system to the manufacturer to have the frequency changed. Some manufacturers offer "frequency-agile" systems, which allow the user to switch to an alternate frequency, saving time, expense, and frustration. These systems usually cost a little more, but the extra expense is worth it when you need to change frequencies and get back on the air quickly. Be aware that some radio stations are part-time, and may create interference that wasn't there when you tested the system.

TRANSMISSION LOSS AND DROPOUTS

Paying attention to the essentials of wireless operation should minimize dropouts—though no system is dropout-proof. Relocating the antenna(s) can help if problems crop up. If they persist, a diversity system may be required.

Problems with intermittent signals when the microphone or transmitter is moved can result from a faulty mic cable or antenna.

FEEDBACK

In addition to avoiding standing in front of a loudspeaker, there are some measures you can take to minimize feedback.

With a lavalier mic, the first step is to put the capsule as close to the person's mouth as possible. For a man, pin it on the tie, up close to the knot. As an aside, it is possible to place a lavalier capsule under a garment, if you wish for it to be completely invisible to the audience. Some frequency response is lost, so that the voice may not be quite as intelligible, and you need to be careful to avoid clothing noise. But it has been done.

For dramatic presentations, a small flesh-tone capsule is sometimes used, with the cord running up the back and through the hair, and the mic affixed to the forehead! This not only avoids clothing noise, it also prevents the resonance of the chest cavity from coloring the sound (though some "tinny"-sounding capsules actually benefit from this resonance).

A unidirectional microphone can help fight feedback, too. Finally, a parametric equalizer (see Chapter 7) placed between the receiver and the mixing console (or in the channel insert) can "tune out" feedback, as well as sculpt the response of the microphone to achieve a natural sound (e.g., to eliminate chest resonance).

THE
YAMAHA
GUIDE TO
SOUND SYSTEMS
FOR WORSHIP
PAGE 60

CHAPTER 6.
MIXERS AND MIXING CONSOLES

FUNDAMENTALS

The terms *mixer*, *mixing console*, *console*, *board*, and *desk* are often used interchangeably. All are used for combining and rerouting audio signals from a set of inputs to a set of outputs, usually with some added signal processing, and level adjustment. What, then, is the distinction?

"Console" is merely an abbreviation of "mixing console." "Mixer" is sometimes restricted to a small unit, either rack-mountable or having fewer than 10 or 12 inputs—the larger units being called consoles—though some use "mixer" for consoles as well. "Board" is a less formal word sometimes used for a console, and "desk" is the British equivalent.

The basic path of a signal in a mixer or console is as follows: input to channel level control to mixing bus (a *bus* is a line that can connect signals from several sources or destinations) to master level control to output (see Figure 6-1). There generally are several inputs, of course, and each can be mixed in at the desired level.

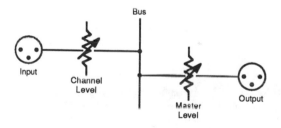

Figure 6-1. Block diagram of basic signal flow in a mixer.

Inputs to a mixer are assigned to different *channels*. (Generally, each input has its own channel, though some mixers may provide two inputs to each channel.) Each channel allows some control over where the signal is directed and in what amounts.

Inputs can be classified by signal level. The most common are *mic level* and *line level*. Actually, each of these covers a broad range of levels, but they do provide a basic way of differentiating between sources.

Mic level, as the name implies, is what a microphone puts out. It is a low-level signal, and and must be boosted by a *preamplifier* (*preamp* for short) before the mixer can handle it effectively. The preamp can be an external device; but unless an input is explicitly identified as a line input, the preamplifier is probably built into that input circuit.

(A phonograph requires a special preamp with what is known as RIAA EQ, a treatment of the signal standardized by the Recording Industry Association of America.)

Line level is a higher level, such as the output of a tape deck or an electronic keyboard instrument. No preamp is necessary before input.

Professional equipment usually provides *balanced* inputs, especially useful with microphones, which help reduce the pickup of extraneous noise by the cable. A balanced input can be created either by the use of a transformer or through electronic circuitry. The latter, sometimes called *differential* inputs, are generally less expensive and massive than transformer-balanced circuits, though transformers generally reject higher levels of extraneous signals (higher *common mode rejection ratio*) than do differentially balanced circuits, and can also provide some protection against *ground loops* between equipment.

The different channels are mixed together on *busses*. A given mixer or console may have a number of different busses, each of which can be accessed via a different *output*. Output jacks are often balanced and transformer-isolated, just as inputs are.

SMALL MIXERS

Several companies make small mixers that fit in standard-size audio equipment racks. These rack-mountable units are 19" wide, and vary in height in increments of 1.75". Some accept mics, some line inputs, others a combination. Sometimes limited equalization (EQ) is provided for each

THE
YAMAHA
GUIDE TO
SOUND SYSTEMS
FOR WORSHIP
PAGE 61

Figure 6-2. A rack-mount mic or line mixer.

applications where compactness and portability are important. The most common powered mixers have 6 or 8 inputs. It is not unusual for such units to offer some kind of equalization on each channel, as well as graphic equalization on the output. They may also provide some additional built-in signal processing, such as reverb.

channel (see Chapter 7 for more on EQ): perhaps a bass and treble control; occasionally multi-band EQ is provided, but often no EQ is available. Sometimes there will be an auxiliary bus for effects or monitoring, but not always. These tend to be very basic units.

In small sound systems, such mixers may be all that is required. They can also be used in larger systems, as *submixers*, mixing a group of mic or line signals together before sending them to the main console. They can also serve as a discrete, if somewhat limited, fall-back system in the event of catastrophic failure of the main console.

Some small mixers may be designed for stand-alone use, not necessarily for rack mounting. These units generally have from 6 to 12 input channels. This type of mixer may look very much like a scaled-down console, and may include some of the same features, such as straight-line *faders* (level controls; rack-mount mixers generally use rotary controls to conserve space), a wrist bolster (arm rest), etc.

A *powered mixer* combines a mixer and an amplifier in one unit. These are often used for PA systems, for small musical groups, and other

The more complex a mixer (or console), and the greater the number of channels, the more critical the performance of a given circuit. With only a few mics, if each mic is a bit noisy (or a bit distorted) the overall effect may not be too bad. Multiply that noise or distortion by 20 or 40 inputs, and the problem cannot be tolerated. In evaluating the performance specifications of a small mixer, the ultimate application must be considered. If it is to stand alone in a small sound reinforcement system, less stringent standards may be just fine. If it is to contribute to a large system (as a submixer), or is to be part of a recording system (where sound quality may be more critical, and where signals go through the equipment several times—not only for recording but also for effects and mixdown), then higher standards are beneficial. It is important, therefore, not to equate size with quality, but instead to evaluate each separately.

Figure 6-3. A typical small, stand-alone mixer.

THE
YAMAHA
GUIDE TO
SOUND SYSTEMS
FOR WORSHIP
PAGE 62

Figure 6-4. A large mixing console.

CONSOLES

A mixing console is a complex audio system. Not only does it preamplify and assign input signals to different outputs, it also allows for a variety of different mixes and special signal routing and processing. It is the heart of the sound system.

SOUND REINFORCEMENT AND RECORDING

The two main applications of mixing consoles—sound reinforcement and recording—have led to the development of specialized consoles. Yet the availability of small, relatively inexpensive general-purpose units underscores the fact that the specialized units differ not so much in signal-handling capability as in the amenities they offer.

For example, a sound reinforcement console may be lightweight and especially rugged to be used by traveling groups. The profile of the unit may be as low as possible, to afford the operator an unobstructed view of the proceedings. A pink-noise generator may be built in for use in testing and calibrating the sound system.

In contrast, a recording console may include especially long faders for fine control of levels. Each channel may include a *direct output*, bypassing unnecessary circuitry to put the cleanest possible sound on tape. Separate monitor controls may be included for the studio and the control room. Different modes of operation may be available to simplify the different aspects of

recording (recording original tracks, overdubbing or sweetening, and mixdown).

STAGE MONITOR

Other specialized consoles are available for such applications as broadcast and video post-production. But, in addition to sound reinforcement and recording consoles, the kind that is most likely to find use in a (large) worship facility is the *stage monitor*, or simply *monitor*, console.

Picture the following situation, typical of many congregations: Music is provided by an electric guitarist, a bass player, a drummer, a keyboardist, and a vocalist. Each musician has at least one monitor speaker directed at him or her, so that all of the musicians can hear what's going on and thus stay together.

But each musician needs to hear different things. In addition to the need for each to hear himself or herself, the keyboardist needs to hear the guitarist; the vocalist needs a mix of the keyboards and bass; the bass player needs to hear the drummer, and vice versa. In short, the need is to send different mixes of sounds to different destinations. This is what a monitor console does.

The signals from the performers typically go through a *stage box*, also known as a *splitter*, which allows each signal to feed both the main console (which provides the "house mix" for the congregation) and the monitor console (which provides the monitor mixes for the performers). The monitor console may have 8 or more master output busses. Each input typically has a

THE
YAMAHA
GUIDE TO
SOUND SYSTEMS
FOR WORSHIP
PAGE 63

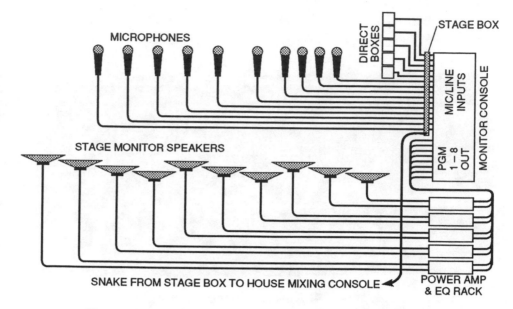

Figure 6-5. Block diagram of a typical monitor system.

separate level control for each of these busses, allowing it to be mixed in to different busses at different levels. Each bus feeds a separate output, which in turn goes to a separate power amplifier (with perhaps some equalization in between; see "Feedback Control and Room Tuning," in Chapter 7), which in turn drives the monitor speaker(s) for a given performer.

AUTOMATIC MICROPHONE MIXERS

In Chapter 5 it was revealed that every time you double the number of open microphones, you must lower the system gain by 3 dB to avoid feedback. Muting microphones not in use, or taking their channel faders all the way down, is one way to keep the number of open microphones to a minimum.

Another alternative is to use an *automatic microphone mixer*. This is a device that automatically mutes any microphone that is not in use. But when someone speaks or sings into a microphone, the channel automatically opens.

Some automatic microphone mixing systems can distinguish between sounds arriving at the front of the microphone and sounds arriving at the back. This helps prevent the microphone from turning on accidentally from incidental sounds nearby.

BASIC FUNCTIONS AND APPLICATIONS OF A MIXER OR CONSOLE

Figure 6-6 shows a block diagram of the rack-mount mixer pictured in Figure 6-2. This unit provides a typical example of the capabilities of a small mixer.

MONO OR STEREO MIX

Microphones or line-level sources are connected to the inputs of the mixer; the block diagram in Figure 6-6 indicates that there are six inputs on this particular mixer, though for clarity's sake only one is shown. *Phantom power* is available for condenser microphones, and can be switched on or off. If dynamic mics or line-level sources are used, it should be turned off. (When combining condenser mics with other kinds of inputs, *isolation transformers* or *direct boxes* can be used to keep the phantom voltage from reaching those sources that don't require it.)

An *input attenuator*, or *pad*, is available on each input channel to adjust the level of the signal that will reach the preamplifier. For a typical microphone, this would be set at –60 dB, and raised if the signal were too weak. For a typical line-level source, it would be set at +4 dB, and lowered if the signal caused distortion. The different level settings not only control the level of the incoming signal, but also the impedance (see Chapter 12) that the mixer presents to that signal—since professional microphones are

THE
YAMAHA
GUIDE TO
SOUND SYSTEMS
FOR WORSHIP
PAGE 64

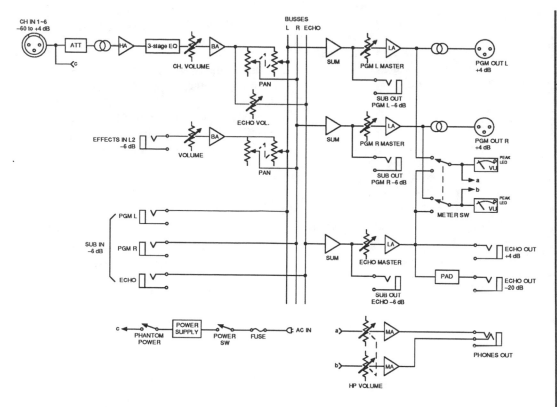

Figure 6-6. Block diagram of a small mixer.

generally low-impedance devices, while line level sources are generally high-impedance ones.

After passing through the *preamplifier*, which boosts its level, the signal goes through *equalization*, or *EQ*, which allows the frequency content to be shaped. Equalization is discussed in depth in Chapter 7.

Next the signal passes to the *channel level* (or volume) control. This is where the level of the channel is controlled, so that the proper balance among inputs can be obtained.

For a basic mixdown, the *stereo bus* is used (sometimes called the *master bus*, here labeled Program Left and Program Right). If you are mixing in stereo, use the *pan* control on each channel to control amount of the signal directed to each leg of the stereo bus, and thus the perceived location of the sound in the stereo field. If you have a monaural (mono) system, use only one side of the stereo bus (left or right), and leave the pan control centered. (The choice between mono and stereo in the worship service is examined in Chapter 9.)

CAUTION: NEVER connect the stereo outputs together with a "Y" cord to achieve a monaural signal. This applies not only to

mixers and consoles, but to all audio equipment. At best, this is a poor way of "mixing" signals; at worst, it can cause distortion and may overtax the outputs.

The signals for each leg of the stereo bus pass through the *summing amplifier* (sometimes called an *active combining network*). Just as it is possible for too high an input signal to cause distortion in the preamplifier, here it is possible that the combined levels of the signals will exceed the capacity of the summing amp. In this type of distortion, called *clipping*, the peaks of the waves are "clipped" off, resulting in the addition of unwanted higher-frequency signal components. The solution here is to lower the levels of the individual channels.

Each leg of the stereo bus has a *level control* (on some mixers, the left and right controls are ganged together under the control of a single knob or slider), to control the output level. After this control, each bus passes through a *line amplifier* and to an *output jack*. From here, connection is made to the power amplifier(s), with the possible addition of signal processing (such as graphic equalization) in between.

Meters give the average level of the output signals on each leg of the stereo bus. Each meter often includes a *peak* LED (Light-

THE
YAMAHA
GUIDE TO
SOUND SYSTEMS
FOR WORSHIP
PAGE 65

Emitting Diode; a small, usually red, "lamp") that illuminates to indicate signal peaks that the needle of the meter itself might not show. Such indicated peaks warn of the possibility of clipping.

ECHO BUS

The *echo* bus, sometimes labeled *effects* or *auxiliary*, is most often used to incorporate external signal processing into the mix. Each channel has a level control, sometimes called an *effect send* control, that determines how much of the signal from that channel is sent to the echo bus. A *master level* (or *master send*) control similarly determines how much of the combined signals on the bus is sent to the *echo out* jack(s). Two jacks are provided on the mixer shown in Figure 6-6, at different levels, to provide compatibility with different equipment.

It bears mentioning here that this bus need not necessarily be used for effects (though the name "echo" indicates its primary use—to add electronic reverb or delay). One alternative use would be to use it to send a signal to a monaural cassette recorder, or to the audio input of a video recorder.

When used for effects, the echo out jack is connected to the input of the signal processor. More than one signal processor can be used if they are connected in series (one after the other). The output of the signal processor(s) is connected to the *effects in* jack on the mixer. A level control, often labeled *effects return*, determines how much of the "effected" signal is returned to the stereo bus. A *pan* control governs the distribution of this signal between the left and right branches of the stereo bus.

This setup is known as an *effects loop*. The signal that goes directly from the channel inputs to the stereo bus is called the *dry* signal, and the signal that is returned from the effects loop is consequently known as the *wet* signal. The send and return controls determine how much of the wet signal appears on the stereo bus, and consequently govern the *wet-to-dry balance*. Notice that the channel send control is positioned *after* the channel level control (this is known as a *post-fader send*); this means that if the level of a channel is increased or decreased, the level of the effect for that channel will increase or decrease proportionally. In other

words, the wet-to-dry balance will be maintained.

Just as the echo out jack can be used for purposes other than effects, so can the effects *in* jack. In particular, it may come in handy as an additional line-level input; its only shortcomings (in this case) are the lack of EQ and the lack of assignability to the auxiliary busses.

MONITORING

A stereo *headphone jack* is provided for *monitoring* (listening to) either the stereo bus or the echo bus. A *meter/monitor switch* governs which signal is sent both to the phones and to the meters. This affords visual confirmation of what you hear. A *headphone volume* control regulates the level of the signal sent to the phones.

INTERMEDIATE FUNCTIONS AND APPLICATIONS OF A MIXER OR CONSOLE

Figure 6-3 depicts a larger mixer than the rack-mount unit just considered. It could be regarded as a small console. The block diagram of this piece of equipment is shown in Figure 6-7, and together with the following discussion it illustrates some intermediate mixing features and operations.

ADDITIONAL INPUT FEATURES

Perhaps the most apparent difference between the kind of mixer being considered here and the smaller one discussed earlier (aside from the physical appearance of the units) is the number of input channels. The block diagram indicates that this particular model is available with 8, 12, or 16 channels. The variable number of channels also points up the prevalence of *modular* design in consoles, which allows input channel "strips" to be added (within limits) and eases the task of maintenance.

Two inputs are available on each channel of this unit: a low-impedance XLR jack, generally used for microphones, and a high-impedance phone jack, typically for line-level sources. In addition to an optional pad on the input, there is also a *gain*, or *trim*, control, which governs the amount by which the preamp boosts the signal. In setting up

THE
YAMAHA
GUIDE TO
SOUND SYSTEMS
FOR WORSHIP
PAGE 66

the levels for the best signal-to-noise ratio, the gain control is turned up if need be, and the pad is engaged if the signal is too high even at the lowest gain setting. A *clip* LED warns of high signal levels that may cause clipping.

A *channel insert* jack makes connection of external signal processing easy. A special cable is used that has one plug on one end—to be plugged into the insert jack—and two on the other—to be plugged into the input and output jacks of the signal processor. The channel insert differs from the effects sends introduced earlier in these ways:

• The effect connected via the channel insert affects only that one channel, rather than a combination of channels.

• The entire signal goes through the signal processor, rather than just part of it. A typical use is to apply *compression* to a vocal source to even out the volume.

• The channel insert occurs before the fader (and before the EQ as well). This means that the level of the signal sent to the signal processor, and returned from it, does not change with movements of the fader.

It might be possible to process a line-level signal simply by plugging the source into the signal processor, and the signal processor into the input of the console. But using a channel insert is much more convenient.

One special-case use for channel inserts is that, on mixers or consoles with only mic inputs, the "in" part of a channel insert jack can be used as a line-in jack.

AUXILIARY BUSSES

In addition to the stereo master bus, this mixer features three *auxiliary busses*. Each channel therefore has three *aux send* controls to govern how much signal from that channel is directed to each of these busses.

The block diagram shows that the Aux 1 send occurs before both the EQ and channel fader (a *pre-EQ, pre-fader* send), while both the Aux 2 send and the Aux 3 send are *post-fader* sends. Note that these settings are established by internal jumper wires (marked "J" on the block diagram), which means that they can be changed—independently for each channel—if need be.

Pre-fader sends are often used to provide a *monitor mix* for musicians. The output of the bus is sent to a separate amplifier and

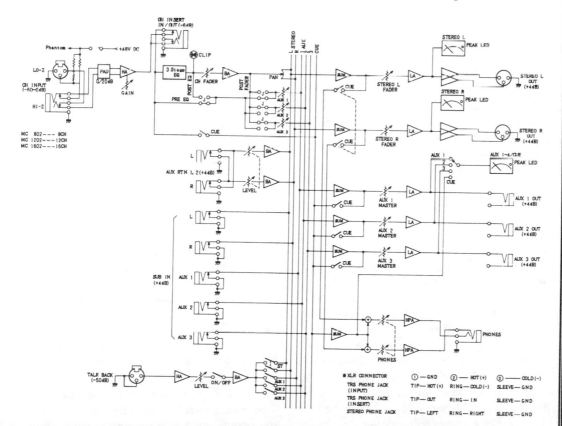

Figure 6-7. Block diagram of a small mixing console.

loudspeaker system, with the speaker(s) typically placed at the musicians' feet. Since this mix is derived before the channel faders, it is unaffected by fader movements, and thus provides a consistent reference. On some mixers, pre-fader sends are labeled *monitor*, *cue*, or *foldback*, indicating this use.

Post-fader sends are most often used for effects loops, as seen previously. The existence of several such busses means the possibility of independent effects, each of which can be fed with different proportions of signals from the different channels.

Notice that the *aux return* jacks are stereo pairs—reflecting the increasing prominence of signal processors with stereo outputs. Notice also that, while the aux out jacks take their signals from the auxiliary busses, the aux return jacks tie into the stereo master bus. It is imperative that a signal sent from a given bus not be returned to that same bus, in order to avoid *electrical feedback*, which is even worse than its acoustical counterpart, the proverbial microphone-in-front-of-the-loudspeaker.

CUE BUS

The *cue*, or *solo*, bus is a special bus with a special purpose: allowing the audio engineer to hear any signal or combination of signals at any point in the mixer or console. It represents an elaboration of the monitor switch found on the rack-mount mixer discussed earlier. Push-on/push-off buttons are used to direct a signal to this bus. Each channel has such a button, as does the stereo master bus and each of the auxiliary busses. Thus the engineer can "zero in on" any signal(s) and hear them via the headphone jack.

TALK BACK

The *talk back* feature allows a microphone to be plugged into the face of the console so that the engineer can make himself heard over the sound system. Switches can direct the output of this microphone to any of the auxiliary busses (for example, to be heard over the stage monitor loudspeakers) or to the stereo master bus (to be heard over the "house" speakers). The on/off button only remains on while it is held down, so that the engineer will only be heard when he or she expressly wishes to be.

THE
YAMAHA
GUIDE TO
SOUND SYSTEMS
FOR WORSHIP
PAGE 68

ADVANCED FUNCTIONS AND APPLICATIONS OF A MIXING CONSOLE

The block diagram for the large console pictured in Figure 6-4 is given in Figure 6-8. The number of busses and other features on such a console makes possible some advanced operations.

ADVANCED INPUT FEATURES

As the block diagram shows, this console is available with 24, 32, or 40 inputs. Each of these has its own switch for turning phantom power on or off. There is also a phase- (actually polarity) invert switch on each channel, indicated by the Greek letter phi: ϕ. This can be used to correct a mic cable that has accidentally been wired in reverse, or to reduce feedback by engendering phase cancellation.

A high-pass filter and four-stage EQ give this console sophisticated control over frequency content. Not only that, but the filter and the EQ can each be switched in or out independently with the press of a button.

MUTING

Speaking of pressing buttons, many consoles have a *mute* button on each channel, to effectively "turn off" that input without having to bring the fader down (and having to try to find the right level again when you bring it back up). As discussed in Chapter 5, the number of open microphones should be kept as small as possible, in order to obtain the greatest gain from the system without causing feedback. So the wise audio engineer will make good use of these little buttons.

On this particular console, the mute capability is carried a step farther. On each channel are eight *mute assign* buttons, which allow that channel to be assigned to any or all of the eight *master mute groups*. In the master section of the console are eight *mute master* buttons. Pressing one of these buttons causes all of the channels that are assigned to that group to be muted (and conversely, all channels that are *not* assigned to that group are unmuted). Thus, for example, switching from having only the musicians' microphones open to having only the pulpit microphone open is reduced to a single operation.

Each channel also has a *mute safe* switch, which, when engaged, prevents that channel from being muted accidentally by any of the master mute groups. If a channel must remain open throughout the service, this switch should be turned on.

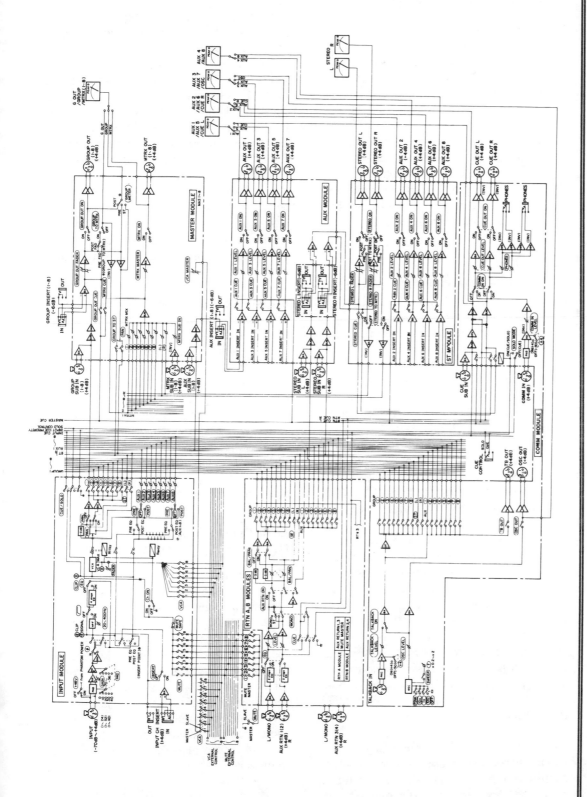

Figure 6-8. Block diagram of a large mixing console.

AUXILIARY

The eight auxiliary busses on this console provide numerous opportunities not only for effects loops, but also for monitor mixes, feeds to recorders or submixers (more on this later), and other uses that might occur in complex mixing situations.

Each send can be set independently as either pre- or post-EQ and either pre- or post-fader (with "off" as a third option) via front-panel switches. The aux busses can therefore be tailored for effects, monitoring, or other uses.

The four sets of aux return jacks can be used as stereo pairs or switched to monaural input. Each of these can be assigned to any of the eight auxiliary busses (if used with an effects loop, be careful to avoid feedback!) or any of the eight group busses.

GROUPS

In addition to allowing the channels to be directly assigned to the stereo master bus, this console also uses an intermediary system of *group* busses, sometimes called *submaster*, or *program*, busses. Each channel has eight *group assign switches*, which allow it to be assigned to any or all of the eight group busses. The level of a channel to all of the group busses to which it is assigned is determined by the channel fader.

Each group, in turn, can be assigned to the stereo master bus. Each group has its own *group fader* to control the overall level of that group, with the stereo master faders controlling the level of the entire mix. This system allows you to group related inputs together—such as all of the choir or drum mics—and then use the group fader to raise or lower the level of the group as a whole, without disturbing the balance established by the channel faders within that group.

Each group has an *insert* available (separate in and out jacks, rather than the one-jack system used on the mixer discussed previously), so that an effect can be applied to multiple channels.

Each group bus has its own *output jack*, making it possible to use a single console to control multiple speaker systems—such as a mono speech system and a stereo music system (see Chapter 9).

MATRIX MIXING SECTION

Besides the group-to-stereo assign switch, each group has a *group-to-matrix assign* switch, which assigns that group to the *matrix mixing section*. Briefly, the matrix section on this console (typical of such sections) consists of ten busses: eight corresponding to the eight group busses, plus two additional busses corresponding to the left and right legs of the stereo master bus (a stereo-to-matrix assign switch governs the last two). If, for example, the group 1 matrix assign switch is on, the signal on the group 1 bus is also sent to the matrix 1 bus. The ten matrix busses can be sent to eight independent *matrix output* jacks. For each matrix output, a set of ten level controls governs the balance of the ten matrix busses. Thus, each matrix output can be fed with a different combination of signals from the matrix busses. If this sounds familiar, it is almost exactly the definition of a monitor console given earlier in this chapter.

Indeed, one use for the matrix section might be to feed the stage monitors. Notice that the block diagram shows that the group-to-matrix assign can be switched to be either before or after the group fader; if pre-fader is chosen, the matrix levels don't change when the group faders are moved (although movements of the individual channel faders would still be reflected in this mix).

The matrix section is essentially a separate, independent mixer within the console, with many potential uses.

USE WITH AN INTERCOM SYSTEM

The small console discussed earlier included talk back capability, so that the person running the console could make himself or herself heard over the sound system. This console extends that capability, providing a special *talk back output* and complementary *communications input*, so that the console can be used with an intercom system. In particular, a wireless intercom allows two-way communication between the console operator and production personnel, whether they are on the platform, in the rafters, or wherever.

THE
YAMAHA
GUIDE TO
SOUND SYSTEMS
FOR WORSHIP
PAGE 70

CUE AND SOLO SYSTEM

As with other aspects of console operation, the *cue system* on a large console such as the one being considered here expands on the capabilities of smaller consoles and mixers. *Cue switches* are provided on all input channels, the group busses, the auxiliary sends, the stereo bus, and the auxiliary returns. A stereo pair of *cue output* jacks allows the console operator to monitor signals via a speaker system (if the console is in a control room, for example) as well as via headphones.

In addition, this system has two modes: In *cue* mode, it functions similarly to the smaller console discussed earlier—pressing any cue switch sends the selected signal to the stereo cue and phones outputs. In *solo* mode, only the selected input channel or aux return signals are sent to the console's outputs. This makes it easy to isolate a given signal for monitoring.

USE WITH OUTBOARD SUBMIXERS

There are times when, despite the size and capabilities of a console, it is advantageous to "off-load" some of the mixing to one or more outboard *submixers*. For example, suppose the worship team includes a keyboard player with several synthesizers and such. If he were using a small mixer such as the one depicted in Figure 6-6, he could balance his keyboards to his liking and then send the combined signal to the main console via the *sub outputs* (or even the main outputs) from his stereo master bus. The console has several *sub inputs* available, which can direct these signals to one of the group or auxiliary busses (alternatively, channel inputs could be used, so that the submixed signal could be directed to several busses).

In return, the console operator can use an auxiliary, group, or matrix output to send a mix to the keyboard submixer (omitting the keyboard signal). The submixer accepts this mix via the *sub input* to the echo bus. (The keyboard signals also feed the echo bus, via the echo send controls on the individual channels.) The *echo output* jack feeds the amplifier-and-loudspeaker system for the keyboard player's stage monitor. Note that no echo effect is actually used here; the echo bus is instead used as an aux mix bus. Figure 6-9 summarizes this setup.

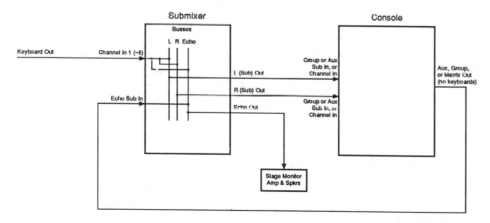

Figure 6-9. Typical use of a submixer with the main console.

THE
YAMAHA
GUIDE TO
SOUND SYSTEMS
FOR WORSHIP
PAGE 71

CHAPTER 7.
SIGNAL PROCESSORS

In a general sense, all of the electronic devices in a sound system can be considered signal processors. But in a more restricted (and more common) sense, "signal processor" refers to a device that changes something about the character of the sound. This chapter explores devices in this second category, describing how they affect the sound and how they can be used in the worship service.

Signal processors can be divided into different categories based on how they affect the program material:

- Devices that affect certain portions of the frequency spectrum (equalizers and filters, as well as crossover networks for loudspeakers).

- Devices that control the volume of the signal (compressors, limiters, and noise gates).

- Devices that control the perceived spaciousness of the sound (reverb and delay).

In addition to these, there are signal processors that are used primarily for special effects. Such devices are less important to sound systems for worship than the other classes of signal processors, which serve to enhance the sound in such a way that no special effect is perceived. Nevertheless, they can fulfill useful roles, particularly where music is concerned.

FREQUENCY PROCESSORS

EQUALIZERS AND EQUALIZATION

As discussed in Chapter 3, the spectrum of audible sound covers a broad range of frequencies. It is often beneficial to be able to control the relative volumes of different areas of the frequency spectrum—to raise the relative volume of a certain band of frequencies ("boost"), or to lower it ("cut," or "attenuate"). This is equalization, or EQ for short.

As you might guess from the name, equalizers make it possible to even out the frequency spectrum, so that the lows, middles, and highs are balanced. But there are reasons for making different frequencies unequal, as well. These reasons include making the spoken word more intelligible, making certain sounds stand out amidst others, and compensating for peculiarities in the acoustics of a room. This is the flip side of equalization.

COMMON TONE CONTROLS

The typical tone controls on a hi-fi amplifier or car stereo constitute a form of equalizer. It generally operates in just two bands: low-frequency (bass) and high-frequency (treble). Figure 7-1 illustrates the appearance of standard bass and treble tone controls, along with a graph of the frequencies that might be affected as the controls are adjusted.

When you turn up the bass tone control, you increase the level of lower frequency sounds (boost them) relative to the rest of the program. This results in a richer or fuller sound, or, in the extreme, in a boomy sound. Conversely, when you turn down the bass tone control, you decrease the level of these same frequencies (cut them), resulting in a thinner or tinny sound.

The graph in Figure 7-1 depicts one particular type of equalization known as a *shelving* characteristic, or shelving curve. For example, look at the shelving type EQ created by the bass control. Below 100 Hz the amount of boost or cut remains constant, as shown by the response plot, which has ceased to slope and is again level. This new boosted or cut level portion of the curve looks like a shelf, hence the term shelving.

THE
YAMAHA
GUIDE TO
SOUND SYSTEMS
FOR WORSHIP
PAGE 72

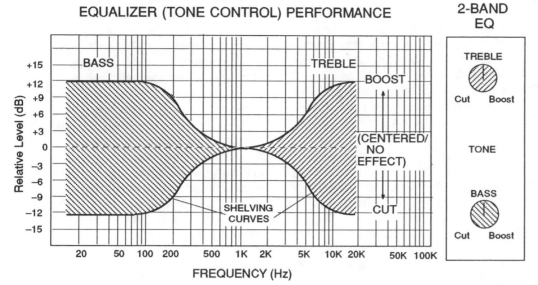

Figure 7-1. Typical bass and treble tone controls and how they alter frequency response.

MULTI-BAND CONVENTIONAL EQUALIZERS

Each input channel on a typical mixer or mixing console may have a two-band equalizer, similar to the hi-fi tone controls described above, but it is more likely to have a somewhat more elaborate equalizer that affords separate, simultaneous control of at least three frequency bands. In the case of a three-band equalizer, the middle frequency band (midrange) will always exhibit what is known as a *peaking* (or peak/dip) characteristic, as illustrated in Figure 7-2.

All peaking equalizers have some center frequency at which maximum peak or dip occurs, and below or above which there is less and less effect until, at some distance from the center frequency (along the frequency axis), there is no effect.

Many mixing console channel equalizers provide two or more midband peaking equalization controls between a pair of shelving high- and low-frequency equalization controls, thus affording a greater degree of control of those frequencies where our ears are most sensitive (500 Hz to 4 kHz). Some manufacturers provide a way to change the actual center frequencies of peaking EQ (or "knee" frequencies of shelving EQ) via switches.

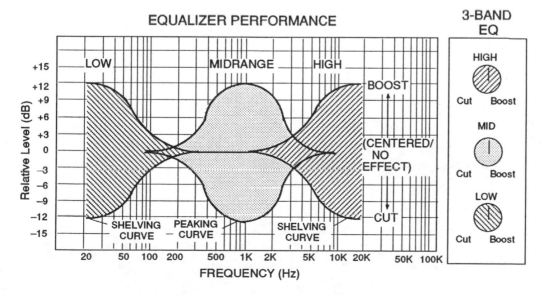

Figure 7-2. Typical three-band equalizer characteristic.

THE
YAMAHA
GUIDE TO
SOUND SYSTEMS
FOR WORSHIP
PAGE 73

SWEEP TYPE EQUALIZERS

The *sweep type equalizer* is much like the multi-band conventional equalizer, except that instead of switching the center or knee frequency, you can continuously adjust it. This provides more precise control over the sound. On these equalizers, each sweepable band has two knobs: one to control the center frequency (for peaking EQ) or knee frequency (for shelving EQ), and one to control the amount of boost or cut. Some such EQs have sweepable center bands and fixed-frequency high and low bands.

PARAMETRIC EQUALIZERS

In all the equalizers discussed thus far, the steepness of the EQ curve has been fixed. The broadness or sharpness of the EQ curve is described by a specification called Q. The higher the Q, the sharper the curve.

Equalizers that provide both sweepable center frequencies and adjustable Q, as well as control over boost and cut, are known as parametric equalizers (because they allow you to adjust all of the parameters of the equalization). A parametric equalizer is illustrated in Figure 7-3.

One of the advantages of parametric EQ is that it enables the frequency needing help to be selected precisely, and the Q to be adjusted, so that a minimal amount of boost or cut can be applied, with correspondingly fewer ill effects on adjacent frequencies where the correction is not needed.

Stand-alone parametric equalizers are available and are especially useful in recording and broadcast applications. In sound reinforcement it is more common to find a parametric equalizer on the input channels of large mixing consoles.

Some people dislike parametric EQ because there are so many parameters that MUST be adjusted, and because it is difficult to make note of specific settings so they can later be duplicated in other mixing situations. If inexperienced operators will be using a mixing console, and will have minimal time to become familiar with it, they may be better off with simpler EQ.

GRAPHIC EQUALIZERS

Unlike typical three- or four-band input equalizers, a *graphic equalizer* can operate on eight or more frequency bands simultaneously. These bands are typically set with center frequencies one octave or one-third octave apart. Most graphic equalizers use the center frequencies established by the International Standards Organization (ISO).

The units are called *graphic* because most have linear slide controls. When they are set they create a visual image that resembles the overall frequency response curve of the EQ (NOT the response of the sound system!).

Graphic equalizers are mainly used to control the output of the sound system, as opposed to the input of individual channels.

THE
YAMAHA
GUIDE TO
SOUND SYSTEMS
FOR WORSHIP
PAGE 74

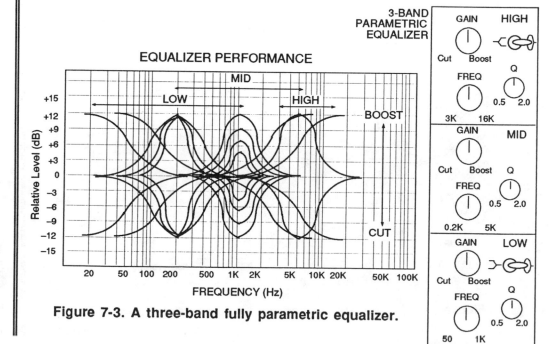

Figure 7-3. A three-band fully parametric equalizer.

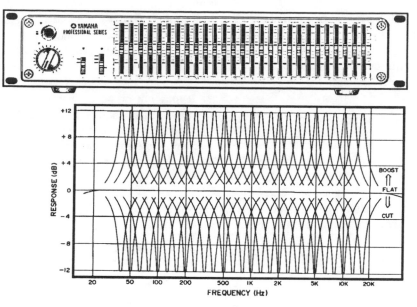

Figure 7-4. A one-third octave graphic equalizer.

(Multiple-band parametric equalizers are also used for output EQ.) Graphic equalizers with one octave bands are useful for general tonal corrections, while those with one-third octave bands are sufficient for most room tuning and feedback control (see "Feedback Control and Room Tuning").

Graphic EQ reduces the effect of resonant peaks and dips in loudspeaker response and, to a lesser degree, in the acoustic environment, reducing the tendency for acoustic feedback to occur.

Another use is to contour the frequency response of the output to obtain the most pleasing sound quality, or improved intelligibility. For example, sometimes the middle portion of the spectrum (1 kHz to 5 kHz) must be boosted to preserve the recognition of vocal consonants and sibilants.

The signal driving each loudspeaker (each main cluster or each monitor mix) usually requires its own channel of graphic equalization, which is installed just after the mixing console output (or in the patch out/in loop of the output circuit), before any electronic crossover or the power amplifier.

Some graphic equalizer circuitry is such that when two adjacent bands are boosted, there remains a large dip between the two band centers. Other equalizers maintain a smoother transition between bands. This latter performance is more desirable, and such equalizers are classified as being *combining* type graphic equalizers.

The graphic equalizer is a useful tool, but it cannot substitute for good acoustics or well-designed amplifier and loudspeaker systems.

DIGITAL EQUALIZERS

Another type of equalizer just recently introduced is the *digital* equalizer. Rather than using analog filters to alter frequency response, these devices use digital signal processing (DSP) techniques to achieve equalization. The advantages of digital equalization include the ability to select different types of equalization. The same device may alternately become a one-octave, ⅔-octave, or ⅓-octave graphic EQ, a parametric EQ, or many other types of filters and tone controls.

Digital equalizers also offer the capability to store and recall various EQ settings. For example, one EQ setting may be used for mid-week prayer service when attendance is light and speech intelligibility is most important. A second "curve" may be used for a standing-room-only choir concert. In addition, it is a simple matter to incorporate signal delay capability into a digital equalizer.

At the same time, digital equalizers may be less intuitive to operate, since a small number of multifunction controls affect a large number of parameters. In addition, the current standard 16-bit PCM analog-to-digital converters deliver dynamic range performance that is somewhat lower than analog equalizers; careful gain-structuring is

THE
YAMAHA
GUIDE TO
SOUND SYSTEMS
FOR WORSHIP
PAGE 75

required. As this book is being written, improvements in analog-to-digital converter technology are taking place, and you can expect dynamic range performance of digital signal processors to improve.

FEEDBACK CONTROL AND ROOM TUNING

Equalization is the LAST step that should be taken in tuning a sound system. Unless a system is correctly designed and carefully set up, the equalization may not accomplish much, and may actually degrade the sound.

There are two basic approaches to tuning the system. One approach is to "ring out" the system, whereby feedback is induced and the equalization is then applied to knock down individual feedback frequencies (nodes). This procedure is described below. Another approach is to measure the frequency response with a device known as a real time audio spectrum analyzer, and adjust the equalization to obtain the desired EQ curve for the room.

Instruction in the use of spectrum analyzers is beyond the scope of this book, and use of such devices is best left to qualified audio professionals.

Ringing out a sound system is accomplished as follows: Turn up the overall gain (volume) of the system, while someone speaks into a microphone. Feedback will first occur at that frequency (or frequencies) where the system has a peak (see Chapter 3 for a discussion of feedback). It typically begins as a slight ringing, and then becomes a loud howl. Identify the feedback frequency, either by ear or using a spectrum analyzer if you have access to one and know how to use it. Locate the corresponding frequency band on the graphic equalizer, and pull that band down until it stops ringing. Then bring up the gain some more, while the same person is talking, until ringing or howling commences again. If it's at the same frequency, pull the slider down a little more; if it's at a different frequency, pull that slider down. Eventually, you'll reach a point where many frequencies all start to howl at once, or where you've already adjusted most of the frequencies that begin to howl as you further raise the gain. That's when you can stop the EQ adjustments. You've gotten all the gain there is. Then back off the gain by 10 dB or so to leave some *headroom*—room between the nominal

(normal) signal level and the peak signal level. When you're done, you may find you've obtained from 3 to 15 dB more usable gain from the system.

It may not be necessary to try to obtain all possible gain before feedback. If you obtain sufficient gain before ringing out every available frequency, stop there. In any case, it's important that the sound still be natural.

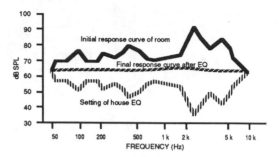

Figure 7-5. Equalization of the frequency response of a room.

Feedback is dependent on the wavelengths of sounds, rather than the frequencies *per se*. This means that the frequencies at which feedback nodes occur may change with changes in temperature or humidity (For example, the warmer the air, the faster sound travels; hence a given wavelength will correspond to a higher frequency.). Such changes may require that the system be rung out again, especially if very narrow band filters (EQ) are used.

The process of "ringing out" should be performed separately for each speaker system—including any stage monitor systems.

HIGH-PASS AND LOW-PASS FILTERS

A *filter*, in signal processing as in the physical world, lets some things pass through it while preventing others from doing so. Audio filters are concerned with passing and attenuating different frequencies.

A *high-pass filter* (also known as a *low-cut filter*) passes all frequencies above its cutoff point without attenuation, whereas frequencies below the cutoff point are attenuated. The cutoff frequency is typically anywhere from 20 Hz to 200 Hz. The slope of the filter (the degree to which frequencies below the cutoff point are attenuated) is given in dB per octave. A slope of 18 dB per

THE
YAMAHA
GUIDE TO
SOUND SYSTEMS
FOR WORSHIP
PAGE 76

octave is considered optimum for many purposes; 12 dB per octave is a shallower slope, and hence does a less pronounced job of filtering; 24 dB per octave is steeper than is generally necessary. (You may read about filter "poles"; a 1-pole filter has a slope of 6 dB per octave, a 2-pole filter has a slope of 12 dB per octave, and so forth.)

High-pass filters reduce rumble, wind noise, and other low-frequency signals. These signals might otherwise use up an inordinate amount of amplifier power, causing distortion and possibly damaging loudspeakers.

Most sound systems reproduce very little below 40 Hz, so a high-pass filter with a 40 Hz cutoff may be used with no adverse effect on the bass response, while eliminating the ill effects of rumble. Such filters are often provided as standard equipment on the electronic crossover network or on a graphic or parametric equalizer, and are even provided on a few power amps. They should be used where available.

If no filter is available in the path from the console to the amplifiers, consider purchasing a separate high-pass filter (cutoff somewhere between 20 Hz and 40 Hz) and inserting it in the signal path ahead of the power amplifier(s).

To eliminate breath and wind noises from microphones, cutoffs above 40 Hz are best. High-pass filters (HPF) and low-pass filters (LPF) are not generally available as stand-alone devices, but are incorporated into mixing consoles or graphic equalizers, and should be used any time you do not hear a loss of desired frequencies when you switch the filter into the circuit. For example, high-pass filters should be used on vocal microphones.

A *low-pass filter* (also known as a *high-cut filter*) does the opposite of a high-pass filter: it attenuates frequencies *above* its cutoff point. These are less common, but still widely found in sound systems. They can be used to roll off (attenuate) unnecessary portions of the frequency spectrum that are above the highest program frequencies, or that exceed the high-frequency response of the loudspeaker or transmission system.

EXCITERS

In 1975, a company named Aphex introduced the first *Aural Exciter*. This unit changed the signal in such a way that, when part of the Exciter-processed signal was mixed in with the direct program, the intelligibility and "presence" of the sound was enhanced. This was achieved without changing the program frequency balance or gain appreciably, as would be the case with parametric or graphic EQ.

A number of other companies have introduced processors that are supposed to perform similar signal manipulation, although Aphex claims exclusive rights to the process and the term "Aural Exciter," and reserves the rights to the technique. Aphex has licensed the "Aural Exciter" process to other manufacturers (including Yamaha), who have incorporated it into their signal processing products.

The key to proper use of any exciter is moderation. Only a small percentage of processed signal should be mixed back into the direct program.

DE-ESSERS

There are situations in which sibilant consonants—S's and T's—are unduly prominent in speaking or singing. This can be caused by improper equalization, in which case equalization can correct it. On the other hand, the required corrective EQ can rob the voice of high-frequency content, and may affect intelligibility. A more selective solution is a sibilance controller, also known as a *de-esser*. This kind of signal processor will pass the signal unaltered unless it encounters high signal levels in roughly the 6 kHz to 8 kHz range, where sibilances occur. Then it momentarily compresses the signal to lower the level of these frequencies. At other times, these frequencies are unaffected.

CROSSOVERS

The primary loudspeakers used in sound systems for worship are composed of low-frequency and high-frequency speakers (drivers) and enclosures, each of which is designed to reproduce only a specific, limited frequency range. To reproduce the entire audio range, such drivers and enclosures are combined into multi-way systems.

Generally, low- and high-frequency drivers cannot be connected directly to the output of a single power amplifier. It is necessary to divide the full-range audio signal into its low- and high-frequency components, directing each only to the appropriate driver(s). This is the function of the *crossover*. Other terms for *crossover* are *frequency dividing network* and *crossover network*, all of which mean the same thing.

Crossovers divide and filter the signal in such a way that, *above* a certain frequency, the input to the low-frequency driver falls off, while the input to the high-frequency driver falls off *below* a certain frequency. The point along the frequency axis of the graph where the two curves meet is called the *crossover point*. Think of a crossover as a traffic cop who directs all the cars carrying low frequencies to the low-frequency amplifier or loudspeaker, and all the cars carrying high frequencies to the high-frequency amplifier or loudspeaker.

Similar principles apply in three-way systems, in which three different frequency ranges are distributed among low-frequency, midrange, and high-frequency drivers.

The rate at which the level to each driver falls off beyond the crossover point is called the *slope* of the crossover. The most commonly used crossover slopes in high-level professional sound systems are 12 dB per octave and 18 dB per octave. (See "High-Pass and Low-Pass Filters," on pages 76–77, for a discussion of filter slopes.)

Two generic types of crossover are in common use in sound systems: *high-level passive* networks, and *low-level active* networks.

Passive, high-level crossovers are made with large coils, high-voltage capacitors, and high-wattage resistors, and are designed to pass high signal levels. They are inserted between the power amplifier output and the drivers. Passive crossovers are most often enclosed in the loudspeaker cabinet, as shown in Figure 7-6, although some are mounted externally.

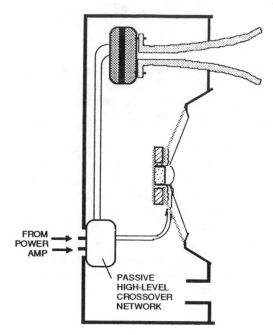

Figure 7-6. Typical location of a passive, high-level crossover network inside a loudspeaker enclosure.

Active crossover networks are designed to be inserted in the signal chain before the power amplifier. They thus work at far lower signal levels than do passive, high-level crossovers. Since active crossovers divide up the total frequency range before the power amplifier, separate amplifier channels are required for each driver or set of drivers. Another term for this type of unit is an *electronic crossover*.

A two-way loudspeaker with an active crossover and two power amplifiers (or two halves of a stereo amplifier), each handling a different frequency band, is called a *biamplified* system. Similarly, a three-way loudspeaker with active crossovers and three sections of power amplifier is a *triamplified* system.

In spite of the fact that they can increase the total cost of a small system, active crossovers are widely used in professional sound because they offer significant advantages in performance. In large systems, with many loudspeakers, they can also offer cost advantages. (See Chapter 9 for more on biamplified and triamplified loudspeakers.)

THE
YAMAHA
GUIDE TO
SOUND SYSTEMS
FOR WORSHIP
PAGE 78

DYNAMICS PROCESSORS

COMPRESSORS AND LIMITERS

Compressors and *limiters* are signal processors that reduce the dynamic range of the signal. The limiter is designed to prevent signals from exceeding a given (usually adjustable) threshold level. This action, because it eliminates the peaks in signal level in a program, is known as leveling, and some limiters are also known as *audio leveling amplifiers*.

The ratio of change in input level (in dB) to the change in output level is known as the *compression ratio*. Most limiters will have a compression ratio of from 8:1 to 20:1 or even higher. If a unit is set to 8:1 compression, then an increase in input level of 8 dB above the threshold level will result in a 1 dB increase in the output level. A few units offer infinite compression, where no amount of increase in input level above the threshold will cause an increase in output level.

Limiters are generally used to process only the peaks of the program signal, which is why they are also known as *peak limiters*. In broadcast, such units prevent overmodulation of the transmitted signal. In sound reinforcement, they can be used to protect loudspeakers—or listeners' ears!

If the threshold is lowered so that most or all of the program is subject to compression, then the device functions as a compressor. Compressors generally use lower compression ratios than limiters, typically 1.5:1 to 4:1. Compression has a number of uses. In tape recording, broadcast, or sound reinforcement, compression is sometimes used to squeeze the dynamic range of a program to suit the medium of storage or reproduction.

For example, in a worship service, a sermon or homily might conceivably cover a broader range of dynamics than the sound system can comfortably deliver to the listeners—the whispers might be too soft, the exclamations too loud. A compressor can reduce the difference between extremes.

Such compression also works well with singing. With instruments such as electric guitar and bass, compression can not only even out the sometimes erratic dynamics of the instruments, but can also add to the apparent sustain of held notes.

Because the circuitry is almost identical, the real distinction between a compressor and a limiter is how the device is used. Many such devices are designed to perform both functions. They have a wide range of adjustable threshold and compression ratio values (and sometimes adjustments for attack and release times), and are therefore known as *compressor/limiters*.

Some compressor/limiters have an additional set of inputs and outputs for what is known as a *side chain*. The signal entering the side chain input can be used to control the compression of the signal entering the main input. This allows for several applications, the most common being *ducking*. Imagine that a musical number is being performed that includes narration. With the music plugged into the compressor's main input and the narration into the side chain input, the level of the music will automatically be reduced when the narrator speaks.

NOISE GATES AND EXPANDERS

A *noise gate* is a signal processor that turns off or significantly attenuates the audio signal passing through it when the signal level falls below a user-adjustable threshold. The idea is that the desired program will pass through unaltered, but low-level hiss and noise (or leakage from other sound sources) will not be heard when the primary program is not present (presumably when the level is below the set threshold).

Some noise gates literally shut off the signal flow when the program is below the threshold level. These will tend to have an audible effect as they cut in and out. This is why other noise gates are designed to merely reduce the signal level by a finite amount (to lower the gain) when the level falls below the threshold. To further reduce the audible effect of this gating, these units may have an automatic or adjustable setting whereby, after the level drops below the threshold, it takes so many milliseconds for the gain to be reduced.

The circuit that reduces gain is an *expander*, although it is not known as such in this case. The noise floor of the program is being reduced, and hence the dynamic range is being expanded.

When the expansion circuit works only below a set threshold, the device is called a noise gate.

There are also signal processors that expand the entire program. Any signals falling below the threshold are expanded downward in level so they become even quieter, and signals above the threshold are expanded upward in level. The net result is a program with greater dynamic range. In this case, the device is called an expander.

Noise gates are useful for automatically muting temporarily unused microphones. (Automatic microphone mixers fulfill a similar function; see page 64.)

Expanders can restore the dynamic range of a signal that has been compressed, such as a tape recording, record, or radio broadcast.

REVERBERATION AND DELAY

Reverberation (*reverb* for short) consists of multiple, blended sound images (not individually discernable echoes) caused by reflection from walls, floor, ceiling, and other surfaces that do not absorb all the sound. Reverberation occurs naturally in most indoor environments, and is most prominent with hard-surfaced environments.

Reverberation can also be created artificially by a number of means. In the past, reverb chambers and units that employed metal plates or springs to simulate reverb were common. Increasingly, these are being supplanted by *digital reverb* units, which produce reverberation effects electronically.

Reverberation is often confused with *delay* (or *echo*), especially since some modern signal processors provide both. Delay refers to one or more distinct sound images (echoes). In fact, true reverberation normally begins with a few relatively closely spaced echoes known as early

reflections. These are caused by the initial bounce back of sound from nearby surfaces. As the sound continues to bounce around, the increasing number of reflections blend, creating the more homogeneous sound field we call reverberation.

Artificial reverberation can be used to provide a more spacious sound in an environment that lacks the desired degree of natural reverberation, such as a small, carpeted church. Organ and choral music, especially, can benefit from this effect. It can also be used with other types of music, and, in moderation, with the spoken word. Indeed, for recording or broadcast, adding reverberation to the "dry" sound from the microphone produces a sound that is more natural and easier to listen to.

Delay, or echo, which formerly was produced by various means, is today created primarily by *digital delay lines* (DDLs). Although they can be used to produce special effects, such as multiple echoes with varying times between them, their chief use in sound systems for worship is to delay the signal to remote speakers.

The following scenario is typical: In a large church, the rear balcony partially blocks the sound of the main speakers from reaching the seats at the back of the main floor (especially the midrange and high frequencies; see the discussion of boundaries in Chapter 3). To compensate, a "fill system" can be aimed below the balcony overhang (see Figure 7-7). Note, however, that this area is physically remote from the main cluster, at a distance D. If you simply connect the fill loudspeakers with the main signal feed, the sound will arrive noticeably sooner than the sound from the main cluster. In order that the listeners perceive the sound as originating up in the front of the room, the feed to the fill system should be electronically delayed so that its sound output coincides with, or actually comes a short while after, the sound arriving from the main cluster.

THE
YAMAHA
GUIDE TO
SOUND SYSTEMS
FOR WORSHIP
PAGE 80

The delay must be adjusted to compensate for the time it takes the sound to travel distance D in Figure 7-7. To calculate the required delay time, use the following formula:

$$\text{Delay (milliseconds)} = 1000 \left(\frac{D \text{ (feet)}}{1130} \right)$$

For example, if D is 100 feet, the required delay is approximately 90 milliseconds. A slightly longer delay is actually preferable, to keep the perceptual image up front. An additional 10–20 milliseconds is suitable; much more than this will result in an apparent echo from the fill loudspeakers.

The preceding formula is based on the speed of sound in dry air, at standard temperature, at sea level (1,130 ft/sec). If it is wetter, warmer, or higher, the sound travels more rapidly, so slightly less delay may be called for. As a rule of thumb you can estimate 88.5 milliseconds delay per 100 feet distance between main and fill loudspeakers, and you'll be close to the optimum value.

Note also that the desired frequency response of the fill system—concentrating on the midrange and high frequencies—helps dictate the choice of speakers and possible use of equalization.

As mentioned above, a delay will typically be set so the sound from the main cluster arrives at the listeners' ears *before* the sound from the under-balcony speaker. This practice takes advantage of a psychoacoustic phenomenon known as the *Haas*, or *precedence*, effect. The human ear will focus on the sound that reaches it first— even if the sound arriving later is louder. This focusing only occurs within a brief time—the later sound must arrive within 30 milliseconds or it will be perceived as a separate event. Thus listeners seated under the balcony will perceive the source of sound to be the front of the church—even if most of the energy reaching their ears comes from the under-balcony speaker.

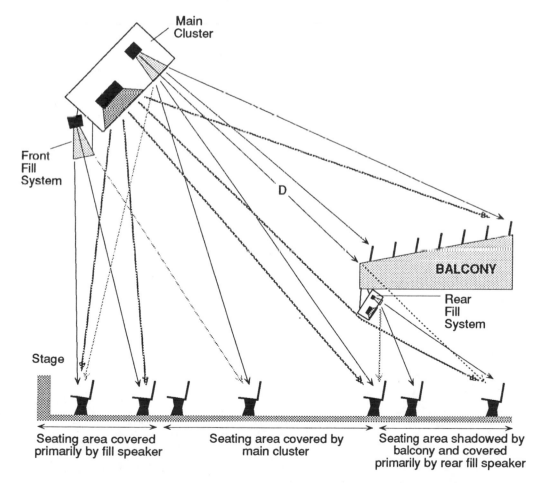

Figure 7-7. Fill loudspeakers used to improve mid- and high-frequency coverage beneath a balcony.

THE
YAMAHA
GUIDE TO
SOUND SYSTEMS
FOR WORSHIP
PAGE 81

EFFECTS

The devices mentioned so far in this chapter can also be used for special effects. For example, digital delays can create a variety of echo effects. Reverberation can be applied to the sound of a musical instrument in such a way that it is an integral part of the sound. Equalization can transform music or speech. But there is another class of signal processors whose entire purpose is special effects.

The following brief discussion will largely examine the effects, rather than the devices that produce them. While, in the past, a separate piece of hardware was necessary to produce each effect, newer *multi-effects units* combine several signal processing and effects functions in a single device. Such units are becoming increasingly more popular and less expensive.

Chorus creates the impression of an ensemble when it receives a signal from a single instrument or voice. A second sound is created from the original signal, and is delayed in time and shifted in pitch. Related effects are sometimes termed *ensemble* or *symphonic*.

Flanging uses phase cancellation (technically referred to as a *comb filter* effect) to produce a sound that can range from hollow or metallic to a distinctive whooshing. The acoustic phase cancellation exemplified in Chapter 1 by the airplane passing overhead could also be termed acoustic flanging. The use of electronic flangers demonstrates that an effect such as phase cancellation, which is generally considered detrimental to sound, has its uses.

Phase shifting, or *phasing*, yields a swooshing sound similar to flanging, only more subtle.

Electric guitar effects include *fuzz* and *wah-wah*, both of which are self-descriptive. The latter is most often produced using a variable control pedal, though some versions respond automatically to the dynamics of the player.

Distortion, *overdrive*, and other similarly named effects attempt to duplicate the sound of a guitar amp (or preamp) that has been turned up so high as to distort the sound of the guitar—without requiring that the volume distort the eardrums of the listeners! The effect is based on clipping the signal.

Pitch shift does what it says: it shifts a signal to another pitch. This can create a variety of effects, ranging from chorus to transposition to automatic harmony, depending on the degree to which the signal is shifted and whether the shifted signal is recombined with the original.

Panning changes the location of the sound in a stereo field by alternately lowering the volume of one channel and raising the volume of the other. *Auto-pan* applies this effect either cyclically (at a controllable speed) or in response to the notes played.

THE
YAMAHA
GUIDE TO
SOUND SYSTEMS
FOR WORSHIP
PAGE 82

CHAPTER 8.
POWER AMPLIFIERS

The audio power amplifier is a component whose function is—as its name implies—to increase the power of an audio signal, so that the signal can drive one or more loudspeakers. In sound systems, the power amplifier is always the final active component in the signal chain, located just before the loudspeakers.

In small portable sound systems, the power amplifier may be built into the mixer, as a convenience. These powered mixers, as they are called, are discussed in Chapter 6.

UNDERSTANDING THE SPEC SHEET

Full comprehension of the function and application of power amplifiers requires an understanding of electrical power and its relationship to voltage, to resistance or impedance, and to current. The details of these relationships, stated by *Ohm's Law* and associated equations, are beyond the province of this book. But some basic understanding may be imparted by way of a classic analogy:

Think of water being forced through a pipe. The greater the pressure being applied, the more water will move through the pipe. The smaller the diameter of the pipe, the less water will flow through it. In drawing a comparison with electricity, the water represents *electrons* (negatively-charged atomic particles), which constitute the electricity itself. The flow rate of the water represents the electrical *current* (abbreviated I), measured in *amperes* (*amps* for short). The pressure represents the *voltage* (sometimes called *electromotive force*, abbreviated E), measured in *volts*. The resistance to flow of the pipe, which decreases as its diameter increases, represents the *resistance* (R), measured in *ohms* (symbolized by Ω); the greater the resistance (i.e., the smaller the pipe diameter), the less current (water) will flow.

Consider the electrical circuit of Figure 8-1. This is a direct-current (DC) circuit, which means that the current flows in one direction only. A DC voltage E from source S (a battery) is applied across a resistance R. This resistance is termed the *load*. The current flow I is represented by an arrow in the diagram. Notice that this is indeed a *circuit*. That is, the current flows "around" from the point of highest voltage (or potential)—the negative (–) terminal of the battery—to the point of the lowest potential—the positive (+) terminal. Should the circuit be broken, the current would cease to flow.

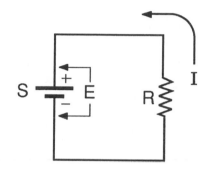

Figure 8-1. A simple DC circuit.

In speaking of alternating current (AC), such as an audio signal, *impedance* is substituted for simple resistance. Impedance, also measured in ohms, is sometimes abbreviated Z, or Z, rather than R. The chief distinction between resistance and impedance is that the impedance of a load (such as a loudspeaker) is different at different frequencies. Nevertheless, loudspeakers are classified by their *nominal* impedance—a single figure, which is used in making calculations about the circuit in which the loudspeaker is used. Figure 8-2 shows a simple AC circuit, which could represent a power amplifier (the AC source) driving a loudspeaker (the load—abbreviated R_L on some amplifier spec sheets).

Electrical power (abbreviated P or P_O), measured in *watts* (W), is the energy used to do the work when an electrical current is made to flow through a load resistance or impedance. Power is proportionate to the square of the voltage or current, which accounts for the different increases in dB of a signal when the power is doubled, as compared to when the voltage is doubled (as discussed in Chapter 3, page 28).

THE
YAMAHA
GUIDE TO
SOUND SYSTEMS
FOR WORSHIP
PAGE 83

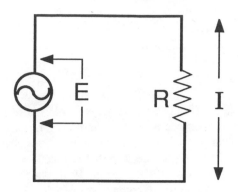

Figure 8-2. A simple AC circuit.

With this rudimentary background, the specifications of power amplifiers can be discussed meaningfully.

POWER RATINGS

The *power rating* of an amplifier states the power that the unit will deliver to a specified load—at a specified distortion level, and over a specified frequency range. The rating most often given is a *continuous average power*, sometimes termed RMS power (RMS stands for Root Mean Squared, which refers to a method for calculating the average power). For stereo amplifiers, a figure of *watts per channel* is given. For example, the power specification for a typical professional amplifier might read:

Power Output Level

Continuous average sine wave power at less than 0.05% THD, 20 Hz to 20 kHz:

Stereo, 8 ohms,
both channels driven..............240 W/ch

Stereo, 4 ohms,
both channels driven..............400 W/ch

Note that, since a 4-ohm figure is given, you can assume that the unit will handle loads as low as 4 ohms. You see, however, that the 4-ohm power figure is somewhat less than twice the 8-ohm figure. This is typical, and indicates protective current limiting, probably due to power supply limitations or component heating restrictions.

Output power specifications must be read carefully to avoid misinterpretation. For example, some manufacturers may provide less complete or less representative statements of output power than that given above (for example, obtaining improved figures by driving only one channel of a

stereo amplifier). If the distortion value, bandwidth, and load impedance are not given, the true performance of the amplifier cannot be adequately predicted.

Manufacturers may occasionally specify *peak power* in addition to average power. This often indicates that the power supply of the amplifier is operating near its limits, and sags under heavy continuous current demand—even though it may be capable of higher current for very brief periods. While such an amplifier may be suitable for home hi-fi use, where the unit's maximum output is rarely (if ever) needed, it won't serve well in a sound reinforcement system.

FTC PRECONDITIONING

A number of years ago, the Federal Trade Commission defined a standard for rating consumer power amplifiers. Such power ratings are derived from tests made after a specific preconditioning cycle. The purpose of the preconditioning is to assure that the unit will perform as specified when it is heated to the highest temperature that it can be expected to reach in normal use.

FTC preconditioning involves operating the amplifier at one third the rated power (typically where maximum heating of the amp occurs), using a 1 kHz sine wave signal, into a resistance equivalent to the rated load impedance, for one hour.

While professional amplifiers are not legally required to meet FTC preconditioning, such an amplifier should reasonably be expected not only to meet but to exceed the FTC preconditioning standard.

If an amplifier has been tested by its manufacturer according to FTC standards, the specifications normally will either indicate "FTC Power Rating" or mention FTC preconditioning by name or by a description of the procedure.

THE
YAMAHA
GUIDE TO
SOUND SYSTEMS
FOR WORSHIP
PAGE 84

FREQUENCY RESPONSE

Frequency response is a measure of how accurately the output of a device reproduces the input across the frequency spectrum. Frequency response is an important specification for devices at all points in the sound chain, from microphones to consoles to signal processors to power amplifiers to loudspeakers. The chain is truly only as strong as its weakest link.

Frequency response is often given as a curve plotted on a graph, as shown in Figure 8-3. The "flatter" the curve (the less deviation from the 0 dB reference point, which represents the input), and the wider the area across which it is flat, the better the frequency response is said to be. (Although the audio spectrum is 20 Hz to 20 kHz, the frequency response graphs of many power amplifiers extend beyond these limits, as a way of ensuring flat frequency and phase response across audible frequencies.)

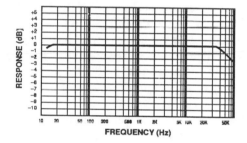

Figure 8-3. Frequency response of a power amplifier.

With power amplifiers, frequency response is often given as a figure, rather than plotted on a graph. (Flat frequency response is easier to design into a power amplifier than, say, a microphone.) For example:

Frequency Response

± 1 dB, F = 10 Hz–50 kHz,
R_L = 8 ohms, P_O = 1 W

As this example shows, a power amplifier's frequency response is generally measured at a 1-watt output level.

A less complete presentation of frequency response is sometimes given in the form of a *frequency range* specification. This gives a range of frequencies between which the response deviates by less than some amount from flat, usually (but not always) within 3 dB.

POWER BANDWIDTH

The *power bandwidth* of an amplifier is a measure of its ability to produce high output power over a wide frequency range. As such, the power bandwidth specification complements the standard power specification described earlier, and can tell more about the performance of the unit.

Power bandwidth is a frequency-related specification, defined as the frequency range lying between those points at which the amplifier will produce at least half its rated power before clipping. It is sometimes specified as a numerical bandwidth (i.e., so many kiloHertz), or may be given in the form of a graph, as in Figure 8-4.

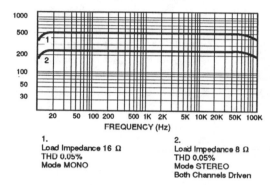

1.
Load Impedance 16 Ω
THD 0.05%
Mode MONO

2.
Load Impedance 8 Ω
THD 0.05%
Mode STEREO
Both Channels Driven

Figure 8-4. Power bandwidth of a power amplifier.

Note that while this figure resembles a frequency response curve, it does not, in fact, represent the frequency response of the amplifier. What it shows is the maximum power output plotted against frequency. There is no assumption that the input drive level is the same across the band.

Power bandwidth can affect frequency response. If an amplifier's power bandwidth is limited—as is the case with most older, transformer-output designs—the amplifier's response may collapse at the frequency extremes when it is driven to maximum power, even though the amplifier might exhibit very wide frequency response at low power levels.

The power bandwidth of modern OTL (output transformerless) transistor amplifiers is generally excellent, resembling that shown in Figure 8-4. Such amplifiers exhibit consistent frequency response at both low and high levels, and consequently reproduce program material at high power with far greater fidelity than many amplifiers that use older technology.

SLEW RATE

Slew rate is a measure of the ability of an amplifier to respond to very fast changes in signal voltage. It is specified in volts per microsecond (1 microsecond = 1 µsec = 1 millionth of a second); the higher the number, the faster the slew rate.

An amplifier's slew rate can affect its ability to render musical transients and complex waveforms with accuracy at high levels. Note that this can be an important specification because sharply rising musical transients usually occur on peaks, where the power demand is greatest.

The higher the amplifier power, the higher the slew rate must be—because the "swing" of the voltage from peak to peak is greater. As a rule of thumb, low-power amplifiers (up to 100 watts continuous power per channel) should have a slew rate of at least 10 V/µsec. High-power amplifiers (over 200 watts) should have a slew rate of at least 30 V/µsec.

The higher the slew rate, the better, up to a point. Too high a slew rate in a power amplifier may be associated with too wide a bandwidth, which can allow the amplifier to pass radio-frequency (RF) signals that only serve to increase distortion, waste power, and overheat drivers. Too high a slew rate may also suggest susceptibility to distortion or current limiting when subjected to the resulting back-EMF (see "Damping Factor," below) from a real-world loudspeaker load.

DISTORTION

Distortion is any unwanted change that occurs in an audio signal. There are many different types of distortion. The two primary types that affect the performance of power amplifiers are *harmonic distortion* and *intermodulation distortion*.

Harmonic distortion is composed of one or more signal components that are whole-number multiples of the input frequency. For example, if a pure 100 Hz sine wave is applied to the input of an amplifier, and the output of the amplifier contains not only 100 Hz, but also 200 Hz, 300 Hz, 400 Hz, and 500 Hz signals, the output can be said to contain 2nd, 3rd, 4th, and 5th harmonics. These harmonics are distortion, since they were not part of the input signal.

In measuring distortion, the relative level of the harmonic components at the output of the device is given, compared to the primary input signal component. This figure is most often given as a percentage of the total signal. Harmonic distortion can be specified for individual harmonics, or as a composite value representing all harmonics. The latter is more common, and is called *total harmonic distortion* (THD).

Harmonic distortion can be caused by clipping (see below) or merely by limitations of the design of the equipment. Many power amplifiers show THD specs of 0.01% or less, although, as with other specifications, a %THD figure is only meaningful when you know the frequency, power, and load impedance used in deriving it. Figure 8-5 shows a THD graph for a typical power amplifier.

THE
YAMAHA
GUIDE TO
SOUND SYSTEMS
FOR WORSHIP
PAGE 86

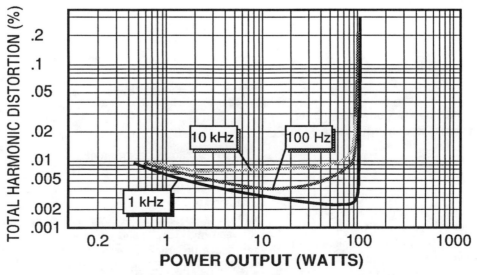

Figure 8-5. THD plot for a typical power amplifier output.

Intermodulation distortion (IM, or IMD) occurs when at least two input signal frequencies interact to form new output frequencies, which are not harmonically related. The standard measurement for IM was devised by the Society of Motion Picture and Television Engineers (SMPTE). It utilizes 60 Hz and 7 kHz sine waves in a 4:1 ratio.

Percent for percent, intermodulation distortion is usually more objectionable to the ear than harmonic distortion.

DAMPING FACTOR

Loudspeakers and dynamic microphones use the same means to accomplish opposite ends. Both feature a coil of wire, placed in the field of a permanent magnet, and physically connected to a diaphragm. In a microphone, moving the coil generates a voltage. In a loudspeaker, applying a voltage (from the amplifier) moves the coil. But Newton's first law of motion states that, once set in motion, the coil tends to continue moving, even after the amplifier has ceased to apply the signal that set it in motion in the first place. The result? The coil, moving in the magnetic field, generates a voltage of its own, as if it were a microphone. This is called *back-electromotive force*, or *back-EMF*.

The ability of the amplifier to allow back-EMF to equalize (by providing a very low-impedance path for back-EMF), and consequently to control the motion of the loudspeaker cone, is called the *damping factor*. It affects the accuracy with which the loudspeakers will reproduce low frequencies. The damping factor is calculated as the ratio of the load impedance to the amplifier's output impedance—the lower the output impedance, the higher (and better) the damping factor. Values of 100 or higher are considered good.

BRIDGED MONO OPERATION

The power specification of a professional amplifier will often include mention of mono operation, as follows:

Power Output Level

Continuous average sine wave power at less than 0.05% THD, 20 Hz to 20 kHz:

Stereo, 8 ohms,
both channels driven.............240 W/ch

Stereo, 4 ohms,
both channels driven.............400 W/ch

Mono, 8 ohms ....800 Watts

The mono specification above refers to the power capability of the amplifier in *bridged* operation, sometimes called BTL (for "bridged transformerless"). Bridging is usually selected by a rear-panel switch labeled Mono/Stereo or Bridge/Normal, and requires special output connections.

CAUTION: Consult the owner's manual of the amplifier in question for the exact details of bridged connection and operation.

When a power amplifier is bridged, both amplifier channels are fed the same signal (usually from the left input). Both halves of the amplifier process the same signal, and the load is connected in such a way as to draw power from both channels. The amplifier effectively becomes a single-channel unit, even though both channels are used—hence the term mono. The RMS voltage driving the load is effectively double what it would be if only one channel were used.

Note that the specification above gives mono output power for 8 ohms only. A load of 4 ohms in this instance would draw too much current, and could damage the amplifier, the loudspeakers, or both.

Bridging must NEVER be confused with mono operation as it is commonly known in hi-fi equipment—in which loudspeakers are connected to each of the outputs on the amplifier.

THE EFFECT OF CLIPPING

When a power amplifier is asked to reproduce levels that exceed its design limits, clipping occurs. Clipping is illustrated in Figure 8-6.

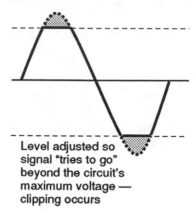

Level adjusted so signal "tries to go" beyond the circuit's maximum voltage — clipping occurs

Figure 8-6. Clipping of a sine wave.

Those portions of the wave that lie beyond the output voltage capability of the amplifier are truncated. The amplifier cannot produce a higher output signal voltage, so it simply maintains its maximum output voltage until the input signal voltage drops to a level that it can accurately reproduce. As a consequence, the wave is flattened on the top and bottom.

Clipping has two basic effects:

*   It greatly increases the distortion. This results in the generation of high-frequency components that lend a harsh quality to the sound, and may endanger high-frequency drivers—particularly in passive crossover systems.

*   More importantly, it dramatically increases the average power applied to the load, which can overheat voice coils on any drivers.

MATCHING POWER AMPLIFIERS TO LOUDSPEAKERS

When choosing an amplifier for a loudspeaker system, the system designer must consider a number of factors.

Unless the system will be used only at low levels, it is important that the power rating of the amplifier not be too low. Otherwise, you won't be able to utilize the full SPL potential of the loudspeaker. An amplifier with inadequate power can, in fact, damage loudspeakers by stressing them more than a larger amp (the smaller amp will be driven into clipping, the dangers of which are discussed in the preceding section). On the other hand, it is unwise to choose an amplifier that is significantly more powerful than the loudspeaker can handle, because it becomes too easy to destroy the loudspeaker thermally (with excess power) or mechanically (with excess excursion—movement of the coil and cone).

The amplifier must also be able to handle the load that the loudspeakers present. In order to avoid excessively loading the amplifier when multiple loudspeakers are connected to a single output, you need to know the impedance of each individual loudspeaker and you must calculate the net load impedance.

IMPEDANCE CALCULATIONS

The impedance of a loudspeaker is the total opposition to AC current flow that it presents to the output of the power amplifier.

The amount of power extracted from the amplifier by the loudspeaker is inversely proportional to its impedance. Think back to the water analogy: The lower the resistance or impedance, the more current will flow—and hence the more power the load will "draw" from the amplifier. For this reason, amplifier power ratings are usually given at two or more load impedances, and the 4-ohm power is usually close to twice the 8-ohm power.

The load impedance seen by an amplifier must always be greater that zero. If it were equal to zero, the amplifier output would be

THE
YAMAHA
GUIDE TO
SOUND SYSTEMS
FOR WORSHIP
PAGE 88

short-circuited and the current demand would be infinite.

Practically speaking, the load impedance on an amplifier should never be less than 4 ohms. While some amplifiers are rated for 2-ohm, operation, it is not advisable to load an amplifier this heavily in a sound-reinforcement system. Not only will the amplifier be stressed, but the loudspeaker cable will have to be exceptionally large, particularly over long runs, since any resistance in the cable will constitute a larger percentage of the load impedance, and will therefore waste a larger percentage of the amplifier's power.

Connecting a single loudspeaker to an amplifier output is a simple affair. (Note, however, that even in simple, one-loudspeaker-per-channel installations, care must be taken that the polarity of all loudspeakers is correct.) What happens, though, when you wish to drive two or more loudspeakers from a given output? How will this affect the net impedance seen by the amplifier?

There are two basic ways to connect multiple loudspeakers to a single output: in *series*, and in *parallel*. These are shown in Figure 8-7.

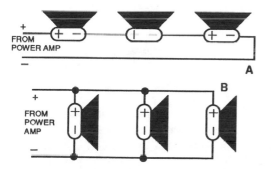

Figure 8-7. Series (A) and parallel (B) connection of loudspeakers.

When loudspeakers are connected in series, as shown in Figure 8-7A, the net impedance is the sum of the individual impedances. For example, if you connect three loudspeakers—with impedances of 8, 8, and 4 ohms, respectively—in series across an output, the net impedance "seen" by the amp will be:

$$Z_{net} = Z_1 + Z_2 + Z_3$$
$$= 8 + 8 + 4$$
$$= 20 \text{ ohms}$$

When loudspeakers are connected in parallel, as shown in Figure 8-7B, the net impedance is a bit more complicated to calculate. It is described by the equation:

$$Z_{net} = \cfrac{1}{\cfrac{1}{Z_1} + \cfrac{1}{Z_2} \cdots \cfrac{1}{Z_n}}$$

Where n = the total number of parallel elements.

If you connect three loudspeakers—with impedances of 16, 16, and 8 ohms, respectively—in parallel across an output, the net impedance "seen" by the amp will be:

$$Z_{net} = \cfrac{1}{\cfrac{1}{16} + \cfrac{1}{16} + \cfrac{1}{8}}$$

$$= \cfrac{1}{\cfrac{1}{4}}$$

$$= 4 \text{ ohms}$$

When you connect only loads of equal impedance, the complexity of the calculation is reduced. In such a case, the net impedance of the load is equal to the impedance of one loudspeaker divided by the number of loudspeakers. For example, four 16-ohm loudspeakers connected in parallel would yield a net impedance of 4 ohms (16 ÷ 4).

Note that the impedance specification of a loudspeaker is typically a *nominal* value. This means that at some frequencies the speaker's actual impedance may be considerably below the nominal figure. A hypothetical speaker with a nominal impedance of 8 ohms may have a minimum impedance of 5 ohms. Connecting three such speakers in parallel will present the amplifier with a load not of 2.67 ohms, but rather with a 1.67 ohm *minimum* impedance.

In summary:

• Series connection raises the impedance.

• Parallel connection lowers the impedance.

THE
YAMAHA
GUIDE TO
SOUND SYSTEMS
FOR WORSHIP
PAGE 89

Parallel connections are generally used in sound reinforcement systems, since if one of the loudspeakers "blows" (becomes an open circuit), it won't cause the other loudspeaker(s) connected to that output to fall silent—as would happen with a series connection. The number of loudspeakers in a parallel connection should be limited so as not to allow too low a net impedance on that output.

LOUDSPEAKER SENSITIVITY

The factor that relates amplifier power to sound pressure level for a given loudspeaker is the loudspeaker's *sensitivity* rating. Unless otherwise noted, sensitivity is generally specified in dB SPL at 1 watt at 1 meter, on axis (directly in front of the loudspeaker).

Consider two loudspeakers with the same power handling capacity, but different sensitivity ratings. Say one is rated at 93 dB SPL (1 W, 1 m), and the other at 90 dB SPL (1 W, 1 m). The difference between them is a "mere" 3 dB SPL. But recall from Chapter 3 that an increase of 3 dB is equivalent to a doubling of power. In other words, it would take *twice* the amplifier power to obtain the same loudness from the speaker with the lower sensitivity. The moral of the story is: All other things being equal, choose the loudspeaker with the highest sensitivity.

Of course, all else is rarely equal. In practice, increased sensitivity is achieved by trading off other desirable characteristics. To increase sensitivity, a loudspeaker designer may have to tighten manufacturing tolerances (increasing cost), or give up extended frequency response, or tolerate higher distortion levels.

FEATURES ON POWER AMPS

Power amplifiers designed for use in a professional audio system are generally simple in appearance compared to many hi-fi amplifiers. Aside from a line-level input and a high-level output for connection to the loudspeakers, they may have a power switch, input attenuation (volume) controls, and, occasionally, meters. Many professional amplifiers omit one or more of even these bare amenities.

METERING

Meters may or may not appear on professional power amplifiers. The most useful are are either peak-reading mechanical meters, or meters with a peak LED, or LED "bar graph" meters with a peak hold. Clip LEDs appear on many power amplifiers to warn of clipping.

INPUT ATTENUATORS

The "volume controls" on most professional amplifiers control the level of the input, rather than only the level of the output. This means they are useful for "padding back" the signal so that it does not cause clipping in the amplifier. Of course, by changing the level of the input, they also affect the level of the output. (Relative to a given input level, this does not affect the power output of the amp.) For this reason they can be used to set the proper level for a group of loudspeakers. On many amplifiers, these controls are *detented* (that is, rather than rotating freely, the control clicks into each position), so that precise settings can be made. They also generally are recessed in the front panel, and frequently are provided with knob-locks, to discourage accidental or casual changes of settings.

PROTECTION SCHEMES

Modern power amplifiers often include elaborate means to protect both the amplifier itself and the loudspeakers connected to it from damage.

When some amplifiers are switched on, a relay, operating on a timed delay, waits a short time to connect the load. This *muting* circuit keeps harmful transients ("spikes," or "pops"), which occur when the amplifier "kicks in," from reaching the loudspeakers. The same relay typically opens immediately when the amplifier is turned off, to similarly protect the loudspeakers.

This relay also comes into play in protecting the loudspeakers from DC voltages, which could damage voice coils. Circuitry in the amplifier will cause the relay to disconnect the load if DC is detected at the outputs.

Thermal protection circuits are sometimes provided, which shut the amplifier down automatically if the operating temperature exceeds a certain limit.

THE
YAMAHA
GUIDE TO
SOUND SYSTEMS
FOR WORSHIP
PAGE 90

Power or *current limiting* protects the amplifier against low load impedances, such as shorted speaker cables (or a group of loudspeakers connected in parallel with too low a net impedance), which could otherwise cause the amplifier to burn out.

A different kind of limiting occasionally provided is *signal limiting*, or *transient suppression*. This acts on the input signal, automatically "turning it down" when it is too high, to keep it from clipping. This kind of limiting is discussed in Chapter 7.

A *subsonic filter* can remove inaudible low frequencies from the input signal—frequencies that waste amplifier power and can also cause clipping.

Power amplifiers with one or more of these protection schemes frequently include LED indicators on the front panel to indicate the status of the various features.

One other means of protecting loudspeakers is not a feature on power amplifiers *per se*, but can supplement them. It involves placing a *fuse* between the amplifier output and the speaker. In order to do its job, the fuse has to be connected to the hot (+) terminal of the amplifier, and must be of a rating that allows it to blow quickly in response to too high a transient peak. When such a fuse does its job, the loudspeaker will be silent until the fuse can be replaced; but this inconvenience is minor compared to having to replace the loudspeaker itself. Fuses are not fool-proof protection. Some transients may damage a driver before the fuse can react. Also, the fuse will pass low and high frequencies alike, and will not prevent a high-frequency driver from being damaged by low frequencies.

POWER AND COOLING REQUIREMENTS

It is typical for a power surge to occur when turning on a power amplifier. This is why muting circuits are useful in protecting loudspeakers; it takes a short time—a couple of seconds or less—for the amplifier to stabilize. In large systems, it is often difficult to obtain a sufficient number of 20-amp circuits to accommodate these surges. Many modern power amplifiers, for example, each require the full capacity of a 20-amp circuit at turn-on, though their operating current requirement is usually

much lower. The solution to this problem is to use a stepped turn-on sequence; in fixed installations, the turn-on sequence can be automated with timing and control circuits.

Power amplifiers should always be the LAST items in the signal chain to be turned on, and the FIRST to be turned off. Again, this offers a measure of protection to the loudspeakers (and the ears) against transients generated by the other equipment when it is switched on and off.

A common problem with high-power amplifiers only shows up when multiple amps are used. When banks of these amps are installed in large sound systems, they draw so much power on loud peaks that the voltage of the AC main sags, causing interaction with the console and other low-level signal processing equipment through the power supplies, and a terrible low-frequency feedback/distortion loop. On many occasions, this equipment can trip the main AC service breakers. Particularly when driving woofers (low-frequency loudspeaker elements), the AC power source must be "stiff." Most manufacturers incorporate current-limiting circuitry in their amplifiers, or install appropriately rated circuit breakers, to avoid such disasters.

The present state of electronic technology, impressive though it is, cannot overcome one fact: Where there is power, there is heat. Power amplifiers can generate a great deal of heat, which is the fact behind FTC preconditioning, thermal protection schemes, and temperature LEDs on front panels.

To help keep amplifiers cool, fans are sometimes incorporated into them. Since fans generate noise, on some amplifiers the fans turn on only when the operating temperature reaches a certain point. Sometimes these fans operate at different speeds, according to how hot the amplifier is. Sometimes no fans are necessary at all; the use of heat sinks or the incorporation of sophisticated convection designs may keep an amplifier cool enough.

Fans or no, all power amplifiers require *air* to keep cool. This means that vents should never be blocked, and that sufficient "breathing space" be allowed above, below, and behind the unit. This is especially important in equipment racks, where the close proximity of several heat-generating devices can exacerbate the problem.

CHAPTER 9.
LOUDSPEAKERS

Loudspeaker is a generic term used to describe a wide variety of transducers that convert electrical energy into acoustical energy, or sound. The term also is commonly used to refer to systems of two or more transducers in a single enclosure, with or without a crossover.

For the sake of clarity, this chapter will use the term *driver* to refer to an individual transducer, and *loudspeaker* to refer to a system. A system consists of one or more drivers implemented as a free-standing functional component—that is, mounted in an enclosure with or without crossover, or fitted with a horn, or otherwise configured for a specific function.

By using an appropriate crossover (discussed in Chapter 7) to combine two or more drivers that reproduce different frequency bands, loudspeaker systems can be created that cover most of the audio frequency range. Such a system is referred to as a *full-range loudspeaker*. It is distinguished from the more limited *full-range driver*, which is a single driver that is intended to, but rarely does, reproduce most of the audio frequency range.

Single-source (*dual concentric*, or *coaxial*) loudspeakers, in which a high-frequency driver is mounted at the center of a low-frequency one, enable all frequencies to emerge from the same place. These professional units, typically used for studio monitors, are not to be confused with coaxial car speakers.

Low-frequency drivers are often called *woofers* (*subwoofers* are sometimes used to reach the lowest audible frequencies). High-frequency drivers are similarly called *tweeters* (*supertweeters* are sometimes used to reach the highest audible frequencies). Midrange drivers are called...midrange drivers (actually, they used to be called *squawkers*, but that term is not used these days).

METHODS OF TRANSDUCTION

As stated at left, loudspeakers convert electrical energy into acoustical energy. There are many ways to effect this conversion, and some esoteric methods have been employed—both in scientific applications and, occasionally, in hi-fi systems. In the down-to-earth world of sound reinforcement and recording, two methods overwhelmingly prevail: the *electromagnetically* modulated diaphragm and the *piezoelectrically* modulated diaphragm. Of the two, the former is by far the more common.

ELECTROMAGNETIC TRANSDUCTION

Electromagnetic drivers are built on the same principle as electric motors: the creation of a magnetic field when electrical current passes through a coil of wire. In fact, electromagnetic drivers are classified as *linear electromagnetic motors*. Look at Figure 9-1. The coil (a), called a *voice coil* in the case of a driver, is placed in a gap in a permanent magnet (b). The permanent magnet sets up stationary lines of magnetic force (c).

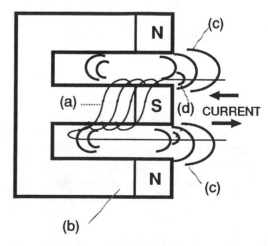

Figure 9-1. Operation of a linear electromagnetic motor.

If a direct current is now passed through the coil, the flow of electrons in the wire creates a second magnetic field around the

THE
YAMAHA
GUIDE TO
SOUND SYSTEMS
FOR WORSHIP
PAGE 92

coil (d). The polarity (north-south direction) of this field depends on the direction of current flow through the wire.

The electromagnetic field interacts with that of the permanent magnet. Assuming that the position of the permanent magnet is fixed, the force resulting from the interaction of the two fields causes the coil to move.

If the flow of current in the coil is reversed, then the polarity of the electromagnetic field is also reversed. This reverses the direction of the force acting on the coil, causing it to move in the opposite direction.

If the direction of the current is repeatedly reversed, the coil will move back and forth within the field of the magnet. The motion of the coil will be a physical representation of the alternations of the current.

This is the principle behind an electromagnetic driver. Alternating current from the power amplifier (i.e., the amplified audio signal) passes through the coil, causing it to move back and forth. The coil is attached to a suitable diaphragm, which couples this mechanical motion to the air.

PIEZOELECTRIC TRANSDUCTION

The piezoelectric (pressure-electric) effect is a property of certain crystalline materials. When such a crystal is mechanically deformed, electricity is generated (Chapter 5 discusses the use of the effect in microphones and contact pickups). On the other hand, if an electric potential is applied across the crystal, it changes dimensions, expanding or contracting in the axis of electrical polarization.

The piezoelectric elements used in audio transducers are generally of the type known as *bimorphs* ("bi-" meaning "two," and "morph" meaning "form"). Bimorphs are elements built in two layers of piezoelectric material, and are also called *benders*. Figure 9-2 shows the type of deformation that bimorphs undergo when a voltage is applied across them.

An alternating current, such as an audio signal, causes an alternation of these motions. As with electromagnetic drivers, the piezoelectric element is joined to a diaphragm to couple this motion to the air.

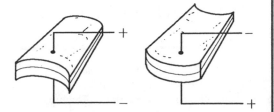

Figure 9-2. Bimorphs as used in piezoelectric drivers.

POLARITY

As mentioned in previous chapters, it is important to the quality (and quantity) of the sound that all loudspeakers be connected with the correct *polarity*—that is, the positive (+) output terminal of the power amplifier must be connected to the positive terminal of the loudspeaker, and the negative (–) terminal of the amplifier to the negative terminal of the loudspeaker. The polarity of the connection terminals on a loudspeaker may be specified in any number of ways. The most common is color-coding, with red for positive and black for negative (though some loudspeakers are just the reverse!).

The polarity of a driver can be checked with a 9-volt battery, as shown in Figure 9-3. (This assumes that the motion of the diaphragm can be observed. For drivers mounted in horns, and high-frequency drivers with small excursions, a device called a phase [polarity] tester may be the only reliable way to test polarity.) When a connection is made so that the cone moves outward, the lead that is connected to the positive terminal of the battery is the positive lead of the driver.

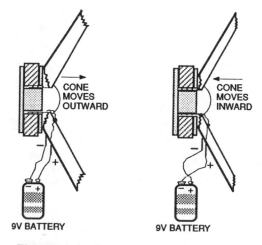

Figure 9-3. Testing driver polarity with a battery.

LOW-FREQUENCY DRIVERS

Efficient reproduction of low frequencies calls for moving a large volume of air. This requires one or both of the following:

• Long diaphragm excursion.

• Large diaphragm area.

For these reasons, low-frequency drivers are generally electromagnetic drivers with *cone* diaphragms. When flush-mounted on the front of the enclosure (i.e., without a horn), this type of driver is also known as a *direct radiator*. Figure 9-4 shows a typical low-frequency driver.

The size of the driver is specified by the diameter of the cone, measured at the base (widest part). Standard sizes for low-frequency drivers in sound systems are 12, 15, and 18 inches (30.5, 38, and 45.7 cm). Because different manufacturers use different sized frames and measure cones differently, not all 12-inch drivers, for example, will be the same actual diameter.

The directional characteristics of a cone driver are dependent on the relationship between the diameter of the cone and the wavelength of the sound that the driver is reproducing. At low frequencies, where the wavelength is long compared to the size of the cone, the driver is omnidirectional—it tends to radiate the sound in all directions. As the frequency rises, the wavelength gets shorter, and the directional pattern of the cone narrows gradually—more of the sound is directed in front of the driver, and less in other directions.

LOW-FREQUENCY ENCLOSURES

Cone-type low-frequency drivers are nearly always mounted in enclosures. Why? Consider what happens when a driver operates: When the cone moves forward, compressing the air in front, it rarefies the air behind. Similarly, when the cone moves backward, rarefying the air in front, it compresses the air behind. The motion of the air behind the cone is called the *back wave*. Left unenclosed, the air would tend to move *around* the cone from front to back or back

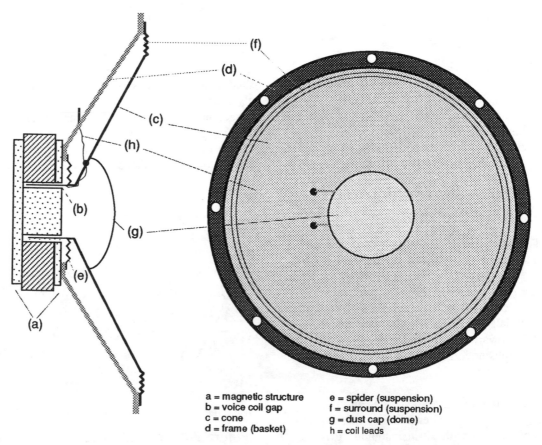

a = magnetic structure
b = voice coil gap
c = cone
d = frame (basket)
e = spider (suspension)
f = surround (suspension)
g = dust cap (dome)
h = coil leads

Figure 9-4. A cone-type driver (cross-section and front views).

THE
YAMAHA
GUIDE TO
SOUND SYSTEMS
FOR WORSHIP
PAGE 94

to front, to equalize the pressure on both sides of the cone. This would effectively cancel much of the power the loudspeaker produced. An enclosure isolates the air in front of the cone from the air behind.

The most common low-frequency enclosures used in sound systems are the *vented* enclosure and the *horn-loaded* enclosure.

VENTED ENCLOSURES

A vented enclosure features an opening, called a *vent*, or *port*. The enclosure is constructed so that the back wave is sent out the port, shifted in phase by 180°, so that it is in phase with the front wave. The two combine constructively, and the result is a higher level of sound.

This reinforcement of the sound occurs at a certain frequency, called the *resonant frequency* of the enclosure. (To a lesser degree, this reinforcement also affects the frequencies around the resonant frequency.) This frequency is determined by the area of the port and the size of the enclosure. Vented enclosures are constructed to be *tuned* to a certain resonant frequency— usually to reinforce the low-frequency response of the driver.

A variation on the vented enclosure uses what is called a *ducted port*, shown in cross-section in Figure 9-6. Ducting also affects

the tuning of an enclosure, and is normally used to extend the low-frequency response of small enclosures.

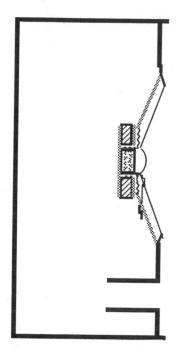

Figure 9-6. A ducted-port low-frequency enclosure.

Vented enclosures, ducted or not, are generally used for direct-radiator, low-frequency systems. Although they extend low-frequency response, there is a trade-off: Below the resonant frequency, the sound level drops off much more rapidly than in a sealed (also called *infinite-baffle*) enclosure.

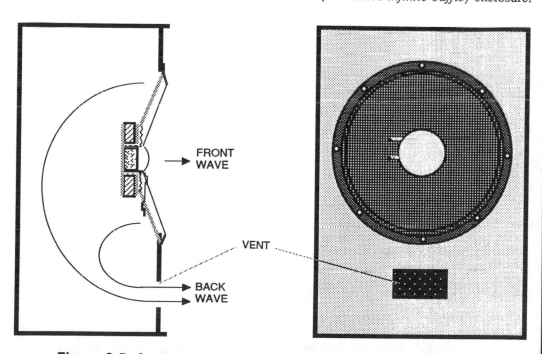

Figure 9-5. A vented, direct-radiator low-frequency enclosure.

LOW-FREQUENCY HORNS

Horn-loaded enclosures can be very efficient, and provide better control of directivity than direct-radiator enclosures. The directional characteristics of a low-frequency horn are determined by the horn rather than by the driver size, and horns with large mouths retain directivity in the low frequencies. Since horn enclosures are more directional than direct-radiator types, they are particularly useful in situations where long throws are required.

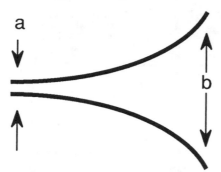

Figure 9-7. Cross-section of a straight exponential horn, pointing out the throat (a) and mouth (b).

The diameter of the mouth of a horn (or the equivalent diameter for a rectangular-mouthed horn) should be at least one quarter the wavelength of the cutoff frequency—the lowest frequency at which the horn can effectively control the driver diaphragm. For this reason, low-frequency horns must, in theory, be very large if their directional control is to extend to the lowest end of the audio range.

When horns are arrayed together, their mouth areas couple acoustically to form the equivalent of a single large mouth. This effect permits the design of individual low-frequency horn enclosures of practical dimensions, which can be grouped together as a block to extend the low-frequency response of the system.

A horn shaped like that in Figure 9-7, if made large enough to be effective at a low frequency, would be unwieldy. For this reason, practical low-frequency horn enclosures are often of the *folded-horn* type. As the name implies, folded-horn enclosures are constructed by folding the horn back on itself to reduce its size. Figures 9-8 and 9-9 show two common folded-horn enclosures, the *W-bin* and the *scoop*. The latter is an approximation of a curled horn.

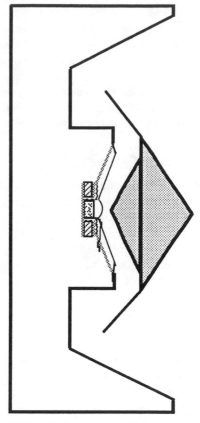

Figure 9-8. Cross-section of a folded low-frequency horn (a W-bin).

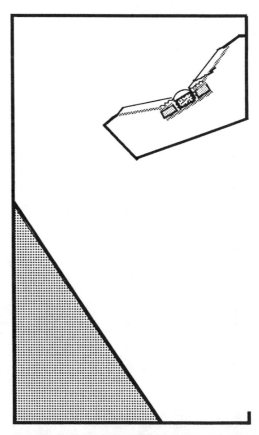

Figure 9-9. Cross-section of a folded low-frequency horn (a scoop).

THE
YAMAHA
GUIDE TO
SOUND SYSTEMS
FOR WORSHIP
PAGE 96

HIGH-FREQUENCY DRIVERS

In sound reinforcement, practical high-frequency loudspeakers are most often horn-loaded. The drivers used at high frequencies are designed to be used with horns, and are called *compression drivers*. A typical compression driver is an electromagnetic linear motor, similar to the low-frequency driver, but with a domed diaphragm rather than a cone. The physical dimensions leave little room for excursion, but not much is needed; high frequencies require less excursion than low frequencies, and the use of the horn also reduces excursion requirements.

Supertweeters, used to extend the high-frequency range of a full-range system, may be either electromagnetic or piezoelectric. Piezoelectric drivers are low in cost, but do not deliver the sound quality of a well-designed electromagnetic compression tweeter. In sound reinforcement systems, they are horn-loaded.

HIGH-FREQUENCY HORNS

Many types of high-frequency horns are used in sound reinforcement, classified by names such as *exponential*, *radial*, and *constant-directivity*. In all of these, the most important attribute is a controlled dispersion pattern. The horizontal and vertical dispersion angles of the horn will usually differ from one another, with good reason. A wide horizontal angle allows coverage of a typical seating area. A wide vertical angle would waste acoustic energy by directing it to undesired areas—into free space or onto ceilings, for example.

DIRECTIONAL CHARACTERISTICS AND COVERAGE

The directional characteristics of a loudspeaker may be specified in a number of ways. The most common method is to specify the angles of horizontal and vertical dispersion, in degrees. These figures normally represent the angle within which the sound pressure level is within 6 dB of the *on-axis* (straight-ahead) level at some frequency.

Some loudspeaker specifications also include values for *directivity factor* (also called *directivity ratio*, or Q) and *directivity index* (DI). These figures apply to families of calculations that are beyond the scope of this book. They are generally used by acousticians and consultants in specifying speech reinforcement systems.

One more method of specifying the directional characteristics of a loudspeaker is the *polar plot*. Figure 9-10 (on the next page) shows typical horizontal and vertical plots for a full-range loudspeaker. The plots are circular, with the loudspeaker at the center and 0° representing the on-axis direction. The concentric circles are sometimes labeled as distances (as in this figure), and sometimes as levels (with the levels becoming *lower* as you move toward the center of the circle). They amount to the same thing: The farther out a plotted line extends, the greater the level of the sound in that direction, and the farther out it will "reach." (Actually, "reach" is a misleading term; it means that the critical distance will be greater since less reverberation will occur, due to a narrower dispersion pattern).

Note that the loudspeaker's directional characteristics are shown in a number of different frequency ranges. This enables you to deduce how the sound will change as you move off-axis, and how the reverberant field may be colored on- or off-axis.

A graphic means of relating the coverage of a loudspeaker to the environment in which that loudspeaker will be used is the *isobar plot* (see Figure 9-11). Here, imagine that you are in the position of the loudspeaker, looking out. The 0° axis is directly in front of you, in the center. Angles to the sides or

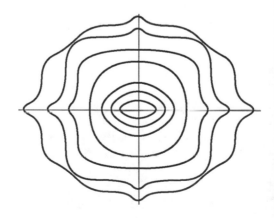

Figure 9-11. An isobar plot for a hypothetical loudspeaker.

up and down increase as they move away from the center. Plotted lines circumscribe areas of equal sound pressure, analogous to the isobars on a weather map. The drop as you move outward from one level to the next is specified—2 dB, for example.

The value of isobar plots lies in using them to *map* the coverage of the driver onto the listening area, to show how well the area will be covered. These techniques have gotten quite sophisticated in the past decade or so, to the point of superimposing isobar plots and architectural maps on transparent spheres to obtain the truest perspective of how the listener areas "appear" to the loudspeaker, or using isobar data in computer programs to make complex calculations that aid the system designer in predicting system performance.

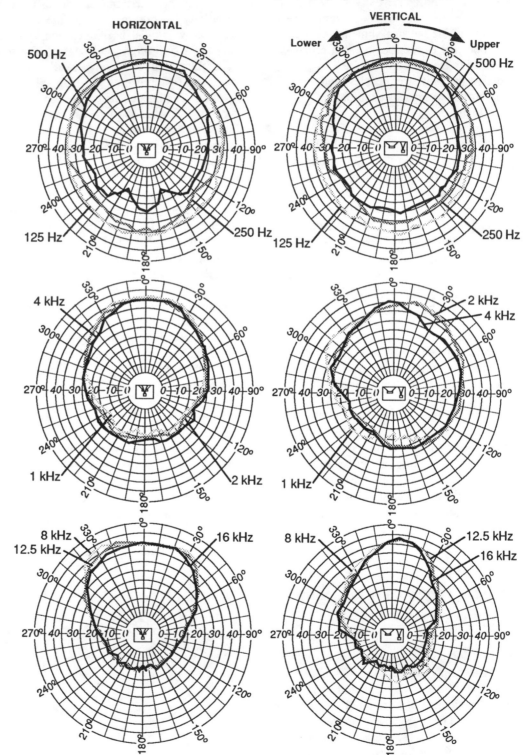

Figure 9-10. Polar plots illustrating the horizontal and vertical dispersion of a full-range loudspeaker system.

THE
YAMAHA
GUIDE TO
SOUND SYSTEMS
FOR WORSHIP
PAGE 98

BI- AND TRIAMPLIFIED LOUDSPEAKER SYSTEMS

Chapter 7 includes a discussion of crossover networks, differentiating between *passive*, *high-level* crossovers (which are placed after the power amplifier) and *active*, *low-level* ones (which are found before the amplifier, and therefore, by necessity, call for a separate amplifier channel for each band of frequencies). The latter are called *bi-* or *triamplified* systems, depending on whether the signal is split into two or three bands. They offer a number of performance advantages over passive systems.

One advantage is increased *headroom*. Most music, especially popular music, is bass-heavy; there is much more energy at low frequencies than at high ones. When both high- and low-frequency material are present in a program, the high-energy bass frequencies can use up most of the power in the power amplifier, leaving little reserve for the high frequencies. The result can be severe clipping of high-frequency material. In a bi- or triamplified system, the high-frequency material is routed to its own power amplifier. The result is an increase in headroom—room above the normal signal level to allow peaks to occur without clipping—that is greater than would be obtained by simply using a single, equivalent, larger power amplifier.

A small bi- or triamplified system is more expensive than a system with passive crossovers, because more amplifiers are required. But a large bi- or triamplified system requires only one crossover network for multiple amplifiers and loudspeakers, whereas conventional systems must have a passive crossover for each loudspeaker—a more costly alternative.

Also, the required power amplifier capacity of a large bi- or triamped system can be less than that of a conventional system (greater headroom can be obtained at lower power levels), which is why the former is often more cost-effective.

PROCESSOR-CONTROLLED LOUDSPEAKER SYSTEMS

Processor-controlled loudspeaker systems are a relatively recent trend in system design. The loudspeakers are designed for use with a special-purpose processor, which takes the place of an active crossover, before the power amplifiers.

These processors not only function as a crossover (some models feature "floating" crossover points, to shift the distribution of the signal among the amplifiers as the frequency content changes), but typically offer sophisticated loudspeaker protection and equalization as well. This can include fast-acting signal limiting, to suppress peaks that would otherwise damage drivers. Connections from the amplifier outputs allow the processor to sense and correct harmful DC voltages and the like.

Some systems also correct the "misalignment" of sounds in time that can occur among multiple drivers.

TYPES OF LOUDSPEAKERS BY APPLICATION

To the layman (or minister!), the variety of different kinds of loudspeakers can be bewildering. After all, don't they all do the same thing? Yes and no. They all change electricity into sound. But different environments and uses call for different characteristics. So a convenient way to make sense of the proliferation of loudspeakers is to classify them by their intended use.

The purpose in making these classifications is to make you aware of the need to use the right tool for the job. If a mechanic wants to remove a hex nut, he should use a wrench; he could get by with a pair of pliers, but the results would *not* be pretty. It's the same with loudspeakers.

THE
YAMAHA
GUIDE TO
SOUND SYSTEMS
FOR WORSHIP
PAGE 99

SOUND REINFORCEMENT

The simplified definition of sound reinforcement stated in Chapter 1 bears repeating here: to distribute sound evenly to all listener areas, and to not distribute sound to any non-listener areas. This requires several characteristics of sound reinforcement loudspeakers:

- A long "throw" for some loudspeakers —the ability to direct sound to the farthest listeners without contributing unduly to the reverberant field.

- A short "throw" for some loudspeakers —the ability to direct sound over a wide angle to nearby listeners without creating interference with the "long-throw" loudspeakers' sound pattern and without contributing unduly to the reverberant field.

- The ability to deliver high sound pressure levels without distortion or self-destruction.

STAGE MONITOR

Controlled dispersion is also important to stage monitors, but for different reasons than with "house" speakers, since stage monitors are placed in close proximity to those who will be listening to them— instrumentalists, song leaders, and other members of the worship team. Controlled dispersion of a stage monitor is important to minimize feedback paths to open mics.

The main distinguishing characteristics of monitor design are visual and functional: Where they can be seen by the congregation, they should be as unobtrusive as possible. For this reason, most stage monitors take the form of "wedges" that sit low on the floor, angling the speaker up toward the performer or minister. Monitors used by touring groups are finished to withstand the loadings and unloadings, and accidental kicks, that attend such use.

RECORDING MONITOR

Monitor loudspeakers for recording engineers primarily need to present the most accurate possible representation of the sound. Flat, smooth frequency response is essential. Small monitor loudspeakers that are mounted on or near the mixing console are referred to as *near-field monitors*, for

they are made for the kind of close-up (8 feet or less) listening that occurs in many control rooms. This kind of loudspeaker can also be used for monitoring at the console in a sound reinforcement system (to hear what's being sent to the various stage monitors, for example); if the console is located on the main floor of the assembly room, one or two of them can be placed on the floor behind the engineer, angled up.

Some designs include compensations for the phase shifts and tiny delays that can occur with crossovers and multiple drivers. These seek to produce what is known as a *phase-coherent wavefront*, which theoretically not only provides the truest sound, but also lessens aural fatigue. This can raise the cost of the monitor, and may not be necessary in sound reinforcement applications.

Many experienced recording engineers avoid the use of extremely "colored" monitors. While such loudspeakers may be very pleasant to listen to in your living room, they don't provide the engineer with the neutral reference needed to produce top-quality recordings. The world may look better through rose-colored glasses, but the picture you paint of it won't be accurate.

HI-FI

The typical hi-fi loudspeaker is made to distribute sound at relatively low levels to a relatively small room. It may find limited application in a worship facility—for piping sound into the cry room, for example—but should be shunned as a "house" loudspeaker in a sound reinforcement system. The demands of live sound reinforcement dictate that some of the subtleties of high-fidelity sound be traded off. Hi-fi speakers lack the sensitivity, power handling, and controlled directivity needed for sound reinforcement. Use of hi-fi speakers in sound reinforcement rarely yields satisfactory results.

PAGING

Paging loudspeakers must do one thing well: reproduce the sound of the human voice. This requires a frequency response from around 200 Hz up to 6 kHz. Fidelity is less important than intelligibility. Compression drivers are sometimes used where high sound pressure levels are required—in noisy environments, or (more likely for a worship facility) outdoors. Indoors, in relatively quiet environments, a paging system can use

THE
YAMAHA
GUIDE TO
SOUND SYSTEMS
FOR WORSHIP
PAGE 100

ceiling loudspeakers, as described under point number 2 in the following section. Some paging systems also distribute background music (as in supermarkets and department stores); these sometimes have wider bandwidth than voice-only systems.

CEILING LOUDSPEAKERS

There are two primary applications for ceiling-mounted loudspeakers in a worship facility, calling for different classes of loudspeaker systems:

1. **In the main assembly room.** It may be that the ceiling is too low to allow a single, elevated loudspeaker cluster at the front of the room, and so loudspeakers must be placed at intervals in the ceiling to cover the seating areas. Or it may be that a "fill" system must be installed on the underside of a balcony, to cover seats where sound from the main cluster is too weak. In either of these cases, the loudspeakers must be capable of delivering high-quality sound—especially if music is an important part of the services. High sound pressure levels generally are not necessary.

2. **Outside the assembly room.** In the foyer or narthex, the cry room, and other such areas, the need for high sound quality is not as great. This, together with the potentially large number of loudspeakers involved, often calls for the use of a *constant-voltage distribution system* (sometimes referred to as *70-volt distributed systems*, though a number of different voltages are available). In such a system, many loudspeakers are connected, via transformers, in parallel, to a single amplifier. Frequency response is limited, both because of the low-frequency limitations inherent in the transformers and because of the limited frequency response of the full-range drivers that typically are used in such systems. The individual loudspeakers are not capable of a great deal of power, but that is not usually a problem in this application.

MONO VS. STEREO IN THE WORSHIP SERVICE

Which is better: mono or stereo? Like so many other decisions, it depends.

If speech is the priority in your worship services, stereo doesn't work well. The spoken signal must be split and fed to two channels of loudspeakers; when the sound from those two channels meets the listener's ear, there is sure to be phase cancellation of the kind discussed in Chapters 1 and 3. So mono systems are preferable for speech.

On the other hand, if the worship team includes a musical ensemble, stereo can benefit the sound of the music, giving it "space." It is easier to hear all that is going on, as well as more aesthetically pleasing, when the sounds are distributed across the stereo field.

Some facilities handle this dilemma by having two sub-systems: a monophonic one for speech and a stereo one for music. It is possible to run them both from the same console, if there are enough output busses.

The arguments against stereo systems include cost: More equipment (especially power amps) is ostensibly necessary for such a system. But some discount this argument, saying that, in a large facility, the different drivers will be driven by separate amplifier channels even in a mono system, in order to control the level in different areas of the room; so the additional cost for stereo may be negligible.

A more difficult obstacle for stereo may be the shape of the assembly room. If the room is fan-shaped (narrow near the front and wide at the back), with a standard stereo configuration (i.e., the left and right loudspeakers separated to provide the best stereo image), the left and right loudspeaker clusters will each reach only one side of the congregation. A possible solution is to employ four clusters—two sets each of left and right channels—with each pair directed toward half of the room. But this poses the same problems as a mono system with multiple clusters: Phase cancellation will occur in those areas covered by both sets of loudspeakers.

Consider this: Many professional sound companies utilize dual stacks of loudspeakers fed with a single mono signal—for some of the biggest-name popular music acts. Stereo may not be appropriate or practical in reaching a large congregation. Mono, with auxiliary effects (reverb or enhanced resonance) channels may actually sound better.

THE
YAMAHA
GUIDE TO
SOUND SYSTEMS
FOR WORSHIP
PAGE 101

CHAPTER 10.
SYSTEMS FOR THE HEARING-IMPAIRED

WHY DO YOU NEED A SPECIAL AUDIO SYSTEM FOR HEARING-IMPAIRED WORSHIPERS?

Most sound system designs for houses of worship now routinely include hearing-assistance systems, to accommodate the special needs of the hearing-impaired. If we take a quick look at the nature and prevalence of hearing loss, you'll see why these systems are becoming so popular. Then we'll take a look at the types of systems that are available, how to select the right system for your needs, and how to properly set it up and use it.

PREVALENCE OF HEARING LOSS

The latest Hearing Industries Association (HIA) estimates on the prevalence of hearing loss range from 14 to 20 million people in the U.S. This means that roughly one out of every 10 to 20 people suffers some significant hearing loss. This number is growing as the population ages. In people over 55 years of age, hearing loss currently affects 15% of the population. In people over 65, it jumps to 24%. Between the time of this writing and the year 2050, the total population will increase about 36%, but the prevalence of hearing loss will rise a predicted 102% as a direct result of the aging population.

THE NATURE OF HEARING LOSS

There are four main types of hearing loss:

1. **Conductive Loss**—Sound is mechanically obstructed in the ear by wax, fluid, or immobility of the bones in the inner ear. Conductive losses generally result in a reduction of sound volume. Conductive losses can often be medically corrected or helped with hearing aids and assistive listening systems.

2. **Sensorineural Loss**—Commonly called "nerve deafness," this type of loss results when tiny hair cells within the inner part of the ear called the cochlea are damaged or destroyed. It is sometimes accompanied by *tinnitus*, or "ringing" in the ears. Hair cells can be damaged by very loud sounds, by constant exposure to noise, by exposure to chemicals or drugs, or by the aging process. There is strong evidence that some hair cells die during the aging process and are not replaced. This is called *presbycusis*. Sensorineural loss is usually a loss of high-frequency sounds, which make speech understandable. The result is a fuzzy, distorted sound, somewhat like listening to a radio tuned slightly off-station. Sensorineural losses cannot be corrected medically, but they can often be helped with hearing aids and assistive listening systems.

3. **Mixed Loss**—A combination of conductive and sensorineural loss that affects the quantity and quality of perceived sound.

4. **Central Processing Disorder**—A relatively rare type of loss that affects the speech processing center in the brain. The listener must isolate desired sounds from others to be able to understand.

In addition to the loss of sound volume or sound clarity, hearing-impaired people also experience a loss of sound *discrimination*. Discrimination is a function in which normal ears work with the brain to allow a person to "tune in" on a particular sound that he or she wants to hear, while ignoring others. When one or both ears are impaired, discrimination deteriorates. The problem intensifies in noisy surroundings.

This is a significant problem for the hearing-impaired in worship facilities because of crowd noises and the large acoustic space. If the room acoustics are poor, good speech intelligibility can be difficult even for people with normal hearing. It becomes just about impossible for people with a hearing loss. The heart of the problem is called the *signal-to-noise ratio*.

THE
YAMAHA
GUIDE TO
SOUND SYSTEMS
FOR WORSHIP
PAGE 102

The signal-to-noise ratio is a way of measuring the level of desirable sounds (signal) versus undesirable sounds (noise). Those sounds that occur closest to a listener are the loudest, and tend to mask other sounds. For the hearing-impaired worshiper, coughing, shuffling feet, and paper rustling compete with hearing the service. A hearing aid won't help, because it amplifies all sounds equally. The hearing aid can't discriminate for the listener.

To solve this problem, you need to deliver the desired sounds directly to the hearing-impaired listener's ears, with as little pickup of background noise as possible. The only way to do this with current technology is to move the microphone that picks up the sound closer to the sound source. A tiny hearing aid microphone, located in a wearer's ear at a distance from the sound source, simply cannot do the job. If you can move the microphone closer to the sound source, the source gets louder and background noises diminish. This is the main principle of a hearing-assistance system.

Hearing-assistance systems are used to deliver sounds directly from the microphones of the audio system to the hearing-impaired listener's ears. This bypasses the distance from the sound source, diminishes background noise, eliminates the effects of room acoustics, and provides the maximum signal-to-noise ratio. If an auditorium has particularly poor acoustics or an inadequate sound system, even people with normal hearing will benefit from using a hearing-assistance system.

In addition to problems with sound quantity, sound clarity, and discrimination, hearing-impaired people cannot tolerate a wide *dynamic range* of sounds. Dynamic range is the difference between the loudest sounds and the softest sounds. Wide dynamic range means that there is a great difference between the loudest sounds and the softest sounds. Narrow dynamic range means that there is little difference between the loudest and softest sounds. Assistive listening systems include signal *compressors* (see Chapter 7) to maintain a relatively narrow dynamic range and to ensure a constant listening level for the users. They also prevent the danger of over-amplifying sounds, which could damage residual hearing.

Because most hearing losses occur in the higher frequencies, some hearing-assistance systems include low-frequency *filters* to reduce low frequencies and emphasize the highs. This may sound overly bright to a listener with normal hearing, but it equalizes the frequency response of the system for most hearing-impaired listeners, preventing the lows from overpowering the highs.

TYPES OF ASSISTIVE LISTENING SYSTEMS

Assistive listening systems can use a variety of technologies to deliver sound from the microphones of the sound system to the listener. Each has its virtues and drawbacks. There is no one system that is perfect in every application, although some are more flexible and desirable than others.

HARD-WIRED SYSTEMS

Hard-wired systems involve running audio feed wires from the PA amplifier (or an auxiliary amplifier) to headphone jacks in selected seats. The amplifier must be of a suitable rating to drive the number of headsets used, and impedance-matching transformers are often used to split the amplifier load evenly. Each user station should have a volume control.

Hard-wired systems are quite reliable, inexpensive, and secure from eavesdropping, although eavesdropping is rarely a concern in worship facilities. They are rarely affected by interference from outside sources or other equipment such as light dimmers. Audio quality can be very good if a good amplifier and headphones are used.

Hard-wired systems can be difficult and expensive to install as retro-fits in existing buildings. Wiring must be concealed and routed to avoid areas of foot traffic. The greatest drawback is that they restrict seating and the number of users. No one wants to sit in the "deaf row" and call attention to oneself. People do not want to have to compete for the selected seats or be separated from friends and family. The finest equipment is of little use if people will not use it. With the availability of wireless systems that allow free seating, hard-wired systems have become obsolete and are usually no longer considered for modern installations.

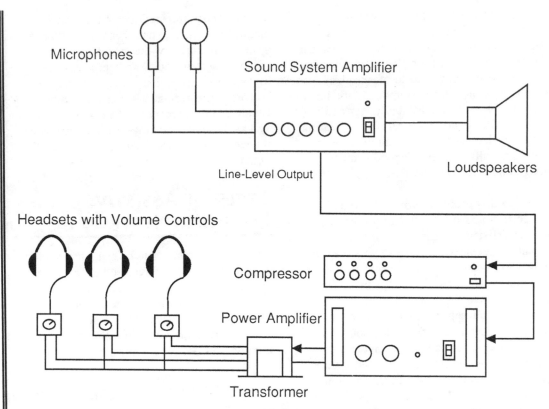

Figure 10-1. Hard-wired system.

INDUCTION LOOP SYSTEMS

Induction loop systems operate on a simple principle of *electromagnetic induction*. An audio amplifier is connected to a loop of wire that is placed around the perimeter of the listening area. When audio signals from the sound system are fed into the loop amplifier, the amplifier drives current through the loop wire, which creates an

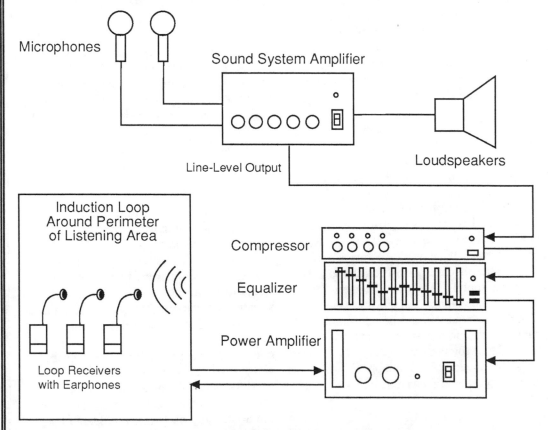

THE
YAMAHA
GUIDE TO
SOUND SYSTEMS
FOR WORSHIP
PAGE 104

Figure 10-2. Induction loop system.

electromagnetic field around the wire that varies with the audio signal. The electromagnetic field can induce an identical signal in a pickup coil contained in a pocket-sized loop receiver or in a hearing aid—hence the name induction loop.

One of the chief advantages of a loop system is that a listener who has a hearing aid equipped with an induction pickup coil (called a telecoil, or T-switch) can hear the loop signal directly with his or her hearing aid. All loop systems are compatible, so a hearing aid or loop receiver may be used with any loop. Because there is no wire between the sound system and the listener, loop systems are wireless and allow freedom of seating. There is no limit to the number of users with a loop system, but each user must have a loop receiver or a hearing aid equipped with a telecoil.

Loops have some disadvantages as well. Only about 10% of the hearing-impaired have a hearing aid with the proper telecoil to pick up the loop signal, and this number is steadily decreasing. The trend in hearing aids is toward ever smaller sizes that do not have room for telecoils and switches to operate them. Telecoil sensitivity and orientation are quite variable, so favorable reception is not assured. It can be difficult to provide uniform coverage with a loop in a large worship area. The strength of the magnetic field falls off rapidly as you move farther from the loop wire. The signal strength is eight times as weak two feet from the loop as it is at one foot from the loop. This can be compensated for by using more powerful amplifiers, which gets expensive, or by looping only part of the seating area, but that introduces seating restrictions.

Loop systems do allow some leakage of the signal into adjacent areas. This may allow eavesdropping, which again is usually not a concern for worship facilities. Routing the loop wire can be a problem in retro-fits. The loop wire must not be placed in a metal conduit, which would shield the loop signal, and foot traffic areas, windows, and doorways must be avoided. Sometimes in new construction, the loop is laid into the floor. This makes it inconspicuous and avoids traffic areas, but it is difficult and expensive to repair or replace.

Induction loops are also susceptible to electromagnetic interference. Room wiring, lighting dimmers, computers, and organs all radiate electromagnetic interference that can create hums and buzzes in a loop system. To overcome this background interference, the loop signal must be considerably stronger than the interference to maintain a good signal-to-noise ratio. This requires an amplifier of 100-200 watts, driven by an audio compressor to maintain constant high power output and stable signal levels for the listeners. The impedance of the loop wire must be carefully matched to the amplifier to prevent it from self-destructing. To obtain sound with good fidelity, an equalizer must be added to compensate for the inherently poor frequency response of an induction loop.

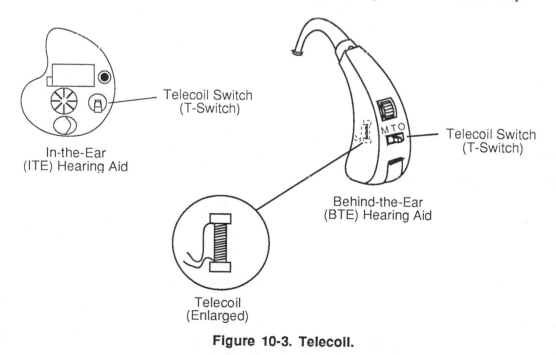

Telecoil Switch
(T-Switch)

In-the-Ear
(ITE) Hearing Aid

Telecoil Switch
(T-Switch)

Behind-the-Ear
(BTE) Hearing Aid

Telecoil
(Enlarged)

Figure 10-3. Telecoil.

THE
YAMAHA
GUIDE TO
SOUND SYSTEMS
FOR WORSHIP
PAGE 105

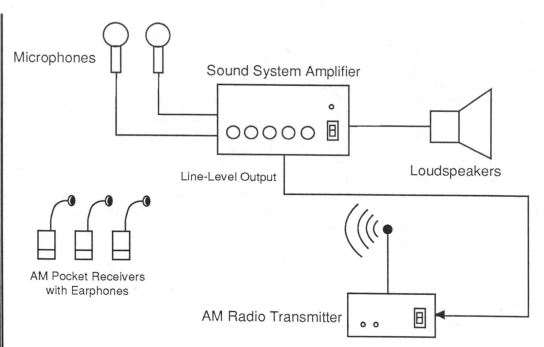

Figure 10-4. AM radio system.

RADIO SYSTEMS—AM

AM systems were the first radio systems used for general-purpose hearing assistance in houses of worship. They operate by connecting a small AM radio transmitter to the sound system and broadcasting the service to portable AM radio receivers. This allows listeners to hear the worship directly from the microphones of the sound system, without seating restrictions. It is similar to setting up a small radio station within the worship facility. AM systems offer an improvement in performance and flexibility over loop systems. There is no limit to the number of users with an AM system, but each user must have a pocket-sized AM receiver.

When using a radio system, the Federal Communications Commission (FCC) determines what operating frequencies can be used, as well as other technical specifications. In 1982, the FCC changed its rules, allowing FM radio technology to be used in worship facilities. Although many AM systems had been sold, manufacturers immediately switched to FM technology because it offered enormous technical and performance improvements. Consequently, there are no new AM listening systems available today that are appropriate for use in worship facilities.

RADIO SYSTEMS—FM

In 1982, the FCC made the 72–76 MHz Auditory Assistance Band of frequencies available for unlicensed FM hearing-assistance systems used in any place of public assembly. As with all frequency allocations, this band is not exclusively for the use of hearing-assistance systems. It is shared with other, licensed business services. To avoid potential interference problems, a number of channels are offered by manufacturers.

FM systems brought a great improvement in performance over AM systems. Allowable transmitting power was great enough to provide uniform coverage in very large buildings. Installation time was reduced with easy-to-install antennas. Sound quality improved as a result of the inherently wider bandwidth and better noise performance of FM operation. FM systems are not as susceptible to interference from light dimmers, organ motors, fluorescent lights, or thunderstorms as were AM systems.

FM systems are preset to a particular frequency. Most manufacturers use a standard frequency to maintain as much compatibility between systems as possible. If the standard frequency cannot be used due to interference from another radio service,

THE
YAMAHA
GUIDE TO
SOUND SYSTEMS
FOR WORSHIP
PAGE 106

alternate frequencies are available. Some manufacturers have offered tunable transmitters operating on the 88–108 MHz FM broadcast band. This allows users to bring their own FM radios to the service. While this seems to be a good approach initially, it does have drawbacks. The quality and performance of consumer radios and earphones are quite variable. Consequently, it is difficult to ensure good system performance for the majority of users. Some users have trouble tuning in the proper program and may end up listening to another program. Interference from strong FM broadcast stations can make reception difficult, and tunable FM transmitters are subject to frequency drift. Tunable transmitters on the FM broadcast band are limited to lower transmitting power than 72–76 MHz auditory-assistance transmitters, so uniform coverage of medium to large facilities is difficult.

With their broad coverage, FM systems allow great flexibility in their use and installation in worship facilities. Installation is inconspicuous, so aesthetic concerns are not compromised. Monitor receivers can be used in cry rooms, nursery areas, offices, kitchens, adjacent chapels,

etc., without wiring. The systems can be used outdoors for special events. Some congregations conduct outdoor services or have handicapped members listen in their cars. Multi-channel systems can be used to provide simultaneous language interpretation as well as hearing assistance. On an installed basis, FM systems are very cost-effective compared to other technologies.

FM systems have relatively few drawbacks. If security is a concern, which is rare in worship services, eavesdropping can occur if the eavesdropper has the right type of receiver. Wireless microphones pose the same considerations, but this has not stopped the steady rise in their use. Interference can occur from other radio services, but this can usually be overcome by changing frequencies. Some other pieces of audio equipment in the sound system can be susceptible to radio interference from the FM transmitter, which usually produces a hum or buzz in the sound system. This is the result of poor design in the susceptible equipment. In most cases, it is NOT the fault of the FM transmitter. A competent installer or technician can easily remedy this problem if it occurs.

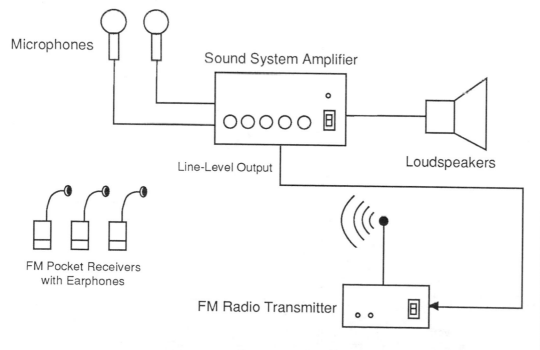

Figure 10-5. FM radio system.

THE
YAMAHA
GUIDE TO
SOUND SYSTEMS
FOR WORSHIP
PAGE 107

INFRARED SYSTEMS

Infrared systems use invisible beams of infrared light to deliver sound directly from the sound system to the listener. The transmission is produced by one or more *emitter panels*, which contain an array of infrared light-emitting diodes (LEDs). The infrared receivers contain an infrared light detector and focusing lens to receive the light signals. Infrared systems are capable of the same excellent sound quality as FM systems.

Infrared light waves have the same characteristics as visible light. Opaque objects, like walls, will block light, so transmission is limited to line-of-sight reception within the walls of the worship facility. Emitter panels are usually aimed in a number of directions, to "flood" the area with infrared light. This helps minimize dead spots produced by shadowed areas behind columns or under balconies.

The ability to confine infrared light makes it ideal for applications where security is a concern. This is not usually a great concern in the worship setting. Because infrared systems do not operate on radio frequencies, they are not subject to interference from radio transmissions. This makes infrared desirable in areas that have adverse radio interference.

Infrared transmission can be affected by strong sunlight, which contains large amounts of infrared light noise. Consequently, infrared systems cannot be used outdoors in the presence of sunlight. If reception is desired in alternate areas, such as cry rooms, nurseries, chapels, or reception areas, separate emitter panels must be installed and wired in each room. Because the infrared emitter panels cannot be concealed, aesthetics or architectural sensitivities may be compromised. Infrared systems are more expensive than FM systems on an installed basis.

INSTALLATION

Most hearing-assistance systems are of straightforward installation. The different types of systems vary in installation time and complexity. FM systems are the easiest and least expensive. Loop and hard-wired are the most difficult and expensive, with infrared systems falling in between.

All systems require a connection to the sound system as a source for the transmitted audio. For facilities that do not have a sound system, most manufacturers of hearing-assistance systems can supply microphones and a self-contained transmitting system.

The most desirable signal source for a hearing-assistance system is a line-level output, such as a tape output jack. The signal must be taken after the mixer to make sure that all microphones in use are connected to the hearing-assistance system. In some

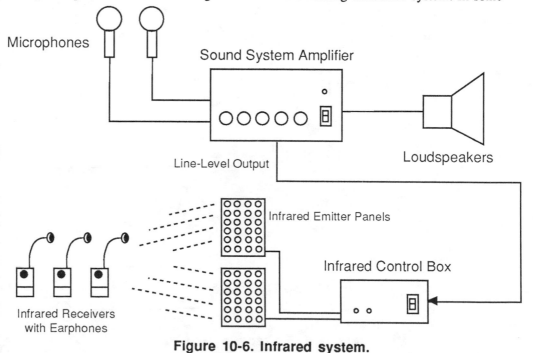

Microphones

Sound System Amplifier

Line-Level Output

Loudspeakers

Infrared Emitter Panels

Infrared Control Box

Infrared Receivers with Earphones

Figure 10-6. Infrared system.

THE
YAMAHA
GUIDE TO
SOUND SYSTEMS
FOR WORSHIP
PAGE 108

installations, it may be necessary to add one or more microphones to provide better pickup of sounds. Most hearing-assistance systems can accept microphone-level inputs, line-level inputs, and speaker-level inputs, but the line-level input produces the input signal with the best quality. Remember the sound quality of the hearing-assistance system depends on the quality of the sound that is fed into it.

Along these lines, it may be desirable to feed a completely different mix to the hearing-assistance system than is fed to the main amplifier/loudspeaker system. This mix, for example, would have a higher ratio of speech and lead vocals to background music or choir. The mix, too, could be signal processed with a greater degree of low frequency roll-off (equalization), although this processing may be built into the hearing-assistance system. It also may be a good idea to use compression in order to keep the levels more uniformly high without excessive peaks (again, this processing may be built into the hearing - assistance system). In setting up such a system, it would be advisable to enlist the assistance of some of the hearing-impaired members of the congregation so that the specific adjustments sound good to them. A non-hearing-impaired sound technician cannot make meaningful judgements in this area.

To ensure easy installation and proper system operation, installers should follow the manufacturer's instructions. Most mistakes are made because installers assume they know how to install the equipment and never consult the installation manuals. Most systems have some simple adjustments for the input level, and some have low-frequency cut adjustments to equalize the system response for hearing-impaired listeners.

SIGNING FOR DEAF WORSHIPERS

Although it is not an audio listening system, another possibility for severely hearing-impaired worshipers is to provide a sign language interpreter. The interpreter listens to the service and translates the words and music into American Sign Language. This would be of use primarily to people who are deaf and understand sign language. There are usually more people with hearing impairments that can be helped by audio amplification systems than there are people who are considered deaf.

Providing a sign language interpreter is an option if the congregation has a significant number of deaf members, although offering this service can often draw deaf people from other areas. Usually a church member who is skilled in sign language volunteers to interpret. If there are no volunteers available, it may be possible to hire an interpreter. Audiologists, speech therapists, and teachers for hearing-impaired students often have sign language skills.

A number of seating arrangements are possible when using an interpreter. It is most important that the interpreter be visible to the "listeners," who read the sign language and lip movements. If the "listeners" are watching the interpreter directly, they must sit together, near the interpreter. Some congregations have used video monitors for the "listeners" to watch the interpreter. This allows more seating freedom.

A third possibility is to use a form of "closed captioning," where the text from the service and music is projected onto a screen or video monitor for people to read. This doesn't require a sign language interpreter, but it does require that the service and music be transcribed into text ahead of time.

USE OF THE SYSTEM

EARPHONES

All hearing-assistance systems are supplied with a standard earphone for listeners to use. The standard earphone type is chosen to satisfy most users, most of the time. All manufacturers offer additional selections to meet a particular individual's needs and preferences. Since hearing loss is unique to each individual, there is no single type of earphone that satisfies everyone. It is a good idea to order a few optional earphones for people who do not like the standard-issue type.

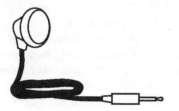

Single "Earbud" Earphone

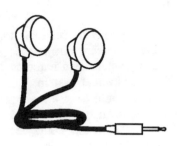

Dual "Earbud" Earphones

Button Receiver with
Custom Earmold

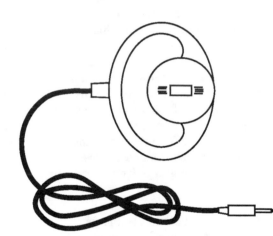

"Surround" Style Earphone

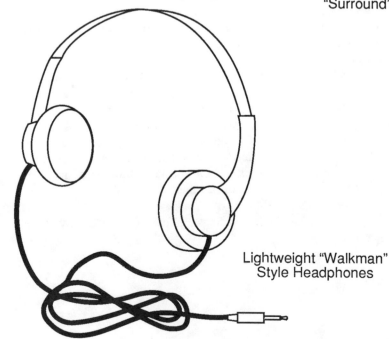

Lightweight "Walkman"
Style Headphones

Figure 10-7. Earphone types.

THE
YAMAHA
GUIDE TO
SOUND SYSTEMS
FOR WORSHIP
PAGE 110

USING THE SYSTEM WITH A HEARING AID

Hearing-assistance systems can also be used in conjunction with an individual's hearing aid. Some types of hearing aids have induction pickup coils built into them, called a telecoil, or T-coil. As was discussed in the section on induction loops, the telecoil in the hearing aid can pick up electromagnetic signals produced by an induction loop. Rather than having a large loop placed around the room, a small loop, called a neckloop, can be placed around the individual's neck, like a lanyard. The neckloop is plugged into the FM or infrared receiver instead of an earphone. The receiver drives the neckloop, which creates an electromagnetic field that can be picked up by the telecoil in the hearing aid. This couples the sound from the hearing-assistance receiver into the hearing aid.

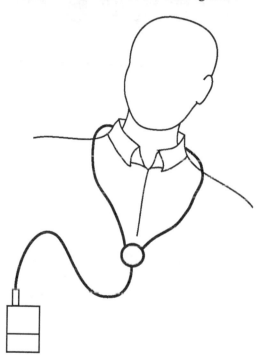

Figure 10-8. Neckloop.

Some hearing aids have a feature called a direct auditory input, which allows a cord to be plugged directly into the hearing aid. In this case, an adaptor cord plugs between the receiver and the hearing aid to couple the sound from the receiver into the hearing aid.

MANAGEMENT OF EQUIPMENT

Worship facilities must implement a receiver management program that fits their needs. Some have regular users purchase their own receiver, taking full responsibility for it, while some share in the purchase price of receivers. Others simply give the receivers to regular users. By having his own receiver, an individual does not have to call attention to himself by asking for one at every service, and he doesn't have to worry about not getting one because they are all checked out. The user is also responsible for battery and earphone maintenance.

Some facilities have a receiver station where users can pick up a receiver and return it. Others have the ushers distribute and collect the receivers. Pilferage is relatively rare, but if it is a potential problem, some facilities will ask for a credit card or driver's license to be held as collateral for the receiver. Most facilities keep extra receivers on hand for guests to use.

There are two options for battery maintenance. If disposable batteries are used, the batteries should be changed on a regular maintenance schedule, running from every two weeks to every month, depending on use. Rechargeable batteries are also available, along with multiple charger cases. These are somewhat expensive initially, but they allow batteries to be recharged after use, rather than replaced. This simplifies battery management and is more economical over the long term.

Most of the earphones supplied with hearing-assistance systems can and should be sanitized after use. For individuals who have their own receivers, this is their responsibility (and probably less of a concern). Some facilities issue earphones to regular users, or use storage boxes marked with users' names. Each user always uses the same earphone. The earphones can be sanitized by wiping them with rubbing alcohol. Some have removable fabric or foam coverings that can be washed. Earphones should never be immersed in alcohol or water, which will damage them.

THE
YAMAHA
GUIDE TO
SOUND SYSTEMS
FOR WORSHIP
PAGE 111

OTHER USES FOR THE SYSTEM

Many facilities are using the hearing-assistance system for simultaneous language interpretation. If your congregation has a large population of non-English-speaking people, these systems can be used by people listening to an interpreter speaking their native language. If two FM transmitters are used, the translation channel can be discrete from the hearing-assistance channel. Additional transmitters can be used for multiple language interpretation so long as receivers are tunable to the correct channel.

PUBLICIZING THE SYSTEM

Once the system is installed, make sure people know it is there to be used! Most systems include a small sign that can be placed near an entrance door to announce the availability of hearing assistance. Additional signs can be purchased for a nominal cost to put at each entrance.

It is also a good idea to announce the installation of the system in the bulletin, and many facilities have a running reminder in the bulletin that the system is available. Some facilities introduce the system to the congregation during a service with an announcement and demonstration. Receivers are passed around the congregation so everyone can try them. This makes people less reluctant to try them in the future, and helps others understand why "that guy" is listening to the "radio."

THE
YAMAHA
GUIDE TO
SOUND SYSTEMS
FOR WORSHIP
PAGE 112

CHAPTER 11.
RECORDERS AND OTHER SOURCES

Microphones and pickups typically serve as the "front end" of a sound system. They convert sound into electricity so that it can be mixed, processed, and amplified before it is translated back into sound by the loudspeakers. But there are times when other input sources are called for:

1. Audio tape recorders.

2. Compact disc players.

3. Video tape recorders or film projectors.

4. Electric and electronic musical instruments.

In these cases, the input starts out not as sound, but as a signal that is either stored in some manner (1–3) or that already exists in the electrical domain (4). This chapter introduces these input sources and discusses their distinguishing characteristics.

A word of warning: Aside from outboard signal processing devices, these input sources offer the greatest potential for mismatches of signal levels between equipment. As mentioned in Chapter 6, the term "line level" actually refers to a range of levels, rather than a single standard. More specifically, audio equipment can generally be categorized by output level as follows:

- Professional equipment generally puts out a signal with a nominal (average) level of +4 dBu.

- Semipro and consumer equipment generally uses an output level of –16 to –10 dBu.

The ramifications of mismatched levels—and how to correct them—are discussed in Chapter 12. For now, you should at least be aware that such mismatches can occur.

AUDIO TAPE RECORDERS

Audio tape recording primarily uses two physical formats: *open-reel* (or *reel-to-reel*) and *cassette*. Cassette enjoys the more widespread use as a playback medium in houses of worship. Many soloists, and even groups, use cassette accompaniment "tracks," as they are called. These instrumental arrangements are frequently drawn from the master tapes of the albums of the artists that popularized the songs in question, so the musical quality is high.

Open-reel machines are used less often as sources in a sound system than cassettes are. Although open-reel tapes offer the potential for better frequency response and lower noise, they are less convenient.

In order to provide the best performance possible, tapes may be recorded using a noise-reduction system—most commonly one of the varieties of Dolby® or dbx® noise reduction. Dolby types A and SR are used most often within professional recording studios on open-reel machines, while types B, C, and S find their way into cassettes and cassette recorders sold to consumers. All work roughly as follows:

There is some noise inherent in any analog recording. (*Analog* refers to the translation of the fluctuating audio signal into fluctuations of magnetic force on the surface of the tape.) Aside from any noise that might be added by the circuitry involved, there is always some amount of *tape hiss*. The Dolby system operates by boosting the high-frequency content of a signal before recording it to tape (*pre-emphasis*), and then lowering it correspondingly on playback (*de-emphasis*). Since tape hiss is most noticeable in the high frequencies, this reduces the presence of tape hiss while bringing the frequency content of the signal back to normal.

Another noise-reduction system is dbx. This is used most often in the professional studio. A consumer version is incorporated into some consumer multitrack cassette recorders and stereo cassette decks. It does

THE
YAMAHA
GUIDE TO
SOUND SYSTEMS
FOR WORSHIP
PAGE 113

not generally find its way into commercially prerecorded cassettes. It combines pre-emphasis and de-emphasis with a system of companding—compression and expanding—similar to that used with many wireless microphones (see Chapter 5). The dynamic range of the signal is compressed before it is recorded to tape. On playback it is expanded, and in the process the low-level tape hiss is forced down in volume. As with Dolby, there are different "flavors" of dbx noise reduction circuits available for different applications.

Both cassette and open-reel machines have line-level inputs and outputs—although, as mentioned previously, professional units will generally put out a "hotter" signal than will consumer equipment.

RECORDING

An entire book the size of this one could easily be devoted to the subject of recording. And although recording technique lies beyond the limits of this discussion, Chapter 13 does examine mixing for the tape and broadcast ministries. For now, a brief look at recording equipment is in order.

There are two main varieties of recording: "ordinary" *stereo* recording and *multitrack* recording. The first of these is what most people are familiar with. Two signals are recorded onto tape simultaneously, representing the left and right channels. These can then be played back as a finished recording. Multitrack recording allows multiple tracks to be recorded independently—a process known as *overdubbing*. The multitrack tape is then "mixed down" to stereo.

It bears mentioning that the frequency response of a tape recording is proportional to the amount of tape used to record the signals. There are two dimensions to this "amount of tape": vertical, which represents the width of the track on which the signal is recorded; and horizontal, which has to do with how fast the tape is moving. Other components being equal (which may not be the case), the faster the tape speed, the better the frequency response. And, other components being equal, the wider the track (the area of the tape being used to record the signal), the lower the level of tape noise relative to the audio level during playback.

Cassette tapes are ⅛" (3.175 mm) wide. Stereo cassettes contain four tracks side by side—two going in one direction, and two going in the other direction (accessible when the cassette is flipped over). Multitrack cassette recorders, which permit overdubbing, may also utilize four tracks (all four to be recorded and played back in the same direction), although recent advances have increased this number to six and even eight tracks on some units. Stereo cassette recorders run at a speed of 1⅞ ips (inches per second; equivalent to 4.75 cm/sec). Multitrack cassette units generally run at twice this speed (3¾ ips; 9.5 cm/sec).

Open-reel machines, on the other hand, are usually run at 15 ips (38 cm/sec) for recordings of music, though they may be twice as fast when quality is paramount and expense is not a consideration (twice the speed means twice the amount of tape is used to record the same length program). For voice, the speed may be cut to half, or even a fourth, of the 15-ips figure. Tapes used for stereo recording are ¼" (6.35 mm) or ½" (12.75 mm) wide. And while some have a four-track format similar to the stereo cassette (called *quarter-track* format), so-called *half-track* machines have only two tracks (so the tracks are roughly twice as wide as those on a quarter-track machine).

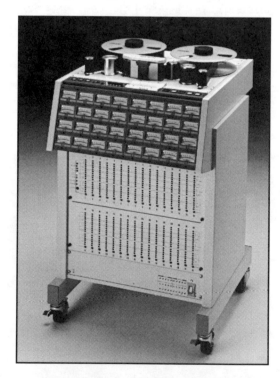

Figure 11-1. A large open-reel multitrack recorder (courtesy of Otari Corporation).

THE
YAMAHA
GUIDE TO
SOUND SYSTEMS
FOR WORSHIP
PAGE 114

Multitrack machines may use tape that is up to 2" (50.8 mm) wide, with as many as 48 tracks on it. (Professional *digital* multitrack recorders record up to 48 tracks on ½" tape.)

So the potential, at least, is for better quality from open-reel recording. Open-reel tapes are also easier to edit, especially when *splicing* (physically cutting the tape apart and putting the pieces back together).

Nevertheless, stereo cassette recorders have gained popularity—in nonprofessional studios, at any rate—even as cassettes themselves have gained acceptance in the consumer marketplace. The quality of sound that can be obtained on cassette has improved over the years, with improved circuitry and noise-reduction such as the Dolby system.

Most worship facilities probably will limit their recording to the stereo variety, preferring cassettes for routine recordings of services and the like—for their ease of use, for the quick and inexpensive duplication they provide (more on this shortly), and because most potential listeners will have cassette players. On the other hand, when recording for broadcast, or for professional duplication (an album of choral music, for example), reel to reel is preferable.

The purchase of multitrack equipment will be economical only for the largest and most active of music ministries. For the rest, either renting the equipment or hiring a professional with his own equipment will suffice for the occasional album.

MONO COMPATIBILITY

When recording for broadcast, or even for distribution of cassettes, a stereo recording may need to be compatible with monaural playback. Most commercial AM radio stations broadcast in mono, and many FM stations do, as well. Furthermore, many mono cassette players are still in wide use, despite the proliferation of stereo players.

What does mono compatibility mean? That the signals from the left and right channels of a stereo signal, when combined, will not introduce phase cancellations. A single input channel on a console, divided between left and right by a pan pot, is mono-compatible. Where mono compatibility should be questioned is in the use of more than one

microphone on a single source. To be safe, keep these two guidelines in mind:

- Use the M-S or X-Y microphone technique when recording in stereo.

- Follow the three-to-one rule in all other cases where multiple mics are used.

Both of these principles are explained in Chapter 5.

CASSETTE DUPLICATORS

There are some stereo cassette recorders on the market that hold two cassettes, side by side. Some of these feature "high-speed dubbing"—the ability to record from one tape to the other at a speed faster than normal (usually twice normal speed). The word "dub," by the way, derives from "double," and is synonymous with "dupe," which is short for "duplicate."

While such units do allow duplication of cassette tapes, their limited speed and capacity make them unsuitable for any but the smallest duplication tasks. For the regular production of multiple copies, dedicated cassette duplicators are well worth purchasing.

Large commercial duplication houses use machines that duplicate the program many times, at 32 to 64 times normal play speed, on large reels of tape known as "pancakes." This tape is then automatically loaded into cassette shells.

For the average worship facility, however, a simpler machine is more practical—one that dubs directly onto cassettes. Such a machine consists of a master unit, which holds the master cassette and one or two additional cassettes, the latter of which will become dubs. Slave units are often available, which can be synchronized to the master unit so that a great number of dubs can be generated at one time.

These in-cassette duplicators often run at 8 to 16 times normal speed, which greatly reduces duplication time. Furthermore, many models duplicate all four tracks in one pass, which saves having to turn the cassettes over to dub "Side B."

Figure 11-2. An "in-cassette" cassette duplicator (courtesy of Otari Corporation).

DAT

DAT is an acronym for Digital Audio Tape. It is not a generic term for digital tape recording; rather, it refers to a specific stereo cassette format. DAT machines use rotating heads to record and play back tracks as a series of angled stripes on the tape, rather than as continuous linear tracks. Because of this technology, borrowed from video tape recorders, DAT is sometimes known as R-DAT (for rotary-head digital audio tape).

DAT cassettes are slightly smaller than standard analog cassettes. And rather than recording in analog fashion (translating the variations in the audio signal into variations of magnetic flux on tape), the sound is recorded as numbers—thus the adjective "digital."

The digital technology behind DAT, which it shares with the compact disc, involves a series of "snapshots" of the sound (called *samples*), taken in rapid succession. Each of these snapshots is translated into a number and stored on tape. On playback, the numbers are retranslated and played back in the proper order and at the proper speed. The result is a recreation of the original sound that can be compared with a motion picture: a series of still pictures that convey the effect of fluid motion.

The advantage of digital recording is that the numbers that represent a sound can be duplicated over and over again without any reduction in fidelity. Compare this to analog recording, in which tape hiss multiplies with each generation of copying (that is, a copy of an original will have more hiss than the original itself, and a copy of a copy will have more still).

DAT offers a further advantage for recording of worship services and music: time. The tiny R-DAT cassette pictured below can provide up to two hours of uninterrupted recording. This is more than enough recording time for even the longest service or choir concert. Since the audio quality of R-DAT equals that of CDs, it is now possible for a skilled mix engineer to create an album-quality digital master recording. With the price of "short run" CD duplication decreasing, you may be able to offer the congregation a compact disc recording of a special musical service.

Figure 11-3. A DAT cassette (actual size).

THE
YAMAHA
GUIDE TO
SOUND SYSTEMS
FOR WORSHIP
PAGE 116

At the time of this writing, a number of professional R-DAT recorders are available in the US. Professional R-DAT recorders are presently available for as little as twice the price of a good professional cassette recorder.

A CD player with a direct digital output can be connected to the digital input of an R-DAT recorder and a perfect copy of the CD can be recorded. As you might imagine, this capability greatly concerns the record industry. Record industry officials, fearing "pirating," copyright infringement, and taping for personal use, have asked Congress to mandate a standard to limit or prevent copying.

The proposed standard is called the Serial Copy Management System (SCMS). It is intended for use on *consumer* (hi-fi) R-DAT recorders. Since the SCMS may also prevent legitimate copying of R-DATs used professionally, recorders for professional applications are specifically exempted (the legislation defines what a professional R-DAT recorder is). An SCMS-equipped recorder will recognize certain instructions (flags) in the digital subcode contained on the CD and will prevent a digital copy of a digital copy from being made. Making a first-generation copy is possible, but the "chain-letter" copying that record industry officials fear is prevented. The flag on the CD may also be set so that no digital copy of the CD can be made.

SCMS effects only the digital inputs and outputs of an R-DAT recorder—it has no effect on copies made using the analog inputs. As we go to press, the SCMS legislation has not been passed by Congress. As a result of this uncertainty, many manufacturers of consumer R-DAT recorders are reluctant to distribute them in the US. Nevertheless, professional R-DAT recorders are currently available and offer the house of worship extraordinary audio performance and convenience at moderate prices.

COMPACT DISC (CD)

The compact disc is another medium of digital storage. It was initially designed for playback only, although recordable discs are in development. Like DAT and analog tape recorders, compact disc players have line-level outputs.

In appearance and use, compact discs resemble phonograph discs. The small (4¾"; 120 mm) metallic platters typically contain selections on concentric tracks, which can be played individually, successively, or (on elaborate CD players) in any order desired. But rather than using a phonograph needle, the CD player employs a laser beam, which reads the digitally encoded information from the reflective surface of the disc. Since there is no physical contact with the disc (in fact, the actual metallic surface is protected by a layer of transparent plastic), CDs don't wear out as phono discs do. And because the recording is digital, the quality of the sound will not degrade over time.

The use of compact discs in worship facilities depends on the availability of suitable material in CD format. Accompaniment tracks have thus far employed analog tape almost exclusively. Occasionally a well-known solo artist will have the instrumental accompaniments from his or her recordings transferred to CD for use in concert tours, but more often, DAT is used.

VIDEO TAPE RECORDERS AND FILM PROJECTORS

While audiovisual presentations are not used in most worship services, they nevertheless have an important place in many congregations—in classes and meetings, for example. Audiovisual materials are usually produced in one of three forms:

- A film strip or slide show with narration (either live or on audio cassette).

- A motion picture.

- A video cassette.

The first of these presents no new audio elements; microphones and cassette recorders have already been covered.

Motion picture projectors can be problematic, because the built-in loudspeakers may be insufficient for the task of making the sound clear to all listening. The problem is that the audio output on these projectors is usually a speaker-level signal, which would overpower a line-level input to the sound system, to say nothing of a mic-level input.

The best solution lies in using a resistive pad to convert the high-level output into one that the console can accept. Alternatively, a knowledgeable person might be able to extract a line-level signal from the circuitry within the projector, bringing it out to a separate jack. A third alternative, while not the most ideal, may be the easiest in some cases: Place a microphone in front of the projector's loudspeakers. But since the loudspeakers are often built into the projector, the microphone will pick up and amplify the projector noise as well as the program material.

Video cassette recorders are more straightforward, since they provide line-level outputs. On the other hand, they constitute one class of devices for which you will hardly be able to avoid a "consumer-level" line out. See Chapter 12 for the best way of dealing with this.

ELECTRIC AND ELECTRONIC MUSICAL INSTRUMENTS

What is the difference between an electric instrument and an electronic one?

In theoretical terms, electric (more properly, *electro-acoustic*) instruments begin with physical vibrations. These vibrations are then converted to electrical impulses by transducers—magnetic pickups, generally, rather than contact pickups or microphones. Electric guitar, electric bass, and electric piano are examples. Electronic instruments, on the other hand, generate sound entirely within the realm of electricity; there is no physical vibration until the loudspeaker is set in motion. Synthesizers, electronic pianos, drum machines, and digital sampling keyboards are examples.

In practical terms, electric instruments tend to put out signals of a lower level than electronic ones. Here a *direct box* is often used to connect the unbalanced output of the electric instrument to the balanced mic input of the console. Where a performer wishes to use his or her instrument amplifier in addition to putting the signal through the sound system, many direct boxes allow such a double connection.

It is also possible to connect an unbalanced instrument output to the balanced input of your mixing console by using a cable with a ¼" phone plug on one end and a male XLR connector on the other (see Chapter 12, Figure 12-3). Since the input to the console is now unbalanced, the length of the total cable run to the console should be less than 30 feet; longer runs will create problems with hum. Also make sure that the phantom power of the channel is turned off before connecting this unbalanced cable.

Signals from electronic instruments can be quite "hot" (high in level), and often require the use of the input pad (attenuation) on the console channel to which they are connected. Even when the nominal output lies within the bounds of safety, transient peaks can send the console input into clipping. Here it may be necessary to have the player keep the dynamic range within reasonable limits (the dynamic response of many electronic instruments can be programmed), and to make sure that, when different sounds are used, they are of similar levels. Failing the ability to have the player limit the dynamics, the sound engineer can save himself or herself many headaches by placing a compressor/limiter on the input channel.

The desire to keep levels under control must be balanced with the knowledge that the higher the volume control on an electronic instrument is set, the better the signal-to-noise ratio will generally be. Make sure the player doesn't "turn it down" so far that you end up with a noisy signal.

THE
YAMAHA
GUIDE TO
SOUND SYSTEMS
FOR WORSHIP
PAGE 118

CHAPTER 12.
HOOKING IT TOGETHER AND
INSTALLATION

Despite the fact that audio signal connection practices are reasonably (though not totally) standardized, improper connection of components remains one of the most common problems in the installation of sound systems. Half of the solution for connection problems is to select components that are compatible electrically. The other half is to connect them properly and consistently. These are the first issues dealt with in this chapter.

Also covered here are more "mundane" matters, such as hanging loudspeakers and mounting equipment.

IMPEDANCE AND LEVEL MATCHING

INPUT AND OUTPUT IMPEDANCES

Impedance is defined as the total opposition to the flow of alternating current (read "audio signal") in an electrical circuit, and is measured in ohms. So much for definitions. But what does impedance mean to the connections in a sound system?

The impedance of an output—of something that supplies audio power—is a measure of how easily the power will flow from that output. This impedance is known as *source impedance*, because it is the impedance of the source of signals.

The impedance of an input—of something to which a signal is applied—is a measure of how much power that input will tend to draw (from a given output voltage). This impedance is known as the *load impedance*, because it is the impedance that determines how loaded down the output will be. (The *lower* the load impedance, the *greater* the load, or draw, on the source.) The load impedance is also known as the *termination*, or *terminating*, impedance.

In most modern line-level audio circuits, it is considered beneficial for the source impedance of the output to be as low as

practical, and for the load impedance of the input to be as high as practical, within limits.

A circuit where the input load impedance is a minimum of some 10 times the source impedance of the output driving that input is said to be a *bridging* input, and the output is said to be *bridged*. (NOTE: This has nothing to do with the bridged mono operation of some power amplifiers.)

In some modern equipment, and in most older equipment, it was desirable for the load impedance of the input to be roughly the same as the source impedance of the output. Such circuits are said to be *matched*.

It is important for you to know whether the output of a particular piece of equipment is supposed to be matched or bridged, or whether that doesn't matter. When there is an impedance mismatch (which means that the source and load are not right for one another, whether matched or bridged), the results can range from improper frequency response to excess distortion to incorrect operating levels to circuit failure.

Unfortunately, equipment specifications are sometimes stated in such a way that it is not clear what the source and load impedances are. Specs such as "Output Impedance" and "Input Impedance" leave the reader guessing whether they refer to the impedance *presented* by that output or input, or whether they refer to the impedance that ought to be *connected* to it. It is essential to know what is what in order for the proper connections to be made. In the absence of a specified load impedance, avoid operating into a load less than the output source impedance of the device.

Too low a load impedance will cause the output to try to deliver more power to the load. With a power amplifier, this could result in overheating and a possible fire hazard, or, at best, automatic shutdown, a blown fuse, or a tripped AC power circuit breaker. With line-level devices, such as preamplifiers and mixing consoles, too low

THE
YAMAHA
GUIDE TO
SOUND SYSTEMS
FOR WORSHIP
PAGE 119

a load impedance will often result in increased distortion, which may be followed by circuit failure as the load is increased.

STANDARD OPERATING LEVELS

There are many ways to specify input and output levels in sound equipment. Complicating the matter, there is no single standard operating level at which all equipment operates. Rather, there are a number of standard operating levels in audio circuitry. It is often awkward to refer to a specific level (e.g., +4 dBu) when one merely wishes to describe a general range of sensitivity. For this reason, most audio engineers think of operating levels in three general categories:

- **Mic Level, or Low Level.** This range extends from no signal up to about –20 dBu (77.5 mV), or –20 dBm (77.5 mV across 600 ohms = 10 millionths of a watt). It includes the output of microphones, guitar pickups, phono cartridges, and tape heads, prior to any form of preamplification (i.e., before any mic, phono, or tape preamps). While some (high-sensitivity) mics can put out a higher level in the presence of very loud sounds, and a hard-picked guitar can go 20 dB above this level (to 0 dBu or higher), this remains the nominal, or average, range.

- **Line Level, or Medium Level.** This range extends from –20 dBu or –20 dBm to +30 dBu (24.5 V) or +30 dBm (24.5 V across 600 ohms = 1 watt). It includes electronic keyboard (synthesizer) outputs, preamp and console outputs, and most of the inputs and outputs of typical signal processing equipment, such as limiters, compressors, signal delays, reverbs, equalizers, and tape decks. In other words, it covers the output levels of nearly all equipment except power amplifiers. Nominal line level (the average level) of a great deal of equipment will be –10 dBu/dBm (245 mV), +4 dBu/dBm (1.23 V), or +8 dBu/dBm (1.95 V).

- **Speaker Level and High Level.** This covers all levels at or above +30 dBu or +30 dBm. These levels include power amplifier speaker outputs, AC power lines, and DC control cables carrying more than 24 volts.

THE
YAMAHA
GUIDE TO
SOUND SYSTEMS
FOR WORSHIP
PAGE 120

WHEN HI-FI AND PRO EQUIPMENT MIX

While some professional sound equipment finds its way into home hi-fi systems, and some consumer hi-fi equipment finds its way into professional sound systems, there are often significant differences in operating levels and impedances that make this a risky proposition.

HI-FI OUTPUT TO PRO EQUIPMENT INPUT

A piece of consumer sound equipment may operate at considerably lower nominal (average) line levels than the pro standard of +4 dBu (1.23 V). This is typically around –16 dBu (123 mV) to –10 dBu (245 mV) into load impedances of 10,000 ohms or higher. Peak output levels in such equipment may not go above +4 dBu. The output current available here would be inadequate to drive a low-impedance input, and even if the professional equipment has a high enough load impedance, the output voltage of the hi-fi equipment may still be inadequate.

The typical result is too-low levels into the professional equipment, and too-high distortion in the overloaded hi-fi output. This can damage loudspeakers (due to the high-frequency content of the clipped waveform), and it can damage the hi-fi equipment (due to overloading of its output circuitry). There are exceptions, but this points out one of the reasons why it's important to read and understand the input and output level and impedance specifications when using consumer sound equipment in a professional application.

PRO EQUIPMENT OUTPUT TO HI-FI INPUT

If a nominal +4 dBu (or +4 dBm) output from a mixing console or professional sound system signal processor (such as a graphic EQ) is connected to a typical hi-fi preamplifier's auxiliary or line input, the chances are excellent that the input will be overdriven. Because the input is expecting to see a nominal –10 dBu to –16 dBu signal, it is going to be driven with 14 to 20 dB too much signal.

Sometimes the hi-fi unit's volume control can be lowered to take care of the excess level, but in some equipment the signal will drive a preamp into clipping before it ever reaches a volume control. This is generally the case in integrated hi-fi amplifiers. If the output level of the professional equipment is lowered, the signal-to-noise ratio may suffer. The impedance mismatch, going in this direction, is not likely to cause any problems for the circuitry itself, but it can cause errors in frequency response.

SOLUTIONS

Simply adhering to the +4 dBu professional standard when selecting equipment helps to avoid problems such as those described above. On the other hand, the quality and utility of some contemporary –10 dBV equipment makes strict adherence to the +4 dBu standard less attractive than it once was, especially since –10 dBV equipment (sometimes called semipro) is usually less expensive than comparable +4 dBu (pro) gear.

There are solutions to this dilemma. Recognizing the market's desire to have the option to use –10 dBV equipment at some places in the signal chain (playback equipment and outboard signal processors are two notable examples), some audio manufacturers supply both +4 dBu and –10 dBV connection points on their equipment. (This is most often true of console manufacturers.) Alternatively, a few companies now offer active interface boxes that convert between these standards. Use of such interfaces is highly recommended, since they offer a simple, quick, and cost-effective fix for level- (and impedance-) matching problems.

DIRECT BOXES AND SIGNAL TRANSFORMERS

Practically speaking, problems at line level are rarely attributable to impedance these days. In the majority of sound systems, impedance-related problems are most likely to appear in the input and output groups of components. At both ends, transducers are used and questions of power transfer come into play.

Chapter 8 deals with the need for proper impedances in output transducers—the connection of the power amplifiers to loudspeakers. It remains to say something here about impedance as it applies to input transducers.

Microphones, guitar pickups, and so on generally are not capable of sourcing much power at all, and so they require relatively high load impedances. (Too low a load impedance would provide too great a power draw from the source.)

Suppose you wish to connect an electric guitar or electric bass directly to the microphone input of a console. The console input load impedance is, say, 3 kΩ—which is fine for low- to medium-impedance microphones. It represents far too great a load for the guitar pickup circuitry, which requires a load impedance of at least 50 kΩ. Moreover, the instrument output is unbalanced, and may be very susceptible to noise. The solution is to use a so-called *DI* (*direct injection*, or simply *direct*) *box*, designed to derive a signal from an instrument directly at its output—before the instrument amplifier. (On the other hand, many guitarists use amplifiers that create some of the character of the sound, so they may prefer that you simply set up a mic in front of the guitar amp.)

The main component of a DI box is a specially designed *signal transformer* that presents a high load impedance to the instrument and provides a low-impedance source to the console. In addition to these functions, DI boxes can provide the following:

- Connection of an unbalanced output to a balanced input.

- Isolation from phantom-power voltages (useful on those consoles that don't have individual phantom on/off switches for each input channel).

- A pad (attenuation) for taming high signal levels.

- A ground-lift switch, to overcome hums caused by ground loops between equipment.

- An additional jack that allows the instrument to be plugged into its own amplifier as well as into the sound system.

Signal transformers can also be used in the connection of low-impedance, balanced microphones to the high-impedance, unbalanced inputs found on some low-end mixing consoles. Other such transformers can connect line-level, or even speaker-level, sources (such as the movie projector output encountered in Chapter 11) to mic inputs, by providing not only impedance matching, but also level matching (voltage transformation), without substantially affecting the inherent signal-to-noise ratio.

If you add a transformer to an input or output circuit, make sure the transformer's characteristics are correctly matched to the circuit. The source impedance and load termination impedance connected to a transformer have a major impact on the resulting performance. The transformer should be capable of handling the levels and frequency range involved. It is best to speak with a knowledgeable audio engineer if you are planning to use any add-on transformer, unless the model is specifically recommended by the equipment manufacturer.

BALANCED AND UNBALANCED LINES

Unbalanced (sometimes called *single-ended*) connections employ two conductors, one at ground potential and the other carrying signal. Unbalanced connections may involve the use of transformers (*transformer-coupled* connections), but the norm is direct coupling. Equipment operating at –10 dBV invariably uses unbalanced connections.

Balanced connections employ at least two conductors, each of which carries the same signal, but with the polarity of one reversed with respect to the other. Balanced connections may or may not be referenced to ground; if not, they are termed *floating* connections. The shield is a third conductor, though it does not carry signal, and it is always connected to ground (but generally only at one end of the cable).

Balanced inputs and outputs are sometimes implemented using a transformer. More often than not, modern professional equipment uses direct coupling. Direct-coupled balanced inputs are sometimes called *differential* inputs. One of the shortcomings of differential circuits is that they may not be floating, so transformers must sometimes be inserted to break ground loops.

Balanced connections are preferred over unbalanced because they are far less susceptible to the pickup of interference.

What happens is that if any external signals—from light dimmers, for example—induce noise in the cable, they do so equally in both signal lines. At the input, since the two lines are of opposite polarity, the noise in the two lines cancels out. Professional +4 dBu equipment usually (but not always) features balanced inputs and outputs.

Particularly for microphones, balanced connections should be used wherever possible. Sometimes this will require the addition of an external transformer at the mixer input, but the advantages of noise immunity and reliability more than justify the added expense. In fact, transformers may be needed even with an electronically balanced input in situations where radio-frequency interference (RFI) or electromagnetic interference (EMI) is severe.

CABLES AND CONNECTORS

Regardless of how high the quality of your mics, mixing console, amplifiers, and loudspeakers may be, the entire system can be degraded or silenced by a bad cable. Never try to save money by cutting corners with cheap cable.

On the other hand, high price alone does not guarantee a good product. There are major differences between similar-looking cables. All wire is not the same, and not all look-alike connectors are made the same way. Even if the overall diameter, wire gauge, and general construction are similar, two cables may have significantly different electrical and physical properties.

For example, almost all audio cables in a sound reinforcement system use stranded conductors, yet many same-gauge wires use a different number of strands. More strands usually yield better flexibility and less chance of metal fatigue failure or failure after an inadvertent nick in the cable.

Even the wire itself makes a difference. Pure copper is an excellent conductor, but lacks tensile strength. Copper/bronze inner conductors are strong yet adequately flexible. Aluminum is strong and lightweight, but has too much resistance for practical use in audio circuits.

THE
YAMAHA
GUIDE TO
SOUND SYSTEMS
FOR WORSHIP
PAGE 122

Conductors may be made well, with low contact resistance (and low tendency to develop resistance over time), or perhaps not. They may be well secured to the cable, with thoroughly soldered shields and inner conductors and good *strain relief* (reinforcement of the cable as it exits the connector, so as not to place undue strain on the conductors), or they may be carelessly put together.

The following paragraphs shed some light on the function and construction of various cables and connectors.

ELECTROSTATIC AND ELECTROMAGNETIC SHIELDING

Shielding for mic- and line-level cables is essential in most applications. Mic and line signals are relatively low in level, and will be amplified. Any noise entering the cable will be amplified along with the desired signal. The purpose of shielding is to exclude *electrostatic* fields, which may be caused by sparks at the armatures of motors or generators, by gas-discharge lighting (neon or fluorescent), and other sources. Radio-frequency interference (RFI) also comes under this heading. Shielding intercepts these spurious charges and drains them to ground so they do not penetrate the inner, signal-carrying conductor(s) of the cable (see Figure 12-1). In the case of an unbalanced cable with a single center conductor, the shield also acts as a return path for the signal.

There are three main kinds of shielding

available: *braided*, *wrapped*, and *foil* (see Figure 12-2). Metal foil provides nearly 100% shielding effectiveness, but will deteriorate if the cable is flexed very much. For this reason, it is best used in permanent, fixed

cable paths. Cables with wrapped shields may offer greater flexibility than similar braided shields, but the wrap will tend to open up with flexing, which not only degrades shielding density, but can also cause *microphonic noise* because of the changing *capacitance* between the shield and the inner conductor(s). For these reasons, braided shields are the most common for mic and instrument connections.

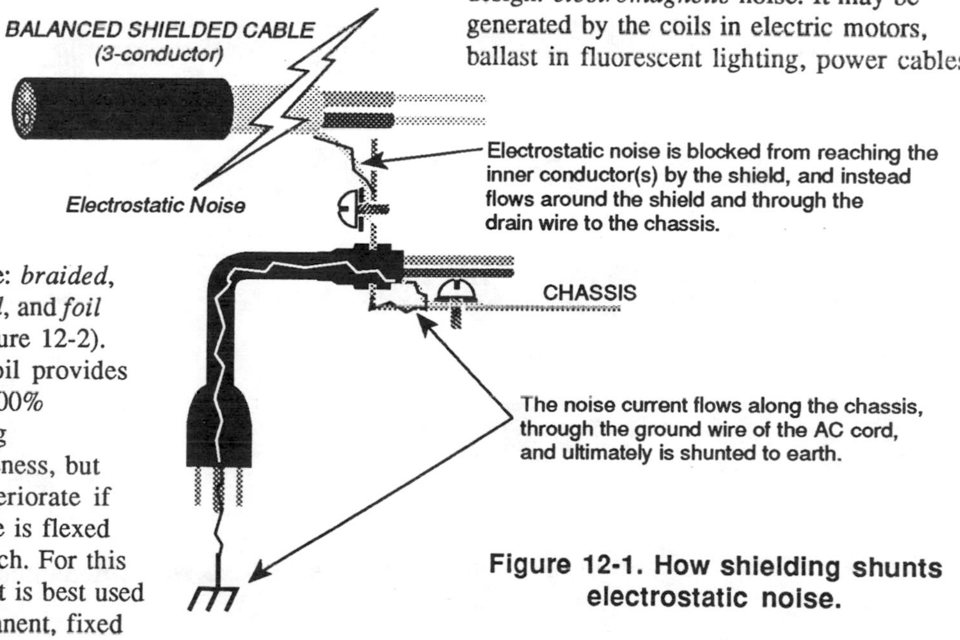

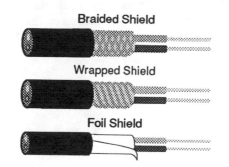

Figure 12-2. Different types of cable shielding.

While shielding is beneficial to the extent that it excludes electrostatic noise, it can also have a negative impact on a cable: it increases the overall distributed capacitance between signal carrying conductors. This, combined with the resistance in the cable (exacerbated if a high-impedance microphone is used), creates a *low-pass filter*, which can cut high frequencies from the signal. For long cable runs, especially, you should choose cable with the lowest possible capacitance per foot (or meter).

In addition to electrostatic noise, there is another type of noise of concern in cable design: *electromagnetic* noise. It may be generated by the coils in electric motors, ballast in fluorescent lighting, power cables

BALANCED SHIELDED CABLE
(3-conductor)

Electrostatic Noise

Electrostatic noise is blocked from reaching the inner conductor(s) by the shield, and instead flows around the shield and through the drain wire to the chassis.

CHASSIS

The noise current flows along the chassis, through the ground wire of the AC cord, and ultimately is shunted to earth.

Figure 12-1. How shielding shunts electrostatic noise.

used for stage lighting, the coils in large rheostat-type lighting dimmers, or the chopping of AC current by silicon-controlled rectifier (SCR) dimmers. (NOTE: If you are installing light dimmers, there are industrial-grade dimmers available that are less prone to produce electromagnetic noise than are simple SCR dimmers.)

Electromagnetic fields are not cancelled by cable shielding—only by a balanced line, with twisted center conductors, and by sheer physical distance from the source. They can also be shielded by running cable in iron pipe conduit!

SINGLE- AND DUAL-CONDUCTOR SHIELDED CABLES

Single-conductor shielded cables are intended for unbalanced connections. Don't use dual-conductor cables, because they can double the capacitance of the cable.

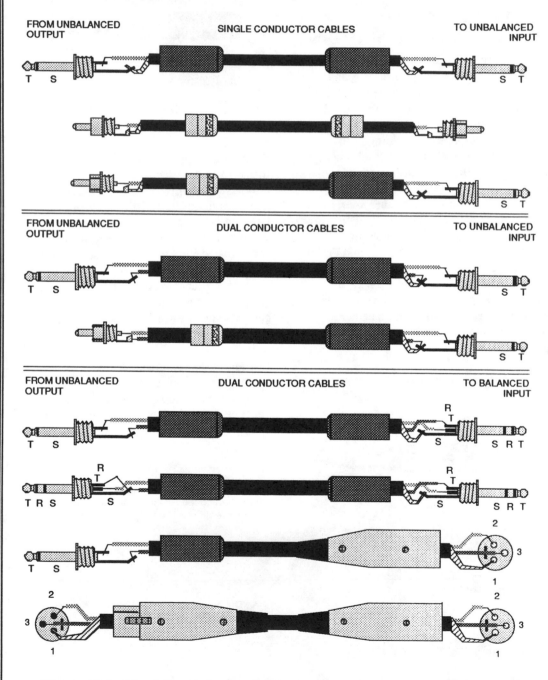

Figure 12-3. Single- and dual-conductor cables for use with unbalanced sources.

THE
YAMAHA
GUIDE TO
SOUND SYSTEMS
FOR WORSHIP
PAGE 124

Dual-conductor shielded cables are primarily used for balanced circuits, although they can be used to good advantage when a balanced output is driving an unbalanced input. Don't use single-conductor cables in balanced circuits, because they will unbalance the connection.

Some single-conductor shielded cables appear to be similar to the coaxial cables used for TV and radio signals, but there are differences. Never use RF (radio-frequency) cable for audio signals.

In dual-conductor cables, the inner pair of conductors is usually color-coded, either black and red or black and white. If black and red, the red wire should be the hot (high, +) side of the pair. If black and white, the situation may not be clear. Many people prefer to make the white the hot side; but in AC wiring the black is hot, so you may find audio cable wired this way, too. It really makes no difference, so long as the cable is wired with consistent polarity between the connectors at both ends.

Figures 12-3 and 12-4 show wiring specifics for various cable and connector types with different combinations of balanced and unbalanced terminations.

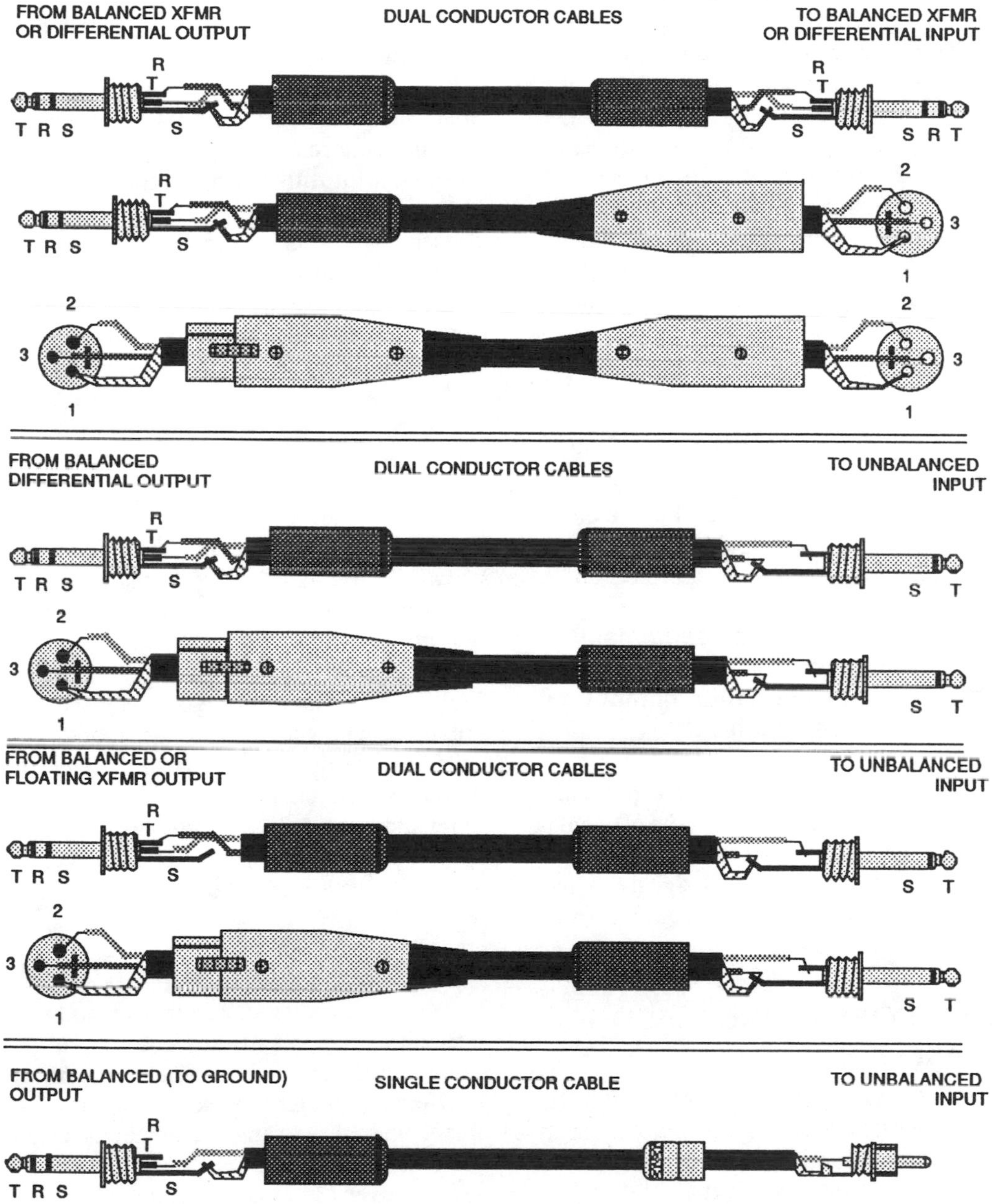

Figure 12-4. Single- and dual-conductor cables for use with transformer- or differentially balanced sources.

THE
YAMAHA
GUIDE TO
SOUND SYSTEMS
FOR WORSHIP
PAGE 125

SPEAKER CABLES

Shielding not only adds capacitance to a cable, but it also adds considerable bulk, weight, and cost. While you should never consider using unshielded cable for microphones or instruments in a sound system, there are applications where no shielding is required. Long telephone lines are one. Speaker cables are another. In speaker cables, the signal is of a sufficient strength that electrostatic noise would have to be very high in level to be audible.

Common speaker cable pitfalls include:

* Using cable that is too small. This puts needless impedance in the signal path. The resistance of a speaker cable will adversely effect the damping factor of a system. For this reason it is best to use heavy cable for low-frequency drivers—especially sub-woofers. See Figure 12-5 for recommended wire diameters. (Keep in mind that the larger the size, the *smaller* the gauge number.) Prefer cable with many fine strands of wire rather than fewer, coarse strands.

Load Z	Length of Run	
	< 100' (30 m)	> 100' (30 m)
16 ohms	16 ga.	14 ga.
8 ohms	14 ga.	12 ga.
4 ohms	12 ga.	10 ga.

Figure 12-5. Minimum recommended wire diameters for loudspeaker connection (lower gauge number is even better).

* Placing speaker cable in close proximity to low-level (mic- or line-level) cables. This risks *crosstalk* between the lines (pickup of the high-level signals by the low-level lines), which can result in electronic feedback.

MULTICORE AUDIO CABLES (SNAKES)

When you have a mixing console with 8, 12, 16, or even 24 inputs located remotely from the platform, a large number of microphone cables must be run over a relatively long distance. For this purpose, many companies supply special *snakes*, which consist of from 8 to 24 (or more) shielded pairs in a single casing.

The multicore cable sometimes terminates in "pigtails"—with each shielded pair separately insulated, strain relieved, and brought to an XLR connector. The other end may terminate in a stage box, which is a junction box that has chassis-mounted XLR connectors. Individual mic cables are then used between the stage box and various mics and instruments. Sometimes a similar junction box is used, in lieu of pigtails, at the console end of the snake.

To minimize crosstalk, don't run mic-level signals and line-level signals in the same snake. NEVER run lines to the stage monitors in the same snake as mic lines coming from the stage. Keep all loudspeaker-level lines as far as possible from lower-level cables.

Some snakes are made with large, locking, multipin connectors that enable them to be 1) fitted with different junction boxes, 2) fitted with pigtails, or 3) extended by connection to another section of multicore cable. This allows some additional flexibility, but also entails added expense. Sometimes consoles are fitted with a mating connector for such a multipin cable; while this speeds setup of a touring sound system, it makes troubleshooting difficult and swapping of lines impossible if a wire should break.

If possible, a snake should have at least one or two spare twisted pairs so that, should one develop a broken wire, the entire snake will not need to be scrapped.

Multicore cables should meet the same criteria of wire gauge, capacitance, and shielding density that you would apply to individual mic cables. Furthermore, strain relief and rugged construction take on added importance because of the size of the cable and the service it is called upon to perform.

CONNECTORS

Ideally, a connector should be easy to use, difficult to accidentally disconnect, and should introduce no resistance and allow no interference to enter the sound system. Depending on the situation, some connectors come closer to this ideal than others. If a system never has to be reconfigured or moved, then soldered, crimped, or wire-wrapped connections would be best. In other systems, other means of interconnection must be used.

THE
YAMAHA
GUIDE TO
SOUND SYSTEMS
FOR WORSHIP
PAGE 126

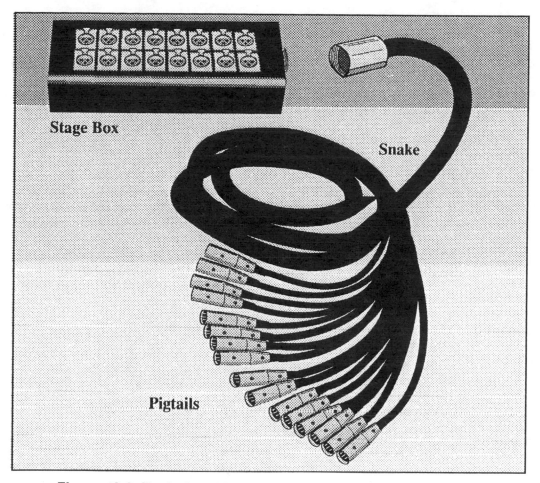

Figure 12-6. Typical multicore snake with stage box and pigtails.

Any time a plug and jack are inserted in the audio path, there will be some additional resistance to signal flow. Even if the contact resistance is minimal when the system is assembled, that resistance increases with aging, as dirt enters, or as corrosion forms. When connectors are regularly mated and unmated, they tend to wipe themselves clean and resistance does not build up excessively. This is why connectors are best avoided in fixed systems, where the regular cleaning action of assembly and disassembly is not present. Where connectors are used in fixed (or semipermanent) systems, it is best to specify gold-plated pins, since these have low initial resistance and don't corrode.

Why use one type of connector or another? Often the choice is made for you by the equipment manufacturer, who may install a specific connector. Sometimes there may be more than one option, and the choice is up to the installer. It helps to know the pros and cons of each connector type in making this choice.

PHONE PLUGS

Phone plugs are so called because they were originally used (and still are in some cases) for patching lines together on telephone switchboards. There are two-circuit plugs (tip-sleeve, or TS) and three-circuit ones (tip-ring-sleeve, or TRS). Figure 12-7 shows typical examples of these two types. Phone plugs are easily wired to the cable, relatively inexpensive, and the mating jacks can be set up to switch circuits when a plug is inserted.

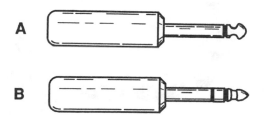

Figure 12-7 Tip-sleeve (A) and tip-ring-sleeve (B) phone plugs.

THE
YAMAHA
GUIDE TO
SOUND SYSTEMS
FOR WORSHIP
PAGE 127

In a balanced audio line, the tip is usually connected to the hot (high) side, the ring to the low side, and the sleeve to the shield ground. If such a plug is inserted into an unbalanced (tip-sleeve) phone jack, the line will be unbalanced, but the polarity will be correct.

Phone plugs can cause pops if inserted when a system is in operation. Another potential problem is that plastic shells (handles) can crack under heavy use. Metal shells are preferable for this reason, and because they electrically shield the connection, too.

Other concerns about phone plugs include the lack of a locking mechanism—which means they can be accidentally disconnected (although some locking phone plugs are now being made)—and vulnerability to internal short circuits. Most phone plug/jack combinations exhibit high contact resistance, although high-current (low-loss) plugs and jacks are available. Brass "military spec" connectors feature lower contact resistance (if regularly wiped clean by usage) than typical nickel- or alloy-plated plugs, though they cost three to five times more.

The three-circuit TRS phone plug has also been called a stereo phone plug, because this is the type of connector used on most stereo headphones. Figure 12-8 shows the connections involved.

TRS jacks are also used for channel inserts or effects loops on some consoles. A special cable is required in these cases, to connect such a jack to both the input and the output of a signal processor. Note that on some consoles the tip is the send and the ring is the return, and on others the reverse is true (the sleeve is the audio common in both cases).

The standard phone plug is ¼" (6.25 mm) in diameter. Similar but slightly smaller *tini* (TT) *plugs* were developed so that patch bays could be miniaturized. Miniature and subminiature varieties also exist, primarily on portable consumer audio equipment.

Avoid handling the plug shaft of a phone plug, and if you do, wipe off finger oils, which promote corrosion. If the connection with a standard phone plug becomes noisy, clean the plug with a brass brush, rubber pencil eraser, or #600 grit emery paper. Clean the jack using a .25 to .30 caliber brass-bristle gun cleaning brush.

Patch Bays

Most connections to audio equipment are found on the backs of the units. Changing connections to such equipment can be inconvenient or even difficult. If you need to make frequent changes, a *patch bay* may be in order.

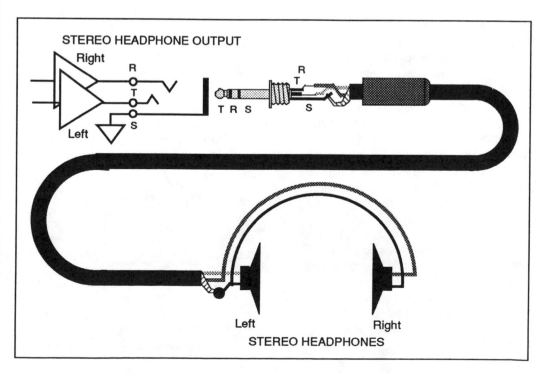

Figure 12-8. A tip-ring-sleeve phone plug wired to stereo headphones.

THE
YAMAHA
GUIDE TO
SOUND SYSTEMS
FOR WORSHIP
PAGE 128

A basic patch bay has two rows of phone jacks on the front—one for outputs and one for inputs. The outputs are generally the top row. Connections from the equipment itself are made to the back of the patch bay, either soldered in or via removable connectors.

Most patch bays in professional sound systems feature *normalled* connections, which means that if no plugs are inserted to the jacks on the front, each output is connected internally to the input below it. These internal connections represent the normal signal connection of the equipment. Inserting a plug into a jack breaks this normal connection, allowing signals to be rerouted as necessary via *patch cords*—short cables with phone plugs on each end.

(In especially large sound systems and recording studios, computer-controlled switching matrices are used as an alternative to patch bays. These allow multiple reroutings to be handled quickly and easily.)

Patch bays can have TS or TRS phone jacks, with the former being used exclusively for unbalanced connections. Do not assume that TRS jacks are for balanced circuits, though usually they are. The TRS jacks in a patch bay may be wired for unbalanced operation, with the tip being the audio common, the ring the audio high, and the sleeve chassis ground. This arrangement avoids pops from static discharge or different ground potentials as a plug is inserted, since the tip (common) makes contact before the signal-carrying ring. CAUTION: If a cable is connected to a patch bay this way, and the other end is connected to an unbalanced tip-sleeve jack, the signal will be shorted out.

In order for patch bays to be most useful, they should be placed within easy reach of engineer while he or she is operating the console.

PHONO (PIN) CONNECTORS

The Radio Corporation of America (RCA) originally developed the pin connector. It became popular for use on the cables that connected phonograph cartridges to preamplifiers. This familiar connector, which has become the standard for most line-level consumer audio equipment, has a protruding pin in the center of a shell (see Figure 12-9). For these reasons, it is known variously as an *RCA plug*, a *phono plug*, or a *pin plug*.

Figure 12-9. An RCA phono pin plug.

This type of plug is used in some professional sound equipment because it is inexpensive and it allows many connectors to be placed in a small area.

Because they are tricky to mate with cables, and because there is a high demand for phono cables in the consumer market, such cables are available prewired with connectors that are encased in molded plastic. As with other aspects of cabling, quality is important. A good cable is not cheap, but an expensive one may not always be good.

One problem with phono connectors is the tendency to develop high resistance where the plug and jack meet. Particularly where connections are not disturbed for years, corrosion at the contact surface can degrade performance. To avoid this problem, select gold-plated connectors, or phono plugs with springy, slightly dished shell fingers that will burnish the surfaces to clean them when the connector is twisted in place. Twist it periodically to clean them.

XLR CONNECTORS

The three-pin XLR connector, also known as XLR-3, was originally introduced by Cannon (now ITT-Cannon), and that company still owns the rights to the term XLR. Other manufacturers offer equivalent connectors, which are usually called XLR-type, XLB, or XL-type.

Both male and female XLR-type connectors are available in in-line (cable-end) and chassis-mount forms. Figure 12-10 shows in-line connectors.

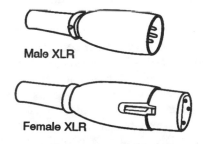

Figure 12-10. Male and female in-line XLR-type connectors.

The XLR-type connector is the most common for balanced connections, for several reasons: It has three conductors, it is shielded, it locks in place, and the ground pin makes contact first, to bleed static from the cable and avoid pops. Other advantages include its abilities to accommodate large-diameter mic cables and to provide good strain relief. Finally, XLR-type connectors have large contact areas, which afford low contact resistance. Their only drawbacks are relatively high cost and the care required to properly attach them to the cable.

LOUDSPEAKER CONNECTORS

Binding posts are common connectors on loudspeaker cabinets (see Figure 12-11). They accept standard banana plugs (Figure 12-12A), either individually or in pairs, as well as spade lugs or bare or tinned wire (Figure 12-12B; it is preferable to pass the wire through the hole in the post, although it can be wrapped clockwise around the post if it is too large for the hole). Binding posts are color-coded with red for the "+" connection and black for the "–" (as a rule; check the owner's manual to confirm this).

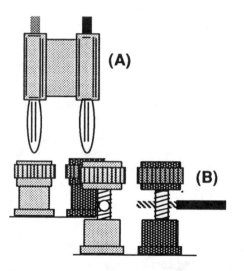

Figure 12-11. Five-way binding posts accept dual banana plugs (A) or bare wires (B), as well as spade lugs and single banana plugs.

Another common connector is the ¼" phone plug. This is a two-circuit connector: the tip is used for the "+" connection and the sleeve for the "–" connection. Phone plugs are less than ideal as loudspeaker connectors because of their relatively high contact resistance, though they may be adequate for small systems. They are also easy to dislodge and prone to short circuits. In addition, if a loudspeaker is plugged in or unplugged while the power amplifier is on, it momentarily shorts the output of the amp; this could contribute to failure of the amp.

XLR-type connectors are also used for loudspeakers at times. Four-circuit XLR-type connectors can be used in a biamplified system (two pins for the high-frequency driver and two for the low-frequency one).

Recently introduced and gaining in popularity is the Neutrik NL-4 connector. While most common speaker connectors were originally intended for other applications, the NL-4 was designed especially for loudspeaker use. The NL-4 has four conductors for use in biamplified systems. Positive locking is achieved in two ways: The connector twists into place, then a ring is screwed down to lock the connector. The NL-4 is made of a rugged polycarbonate and is easy to assemble. One of the two available chassis-mount connectors will fit an XLR chassis cutout. Several manufacturers use the NL-4 on their high-end sound reinforcement loudspeakers.

NOTE: "Sources of Audio Peripherals," on pages 183–185, includes listings for makers of connectors.

POLARITY

In all connections in a sound system, it is important that the "+" and "–" wires of all outputs be connected to the corresponding wires of the inputs of the devices that follow in the signal chain. If the two are reversed, problems with phase cancellation and the intelligibility of speech can result. (With some circuit components, reversal of polarity can result in failure to operate or even destruction.)

Figure 12-12 summarizes the polarity normally found with various connectors. Note that there can be exceptions. Some loudspeakers, for example, reverse the usual color-coding. And some XLR-type connectors, particularly on older European gear, reverse the functions of pins 2 and 3. Possible solutions to the latter case include 1) rewiring the connections on the device (only if you're certain); 2) using a polarity-inverting cable, in which the wires connected to pins 2 and 3 on one end are swapped at the other end (*causes* polarity inversion if accidentally used with normal gear); or 3) engaging the phase (polarity) inversion button on the console input (the easiest).

THE
YAMAHA
GUIDE TO
SOUND SYSTEMS
FOR WORSHIP
PAGE 130

	Unbalanced		Balanced		
	Hot (+)	Cold (−) (Common)	Hot (+)	Cold (−)	Shield (Ground)
Phone (TS)	tip	sleeve	—	—	—
Phone (TRS)	—	—	tip	ring	sleeve
Phono (Pin)	tip	collar	—	—	—
XLR-type	—	—	pin 2	pin 3	pin 1
Binding Posts	red	black	—	—	—

Figure 12-12. Polarity of common connectors.

SYSTEM GROUNDING

Ground is the electrical reference against which potentials (voltages) are expressed. In a practical audio system, a number of different independent references exist in various local subsystems. These may or may not be at the same electrical potential. If handled properly, they need not be at the same potential.

Three specific kinds of ground references can be distinguished in discussing audio connections:

- **Signal Ground**—the reference point against which signal potentials in a specific piece of equipment or group of components are expressed.

- **Earth Ground**—the local electrical potential of the earth. In practice, earth is the potential of the central, rounded terminal in a U.S. standard three-prong 120-volt outlet. Earth is sometimes obtained from a metal cold water pipe (though the use of nonconductive plastic pipe has rendered this increasingly unreliable), or from a chemical earthing rod sunk into the moistened ground.

- **Chassis Ground**—the chassis connection point of a specific component. In equipment fitted with a three-prong AC plug, the chassis is normally connected to earth, with provision to connect signal ground to earth as well. Equipment having a two-prong AC plug will normally have the chassis ground connected to signal ground.

Connections among these various reference points are a crucial factor in assembling a successful audio system.

THE IMPORTANCE OF PROPER GROUNDING

The main reason to ground a system is for safety; proper grounding can prevent lethal shocks. The connection between chassis and earth ground is sometimes called a safety ground, for it is instrumental in achieving this purpose.

The next reason for grounding a system that includes AC-powered equipment is that, under some conditions, proper grounding may reduce the pickup of external noise. While proper grounding doesn't always reduce such noise, improper grounding can increase it.

Low-level audio signal lines are invariably shielded, to intercept electrostatic noise. A major goal of grounding technique is to keep these unwanted signal currents that are induced in the shield away from the signal conductor(s), draining them to ground as directly as possible.

GROUND LOOPS

The ground on an AC power cord (the green wire and the third pin on the AC plug) connects the chassis of electronic equipment to a wire in the wall power service that leads through building wiring to an earth ground. The earth ground is required by electrical codes everywhere. But it can contribute to *ground loops*.

A ground loop occurs when there is more than one ground connection path between two pieces of equipment. The duplicate ground paths form the equivalent of a loop antenna, which very efficiently picks up interference—notably, AC line-frequency hum. Figure 12-13 shows a typical situation in which a ground loop occurs. The earth ground path and duplicate signal ground path (through the shield of a cable) form a loop.

Normally, this kind of ground loop should not cause any noise in the audio circuits if 1) the circuits are truly balanced or floating, and 2) the audio common (the return path of the audio-signal circuit) is maintained separately from the chassis ground within the equipment. If one of these conditions is not met, then instead of going directly to earth ground and disappearing, these circulating ground loop currents infest the signal-carrying lines, producing hum and noise that are amplified along with the rest of the signal.

Ground loops are often difficult to isolate, even for experienced audio engineers. Sometimes, in poorly designed sound equipment (including some expensive equipment), ground loops occur inside the chassis, even though the equipment has balanced inputs and outputs. It's best to avoid this kind of equipment. It's also best to avoid unbalanced equipment (unless the equipment is all going to be very close together, connected to the same phase leg of the AC service, and not subject to high hum fields).

If you encounter a hum-producing ground loop, you may be tempted to break it by "lifting" the earth ground of an AC power cord—using a three-prong-to-two-prong adapter plug, or even chopping off the ground prong from the three-prong plug. NEVER do this! Earth ground is provided for the safety of all concerned, and that safety is a moral, not to mention legal, obligation by which a house of worship ought to abide.

A better solution is to disconnect the shield from ground at one end of the audio cable in the loop in question—creating what is known as a *telescoping shield*. As mentioned earlier in this chapter, some direct boxes include "ground lift" switches that accomplish this. This solution is easier to implement in fixed systems, where you can "set it and forget it," than it is in portable or changeable systems, where the frequent reconnection of equipment makes tracing down ground loops and keeping track of special cables more difficult.

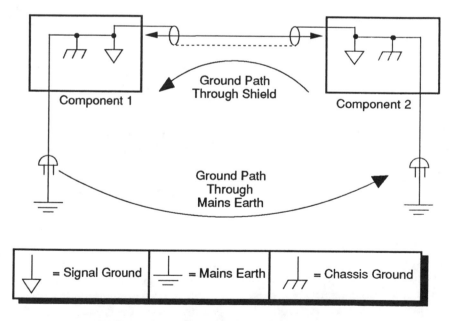

Figure 12-13. Formation of ground loops.

THE
YAMAHA
GUIDE TO
SOUND SYSTEMS
FOR WORSHIP
PAGE 132

AC Power

Check the following aspects of the AC power source before plugging equipment in. This list applies to both fixed and touring systems; if need be, obtain the services of a qualified electrician to verify them.

- **Correct voltage and frequency.** The AC standard for the USA and Canada is 110 to 120 volt, 50 or 60 Hz AC. Elsewhere, it's 220 or 240 volt, 50 or 60 Hz AC. Be sure the power source matches what your equipment expects. More than a 5-10% difference from the specified figures can damage equipment.

- **Stiffness of voltage supply.** Some lines are "soft," meaning they drop in voltage when the line is loaded with excessive resistance or too high a current load. Check the voltage once all equipment is turned on.

- **Properly wired outlets.** The standard three-prong outlet used in the USA and Canada should be wired with the hot wire on the right slot, the neutral on the left (wide) slot, and the earth ground in the center hole underneath. Make sure all of these are connected correctly, and that the earth ground is good. For two-prong outlets, establish a good earth ground with the center screw on the outlet plate, a cold water pipe, or a chemical earthing rod.

- **Sufficient number and capacity of AC circuits.** Be sure that there is enough current available to supply the requirements of your equipment. If you distribute your equipment intelligently, you can avoid blowing fuses or tripping circuit breakers at every turn.

- **Integrity of the power source.** Make every effort to assure that your power source is clean and reliable. Synthesizers, computers, and other digital equipment, in particular, normally require a filtered power source with surge protection, in order to avoid glitches, system hangups, and possible component damage. A higher order of protection is provided by power line isolation transformers, which not only exclude noise and distortion in the AC signal, but also hold the voltage at a nearly constant value, despite fluctuations of the AC source.

Console Placement

A sound reinforcement engineer must be in a location similar to that of the congregation so that he hears the same sound they do. It may mean sacrificing some real estate in the pews, and may ruffle the architect's feathers, but the proper position for the PA engineer is on the main floor, usually ⅔ of the way back from the main platform, near (though not at) the center of the room. A console so placed need not be an eyesore; in fact, as long as the engineer doesn't stand up during the service, the congregation probably will soon forget he or she is there.

Many houses of worship banish the sound man and his gear to a balcony "sound booth." This forces the sound man to apply bandaid fixes to his listening problems. One solution to this is to set up a separate, personal monitoring loudspeaker, "flown" out in front of the mixing location; the audio feed to this monitor is signal-delayed, equalized, and level-matched to provide a fair representation of what a listener on the main seating floor would hear. This can provide a workable arrangement, but the engineer will never be able to provide anything better than an interpretive mix. He will still have to make periodic trips to the main seating area to hear what the congregation there is actually hearing, and then trudge back up to the console to make adjustments accordingly.

Some houses of worship make the mistake of putting the console in a closed room looking through what amounts to a hole in the wall. And the worst possible arrangement is a closed room with the front sealed off by a window. In this predicament, the only way the engineer can hear what is happening in the room is to hang a mic out there and feed it over a little monitor speaker in his booth. Expecting the engineer to be able to make proper mix decisions for the PA system with this arrangement is nothing short of ludicrous. If you are in such a glass cage now, the first thing to do is to remove the glass. The second thing to do is to start negotiations immediately to get your PA console on the main floor where it belongs.

In poor mixing locations, many engineers try resorting to headphones in order to hear what they need to hear. It won't work. An engineer can use headphones to help clarify a problem he encounters, but he should not rely on them as his main listening reference.

The
YAMAHA
GUIDE TO
SOUND SYSTEMS
FOR WORSHIP
PAGE 133

HANGING LOUDSPEAKERS

The subject of hanging loudspeakers is another one that could easily fill a book this size. This section attempts to at least make you aware of some of the different considerations involved.

POSITION

The best placement of loudspeakers is generally up front and overhead. Benefits of such positioning include:

- Providing the smoothest coverage from front to back. It makes the ratio between the distance to the nearest listener and the distance to farthest listener as small as possible, so that the difference in volume of what they hear is as small as possible.

- Directing as much sound as possible at the congregation, but as little as possible at the back wall. (Ideally, you would aim at the farthest listener, and "soften" the back wall to minimize focused reflections. In many cases, however, it is more practical simply to aim about ⅔ of the way back.)

- Removing the loudspeakers as far as is practical from the microphones—thereby helping to increase the gain before feedback.

Single-point placement is best. This means that there should be one central speaker cluster if at all possible, rather than two on opposite sides of the room. By now you're probably familiar enough with the words "acoustic phase cancellation" so that no more need be said on this point.

If a single cluster is not possible—either because it is visually intrusive (see below) or because it does not provide adequate coverage, then two or more clusters may be necessary. But one should be larger, and designed to provide most of the coverage, with the other merely filling in where the main cluster can't.

Be aware that placing loudspeakers near, or especially on, boundaries (walls, ceiling) can reinforce bass frequencies, which may lessen the power necessary for low-frequency drivers and amplification. What happens is that high frequencies tend to be directional, emanating in the direction in which the driver is aimed, while low frequencies tend to be omnidirectional—especially in direct-radiator enclosures. These low frequencies bounce off of nearby boundaries and reinforce the direct sound.

HIDING LOUDSPEAKERS

Ideally, a worship facility should be designed with the sound system in mind, so that loudspeaker clusters are made a part of the decor rather than an intrusion on it. But in the real world, most sound systems are designed for existing facilities, where making the loudspeakers "fit in" visually can be more difficult.

In some cases there may be a desire to hide the loudspeakers, to conceal them from the congregation. Fine, as long as they are hidden visually, but NOT acoustically. Special enclosures can be made, innocuous grille cloth employed, recessed chambers installed in a wall or ceiling in order to keep the speakers out of sight. But nothing should keep them out of hearing; they should not be placed behind pillars or obstructed in any other way, or you will defeat the purpose of having them in the first place.

The visual lines of some assembly rooms are such that an elevated central cluster would do them violence. Very well; use two clusters, following the guidelines given in the preceding section. But do not utterly sacrifice acoustical performance at the altar of visual aesthetics. Sight and sound are both important to worship.

SAFETY

Safety is the top priority in hanging loudspeakers—safety in both the act of hanging them and in the assurance that they will remain hung! It can literally be a matter of vital (life-or-death) importance, and so it is more important than good sound, proper coverage of the seating areas, and visual appearance, though it need not and should not exclude those factors. What follows are a few thoughts on hanging loudspeakers safely.

Somewhere in your congregation, there probably is someone familiar with structural engineering—either an engineer by profession or one by avocation. The *least* you can do is have that person or persons look at your plans to see whether they are adequate

THE
YAMAHA
GUIDE TO
SOUND SYSTEMS
FOR WORSHIP
PAGE 134

to keep the loudspeakers aloft. There is a difference here between listening to everyone's idle opinion and seeking out the advice of knowledgeable people.

Since safety is fundamentally a matter of obtaining reliable information (and acting on that information), you might wish to study books such as the *Handbook of Rigging* (see "For Further Reading," on page 182.

If you're installing a large cluster, consider hiring a rigging professional. Find out who handles the "flown" speaker and lighting systems for concerts that play in your area, and whether they or someone they can recommend has experience with worship facilities. On the other hand, if your sound system is large, there already ought to be professionals involved with the installation.

NEATNESS COUNTS

Neatness is the mother of many virtues in sound system installation, including safety, reliability, freedom from noise, ease of troubleshooting, and (in portable systems) speed of setup and teardown.

Rack-mount equipment should be installed in logical order, so that connections between units can be as short and direct as possible, with as little crossing of wires as possible. Mounting hardware should be uniform, so that a single set of tools can be used to mount or dismount any piece of gear.

Cables within racks should be grouped together where possible—especially cables of the same kind, such as line-level connections to the console. Cable ties should be used at regular intervals to hold these bundles together, and clamps should be used to hold them to the rack itself.

Dissimilar lines should be kept as far apart as possible. Mic-level, line-level, speaker-level, and AC power lines should be separated from one another.

Cables should be routed away from areas of foot traffic, kept from unnecessary twists and turns, and protected from any sharp edges or corners. Proper strain relief should be employed to protect wires from pulling out and from sharp bends.

Leave a *service loop* on cable bundles—a small additional amount of slack that allows a rack or piece of equipment to be moved for easier access during service.

Labels should identify all cables and wires, so that signals can be traced and connections restored if problems call for the system to be "operated upon." Patch bay outputs and inputs should be clearly labeled.

System diagrams and other documentation should be made or obtained, maintained, and kept readily available at all times.

ROOM EQUALIZATION AND SPEAKER BALANCING

If you already know how to set room equalization curves and balance loudspeaker systems, you don't need this book to tell you how. If you DON'T know how to do those things, it might be dangerous for this book to try to tell you how. These are tasks for professionals, with professional equipment, such as real-time spectrum analyzers and pink-noise generators. But perhaps a few words are in order, just to demystify these topics for you.

Chapter 7 explains equalization and equalizers, and tells how to "ring out" a room or a monitor system with graphic EQ. Setting the room EQ is similar. It involves using graphic EQ to compensate for any unevenness in the frequency response of the room. Where the room tends to emphasize a frequency, the EQ de-emphasizes it, and vice versa. The desired result is to obtain a smooth, flat frequency response, to reproduce sounds as accurately as possible.

Some have suggested that room equalizer(s) should be kept in a locked cabinet, away from the Wilburs of the congregation. That's not a bad idea. Along the same lines, some equalizers are set by remote control, from a computer running special software. Once the computer is disconnected, the unit is safe from tampering hands.

Once loudspeakers are positioned and aimed properly, they must be balanced to provide smooth coverage of the seating areas. There should be no jumps in volume if you move from an area covered by one loudspeaker to one covered by another. This balancing is done simply by adjusting the input attenuators on the amplifiers in question. Again, these controls are often made to resist accidental or casual changes of setting.

CHAPTER 13.
SYSTEM OPERATION

SYSTEM FLOW LOGIC

In order to be able to operate a sound system effectively, it is important to understand the various paths that the signals travel within that system. Figure 13-1 represents the signal flow logic of the house sound system for a fairly typical 5,000-seat house of worship. For clarity, the signal flow for the stage monitors is not shown.

The main output of the console is fed to an equalizer for the initial shaping of the room EQ. It then goes to a narrow notch filter to resolve particularly difficult feedback nodes. A peak limiter is next, to provide protection for the loudspeakers. The output of the limiter then feeds a three-way electronic crossover.

The low band of the crossover feeds two separate power amplifiers, with the channels shown powering individual 18" subwoofers. The mid-band output of the crossover feeds two power amplifiers, and each output of those two amps drives a separate low-

frequency speaker enclosure with two 15" speakers in each box.

The high band of the crossover feeds two more power amplifiers, and each output of those amps drives a pair of high-frequency driver/horn combinations. On each amp there are a pair of short-throw horns and a pair of long- (or mid-) throw horns.

The main output of the console is also paralleled over to the second channel of the EQ, which will eventually drive a set of three secondary clusters, flown roughly half the way back into the room. Since the speakers are offset from the main system, the signal next goes through a signal delay. From this point on the signal flow closely matches that of the main speaker system, except that there are only three clusters here, while there are four clusters in the front (main) speaker system. The crossover points are the same in each system.

Note that this signal delay has two outputs. The second output (with its own delay setting) is fed to the input of another EQ (at

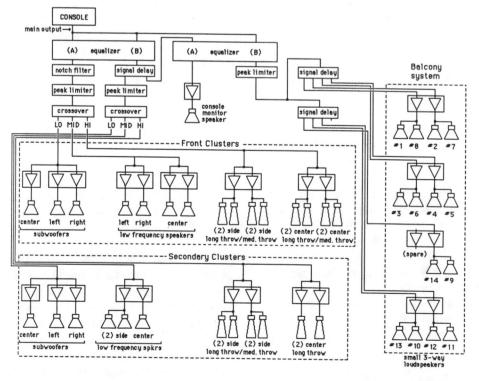

Figure 13-1. Signal flow logic for a hypothetical house of worship.

THE
YAMAHA
GUIDE TO
SOUND SYSTEMS
FOR WORSHIP
PAGE 136

least one recently introduced signal delay includes digital-domain equalization, eliminating the need for the additional EQ), and then through a power amp to a small two-way speaker (15" woofer plus a horn). This speaker is used as a "personal monitor" for the house mixing console location. In this case, the poor guy is stuck in the balcony, away from all the action on the main floor, and therefore needs a reasonable listening reference from which to base his mix decisions. Note that the signal to this speaker is delayed, equalized and level-matched to provide a reasonable approximation of the sound the congregation will hear on the main floor.

Now that the main floor seating area is covered, next are the congregation seating areas in the balcony. The balcony runs the length of the room on both sides and in the rear, and accounts for 2,000 of the 5,000 total seats available. Needless to say, it would be careless to not cover them adequately.

The balcony signal flow parallels off of the main house output, flows through the remaining channel of the EQ for shaping, through a peak limiter for speaker protection, and then to a pair of 1-input/4-output signal delays. There are fourteen three-way loudspeakers flown in strategic locations out in front of the balcony. They are delayed in seven zones or groups, as indicated by the flow chart.

The stage monitor system is fed from six auxiliary mixes at the house mixing desk. Each of the six feeds has a separate ⅓-octave graphic EQ for feedback control, and power amp(s) to drive the speakers. Individual channel outputs are located in stage plates across rear of the stage.

SETTING GAIN STRUCTURE

The subject of setting gain structure is probably misunderstood by more operators of sound systems than any other. Few system operators bother to take a methodical approach to adjusting the system gain structure; rather, they rely on random knob twiddling until they achieve something approaching adequate system operation.

By understanding and applying the basics of proper gain structure to your sound system, you can enjoy the maximum dynamic range

and the minimum level of noise of which your system is capable. You just may discover that your "noisy" mixer or signal processor is far more capable than you thought.

THEORY OF PROPER GAIN STRUCTURE

Electrical *gain* is the difference between the input signal level and the output signal level of a system or system component. It will typically be expressed in dB. There are two basic guidelines in setting system gain structure:

1. **Everything clips at (or about) the same time.** If some component in your system (for example, the power amplifier) is driven into clipping while other components are operating far below maximum signal level, you are certainly sacrificing dynamic range and increasing system noise.

2. **Take as much gain as possible as early as possible.** The total gain of a sound system (the amount of signal boost from mic input to speaker output) will be about the same for a properly or improperly gain-structured system. A typical house of worship requires up to 120 dB of gain. The critical element in gain structuring is *where* in the system that gain is taken. If you take the gain toward the output of the system, all the noise from the previous stages will be boosted with the signal. If you take the gain toward the input of the system, there will be less noise to increase, and so system noise will decrease.

Figure 13-2 illustrates the dynamic range of a professional mixing console. The key elements are:

- The *noise floor* is the point at which the signal gets lost in the noise generated by various electronic components. (While professional equipment is low in noise, current electronic technology cannot deliver totally noise-free performance.)

- *Nominal* is the average level of the signal. A musician might think of nominal as being *mezzo forte* or *forte*. Output meters of a properly gain-structured mixing console will read "0" when the program material is at nominal level. The output of a professional mixing console will then be at +4 dBm (see pages 27–28 for more discussion of dBm).

- *Peak* is the onset of clipping (see Chapter 8). Before the signal reaches this level, the peak LED on most mixing consoles will light. When clipping is exceeded, distortion will become increasingly audible.

- *Headroom* is the difference between peak and nominal. Headroom may be thought of as a safety margin that allows room for all those dynamic peaks that give impact to music.

- *Signal-to-noise ratio* (S/N ratio) is, as the term implies, the ratio of signal to noise; it is at the heart of gain structuring theory. Put simply, your goal is to set the dynamic "window" of your system to maximize the S/N ratio. This can be done by operating the system *near* (but not *into*) clipping.

ADJUSTMENT OF AMPLIFIERS, CROSSOVERS, EQUALIZERS

WARNING: If your system was installed and adjusted by a knowledgeable contractor or consultant, adjustments of amplifiers, crossovers, and equalizers have been completed. We strongly discourage tampering with the settings of a professionally tuned system, which were carefully arrived at. Ill-advised readjustment may make necessary a complete retuning of the system by the contractor or consultant, who will be completely justified in charging for this service.

If, on the other hand, your system was never properly gain-structured, read on. Another word of caution: This procedure may be time-consuming. Don't attempt to restructure your system gain 30 minutes before a service, or you may find yourself in a very awkward situation.

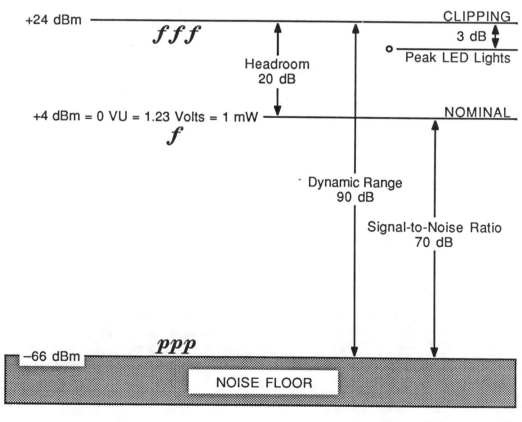

Figure 13-2. Dynamic range of a professional mixing console.

THE
YAMAHA
GUIDE TO
SOUND SYSTEMS
FOR WORSHIP
PAGE 138

Make sure the amplifiers are switched off and perform the following steps:

1. **Mute all console inputs and outputs and set them to minimum.** This will prevent any feedback surprises.

2. **Set the input level controls of the system equalizer(s) to maximum.** An equalizer will usually be operated at "unity gain" (no increase or decrease in gain through the unit). While you're at it, check the back panel of the equalizer to see if it has any input or output level switches. If so, set them to the +4 dB position. (This applies to equalizers used on the console's primary outputs. Equalizers used at other points—such as inserts—should be set to the input and output levels to which they are connected. Consult your owner's manuals.)

   Cutting and boosting the frequency bands of an equalizer can decrease or increase its effective gain. It is possible that extreme boost of one or more bands could cause the output stages of an equalizer to be overdriven. Since the peak LED on most equalizers monitors only the input signal level, you will need to rely on your ears to detect this problem. A system that requires extreme equalization may have problems elsewhere.

3. **Set the input and output level controls of the electronic crossover (if any) to maximum.** (There is an equally valid approach that differs somewhat on this point.) This is a good time to verify the crossover frequency and slope settings.

4. **Set the input controls on the power amplifier(s) to midpoint.** This setting is only temporary and will allow you to hear the system while making other adjustments.

5. **Connect a CD player, cassette deck, or other source to a channel(s) of the console. Take that channel's fader(s) to nominal (about ⅔ of the way to the top). Turn on the channel.** Adjust the channel's input gain trim and pad as needed. Mute all other input channels.

6. **Power up the audio source, console, signal processors, and power amplifiers—in that order.**

7. **Turn on the console's master output and increase the level of the channel fader until the output meter registers 0 VU when the music from the source is at an average (nominal) level.**

8. **Check the clip LED (if any) of the equalizer.** If it lights for more than an instant during brief dynamic peaks, reduce the equalizer's input level control.

9. **If your system is not bi- or triamplified, go to step 14.**

10. **Check the clip LED (if any) of the crossover.** If it lights for more than an instant during brief dynamic peaks, reduce the crossover's input level control(s).

11. **With the source still playing, adjust the input level of the low-frequency amplifier until the sound from the speakers reaches the desired level.** When the output meters on the console are at 0 VU, the sound pressure level should be near the average level at which you operate the system.

12. **Adjust the input level of the mid-frequency amplifier until the sound from the speakers reaches the desired level.**

13. **Adjust the input level of all remaining amplifiers until the sound from the speakers reaches the desired level.** Walk around the area covered by the various speakers and listen critically. Set the relative levels of the various amplifiers to balance the highs, lows, and mids. Balance the long-throw system with the main cluster. Think of this as the first coarse step in equalizing the system. Some amplifiers have calibrated, detented input level controls to make precise adjustment easy and repeatable.

   Once you have established the basic level of the amplifiers, balance highs, lows, and mids using the output controls provided on most crossovers.

14. **If your system is not bi- or triamplified:** With the source still playing, adjust the input level of the amplifier(s) until the sound from the speakers reaches the desired level. When the output meters on the console are at 0 VU, the sound pressure level should be near the average level at which you operate the system.

15. **Repeat this procedure for each stage-monitor send and for any amplifier-and-speaker systems covering cry rooms, foyers, etc.**

At this point the system should be properly gain-structured from the mixing console output to the speakers. Due to variations in equipment input sensitivity and output level, you may need "fudge" a bit on some settings. Listen carefully for distortion. It could be that your semi-pro EQ can only handle +18 dBu peaks at the input, while your console can produce +22 dBu or more. If so, you must be aware of it and back off on the console output slightly.

Probably the most widespread misconception in audio is that power amplifiers should always be operated with the input level controls "wide open." If input level controls should always be set at maximum, then there would be no need to have them on the amplifier. If there were no need for input level controls, why would amplifier manufacturers go to the needless expense of including them? In fact, the input level of an amplifier is an important control in system gain structuring.

Many sound system operators (and some sound equipment salespeople) believe that turning down the amplifier's input level control "turns down the amp's power." In fact, the input level control on an amplifier simply varies the amount of electrical input needed to drive the amp to full power. That 200-watt amplifier will still produce 200 watts even if the input sensitivity is reduced—it will just need a little more voltage from the console to do it.

With the input level set "wide open," most amplifiers can be driven to full output by 1.25 volts (this will vary between manufacturers). A mixing console can produce 12 volts or more at the output. If input level control on the amplifier is set "wide open," any voltage above 1.25 volts will drive the amplifier into clipping. This

means that the operator will have to adjust the mixing console so the output never exceeds 1.25 volts (which roughly equals 0 VU and also roughly equals +4 dBu). As a result, as much as 20 dB of console headroom may be wasted, and the S/N ratio will be decreased by 20 dB.

SETTING THE GAIN STRUCTURE OF THE CONSOLE

NOTE: In the following examples are several references to drum mixes. While drums are used mostly in youth ministries or contemporary styles of music, the drum mix is particularly demanding and serves well as an illustration. The basic principles discussed are equally applicable to the sound reinforcement needs of more traditional styles of worship.

With all mics plugged into the console and everything wired up, you are ready to start setting the gain structure of the console.

1. **Set the controls on the console as follows:**

   Channel On/Off (or Mute):
   　Off (or muted)
   Input Gain (Trim):
   　Minimum (fully counterclockwise)
   Channel Faders:
   　Minimum
   Pads:
   　Off
   Subgroup Master Faders:
   　Nominal (about ⅔ open)
   Master Faders:
   　Nominal (about ⅔ open)
   Aux, Effects, Monitor Sends:
   　Minimum (fully counterclockwise)
   Aux, Effects, Monitor Masters:
   　Minimum (fully counterclockwise)
   Aux, Effects Returns:
   　Minimum (fully counterclockwise)
   Channel-to-Bus Assigns:
   　Assigned as needed

The bottom of a fader's throw provides maximum attenuation, and is often labeled "−∞" (minus infinity). The top of the fader's throw typically means no attenuation. The console manufacturer will indicate the optimum (or nominal) starting point by marking it with a heavy line, or by a "grayed" area, or sometimes with a "0." This position is typically up about ⅔ of the fader's throw from the bottom of its travel.

THE
YAMAHA
GUIDE TO
SOUND SYSTEMS
FOR WORSHIP
PAGE 140

2. **Turn on channel 1 and ask the performer who will be using the mic on that channel to play or sing for you.** If it is a kick drum, ask the drummer to play solid, steady beats until you say to stop. Whatever the instrument or voice, ask the performers to sing or play at the loudest volume they expect to use during the service. (They will always sing or play louder during the actual service, but at least you will have a head start.)

3. **Watch the channel clip (or overload) LED while gradually rotating the input gain control.** You may also want to use the console's cue (sometimes called PFL, or solo) system and headphones to listen for clipping distortion. The objective is to find the point at which the clip LED lights, and then reduce the input gain slightly. If you have rotated the gain fully counterclockwise (to the least sensitive position) and the clip LED remains lit, it may be necessary to engage the pad. This accomplished, you can now slowly bring the channel fader up until the level of the instrument or voice in the speaker system is about right.

4. **Once you are satisfied that your gain structure for that channel is set, move on to channel 2.** Continue through the process until all channels are set.

5. **After you have set the basic gain structure, ask the drummer (if any) to play the entire set while you work on the overall drum sound.** Now invite the rest of the performers up to play.

6. **Check the console's group meters and master output meters.** When the instruments assigned to the group are playing at an average level (*mezzo forte* to *forte* for you musicians), you should see an indication of 0 VU on the meter. You should see the peak LED flicker occasionally on extreme dynamic peaks (*fortissimo*).

   If the signal on a subgroup or master is too high (meter needle banging the right peg, peak LED continuously lit), you may need to reduce the channel faders or subgroup faders slightly.

If the signal is too low (meter barely twitching, peak LED never flickers), bring the channel faders and/or subgroup faders up. Use the master faders to set overall system volume.

There is an exception to this rule: On most powered mixers (one-piece units including mixer, equalization, and power amplification), the meters are not monitoring the output of the mixer section. Rather, they are monitoring the output of the power amplifier. Since most houses of worship using powered mixers are not using anything near the full rated power, the meters will generally not reach a high level.

7. **Go back and check the channel input peak LEDs.** The performers will probably be working at slightly different (usually higher) levels than during the individual sound checks. Some trimming of input gain will be needed.

8. **Start working on "getting your mix together."** Boosting the EQ on a channel may cause some clipping in that channel. Since the input clip indicator on most consoles is before the EQ section, it will not indicate clipping that occurs after the EQ. Some consoles have an additional post-EQ clip indicator. Otherwise you'll need to use your ears and the console's cue system to detect clipping. Should EQ boost result in clipping, simply trim back the channel's input gain.

EFFECTS DEVICES

Effects devices such as digital reverbs are also part of the discussion of gain structure. Once again, the objective is to use as much of a device's dynamic range as possible. The following steps use the example of adding reverb to a soloist's voice. The digital reverb is being fed from one of the console's Aux busses. The stereo outputs of the digital reverb are being returned to the console's Aux Return.

1. **Match the input and output levels of the console with the input and output levels of the digital reverb.** Many signal processors have inputs and outputs that can be set (via rear-panel switches) to match the inputs and outputs of either professional sound

reinforcement equipment (+4 dBu) or instruments and home recording equipment (–20 dBu).

Check the owner's manuals for your console and signal processor. Match (as closely as possible) the input level of the processor to the output level of the console. If the nominal Aux Send level of your console is +4 dBu, set the processor input level to +4 dBu. If the nominal input level of the console's Aux Returns is +4 dBu, set the processor output level switch to +4 dBu.

2. **Ask the vocalist(s) to sing into the mic, and bring the Aux Send control(s) of the vocal channel(s) up to nominal (about 2 o'clock).**

3. **Check to make sure the Aux Send master is set at nominal.**

4. **Rotate the reverb processor's input level control while watching its input meter.** When the vocalist hits a dynamic peak, the top segment of the LED meter should flicker briefly.

5. **Slowly increase the level of the Aux Return until you hear the desired amount of reverb in the mix.**

6. **If more than one vocal channel is being processed,** balance the amount of reverb on the various channels using the channel Aux Send controls.

7. **Control the overall amount of reverb with the Aux *Returns*.** Never decrease the overall reverb by reducing the Aux *Send* level; this allows all the residual noise from the reverb to remain in the mix. The Aux Send level should only be reduced if the reverb processor is being overdriven.

AN EXAMPLE SYSTEM

Figure 13-3 illustrates the gain relationships within two simple, identical sound systems. Each system consists of the following elements:

- The hand-held *microphone* as used in this application will produce a nominal output level of –60 dBm. Peak output of this microphone will never exceed –40 dBm. The difference between peak

and nominal (20 dB) is known as headroom (for many speech applications it's possible to get by with as little as 10 dB headroom, but we're going to be conservative here). To keep this explanation simple, let's assume the microphone and cable are noiseless.

- The output of the microphone is fed to the *mixing console*. Our simple 8-input console has a maximum input sensitivity of –60 dBm. This means that the console has enough gain to raise the –60 dBm input signal to +4 dBm (the nominal output level of the console). Clipping of the console's output stage will take place at +24 dB. All mixing consoles generate some noise, and our hypothetical console is no exception. With one channel fader and one master fader at nominal, –60 dBm of noise will be present at the primary output.

- Next in the signal path is a *graphic equalizer*. This particular equalizer will accept up to +24 dBm at the input without clipping. Like the mixing console, the equalizer will inevitably produce some noise—let's say about –80 dBm.

  Equalizers are usually used as "unity gain" devices (no effect one way or the other on gain), although most have the ability to reduce (attenuate) the signal level at the input. Some equalizers have a small amount of gain available to "recover" the signal level should it be reduced by the cutting of several frequency bands. Boost or cut of various frequencies will play a role in the overall system gain structure. However, the gain or loss caused by equalization is usually not significant unless a large number of bands are drastically cut or boosted. (The need for excessive adjustment of a graphic equalizer is often an indication that some other problem exists in the design, setup, or adjustment of a sound system.)

- The output of the graphic equalizer drives the input of a 200-watt *power amplifier*. An input level of 0 dBm (.775 volts) will drive the amplifier to its rated output (200 W). The amplifier is also equipped with input level controls that allow adjustment of input sensitivity.

THE
YAMAHA
GUIDE TO
SOUND SYSTEMS
FOR WORSHIP
PAGE 142

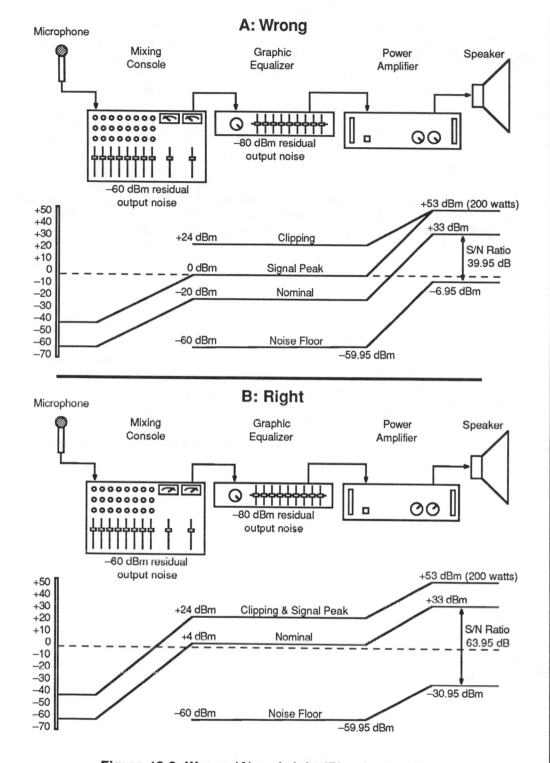

Figure 13-3. Wrong (A) and right (B) gain structure.

So we have two identical sound systems. Both provide 93 dB of gain from microphone input to power amplifier output. Neither system will be driven into clipping during normal operation. Both amplifiers will be driven to their rated 200-watt output during dynamic peaks. Yet one system has a signal-to-noise ratio that is 24 dB better than the other! Why is the noise performance of one system more than 200 times better[*] than the other? The answer lies in proper gain structuring.

---

[*] Recall from Chapter 3 that an increase of 3 dB represents two times the power. Since 24 dB represents eight of these 3 dB increases (24 = 3 x 8), the S/N ratio is 2^8, or 256, times better.

In the Figure 13-3A (the "wrong" system) we see a system with the most common gain structure mistakes. The operator has set mixer gain so the VU meter rarely (if ever) comes close to the 0 VU mark. The amplifier input level control was set "wide open," just as the salesman recommended. Of course, that means that the amplifier will be driven to clipping when the console output is at 0 dBm. Our hypothetical system operator can clearly hear the clipping, so what does he do? Why, turn down the mixer's input gain trim, of course. Turning down the input gain will bring down the level of the signal but will have no effect on the mixer noise, since it is mostly generated *after* the input gain trim.

The equalizer is properly set in both examples at unity gain (no increase or decrease to the signal level). Noise from the equalizer (–80 dBm) will be added to –60 dBm of noise from the console, resulting in –59.95 dBm of noise at the equalizer output. (Don't worry about the math used to arrive at this figure; just pay attention to the results.)

The power amplifier is the key to understanding why it is best to take the gain increases as early as possible in a system. With the input level controls set "wide open," the amplifier will increase the level of any signal by 53 dB. The 0 dBm peak signal, –20 dBm nominal signals, and –59.95 dBm noise will all be increased by 53 dB. As a result, the system noise is less then 40 dB below the nominal signal level and will be very audible.

Contrast this with the identical system in Figure 13-3B (the "right" system). Using proper gain structure techniques, this system operator has taken as much gain as possible as early as possible. The –60 dBm (nominal) microphone output is boosted to +4 dBm at the console output. Since the gain was taken early (before most of the noise-producing components of the mixer) residual output noise of the mixer remains at –60 dBm. Dynamic peaks from the microphone will drive the mixer to +24 dBm at the output, but that is a level that this mixer can handle without clipping.

Once again, the equalizer is set at unity gain and makes its small contribution to increasing the system noise.

The big difference here is in the setting of the amplifier input level control. Using good gain management, our hypothetical system operator decreased the input sensitivity by 24 dB. Now the peak output of the equalizer (+24 dBm) will just drive the amplifier to its full rated output of 200 watts. The amplifier will still produce 200 watts of output power, but overall gain is 24 dB less than in the previous example. With less gain after the noise-producing components, the residual output noise of the system is reduced to –30.95 dBm, an improvement of 24 dB.

Of course, there is always a difference between theory and the real world. In actual practice it may not be necessary to decrease the input sensitivity of the amplifier quite this much. Signal levels to the amplifier may be reduced (slightly) by long cable runs, and the amplifier's gain must be used to recover the loss. Also, some amplifiers can actually produce momentary peak output levels well in excess of their rated power. To take advantage of this capacity, allow 3 to 6 dB more amplifier input sensitivity. If this were a real system, optimum performance would probably be reached with the amplifier sensitivity set so that a +18 dBm input will drive the amp to 200 watts at the output.

LEARNING HOW TO MIX

Admittedly, audio equipment is often built with a confusing array of blinking lights and wagging meters. All of them mean something; some are more important than others. In learning how to operate the sound system, and how to mix, an understanding of what those lights mean and how to read those meters will help.

THE VOLUME INDICATOR

One of the most common indicators used in audio is the *VI* (*volume indicator*) meter, also called a *VU* meter. The meter has a needle that swings in response to the audio signal feeding it. If the needle is at its "at rest" position on the far left, little or no signal is present. The presence of an audio signal will cause the needle to swing towards the right. How far it swings to the right is determined by how strong the signal is.

THE
YAMAHA
GUIDE TO
SOUND SYSTEMS
FOR WORSHIP
PAGE 144

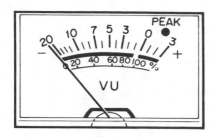

Figure 13-4. A VU meter.

The face of the meter has markings on it that you can read to determine how strong (or weak) the audio signal is. Many meters have two scales printed on them, one marked in Volume Units (VU) and the other in Percent of Modulation. The latter is a broadcast term. Most sound reinforcement and recording engineers live by the VU markings.

When the needle barely moves around the "–20 VU" marking, this means that there is little signal present. An optimum signal strength is at the "0 VU" position, optimum because this will provide your best S/N ratio. The scale at zero and below is colored black, and indicates that this is a "safe" operating range. If the audio signal is too strong, the meter will go into the red side of the scale. If the needle begins to swing into the red portion of the scale (+1 VU to +3 VU), the engineer should exercise caution. If the needle starts to bang against the meter rail on the far right, it is likely that you will start to hear distortion.

Seeing the needle on your VU meter swing up to +1 VU or so is no cause for panic. If you notice frequent swings up to +2 VU or more, you may want to respond by pulling back a mic trim or a group of faders or a submaster—wherever you think the source of the "too strong" signal is. This may require a trial-and-error search at first. With experience, you will find the culprit more quickly.

To properly understand and read a standard VU meter, you need to know about the *ballistics* of the meter—how quickly the meter responds to the audio signal feeding it. A typical VU meter is designed to respond very much like our human hearing does. It senses and displays an "average" of what is fed to it.

The meter is also designed to have a "10 dB meter lag." It is essential that you catch this point. Let's say that the signal feeding the meter is from a microphone placed at a snare drum or piano. You have properly adjusted the gain structure so that when a note is struck sharply, the meter will rise quickly to 0 VU and then fall off. That 0 VU average typically corresponds to a +4 dBu peak level. However, because of the sharp attack of that sound and the 10 dB meter lag, the actual signal that went through the circuit can be as much as 10 dB hotter: 10 dB + 4 dB = +14 dB.

Now the subject turns to *headroom*, which is the "distance" available above the average (0 VU) level before distortion occurs. Most professional-grade audio equipment can handle the level of +14 dB encountered in the preceding situation. A typical maximum output level for balanced outputs is around +24 dBu, which in this example leaves you only 10 dB of headroom at best. A few instruments exhibit transient peaks of 15 to 20 dB above nominal level, so you could run out of headroom with the VU meter showing zero or less!

If you are careless and don't keep an eye on your VU meters, you could easily run into distortion. Since your goal is to faithfully reinforce or reproduce the signal coming off the platform, distortion is something you want to stay clear of, not invite. Forget the motto "if all else fails, read the directions," and consult the owner's manual for your console for any particular quirks it may have.

Some engineers almost take pride in their neglect of what the meters are trying to tell them, even going as far as to put tape over the meters so they can't be influenced by what they see, trusting their ears to warn them of distortion. That is a dangerous way to operate—dangerous in that such an engineer must have both an acute sense of hearing and an outstanding monitoring system in order to hear that distortion. Not only is that a foolish practice, it is doubly foolish for budding engineers working on medium-priced sound reinforcement gear.

THE
YAMAHA
GUIDE TO
SOUND SYSTEMS
FOR WORSHIP
PAGE 145

PEAK AND SIGNAL LIGHTS

To aid the sound man in knowing more precisely when he is approaching clipping distortion, many console manufacturers have added a *peak* light on each channel. You will often see them installed within the face of the standard VI meter. Peak lights installed on individual channels reflect the overload status of those channels, and peak lights installed within the VI meter reflect the overload status of the signal assigned to that meter. The sensitivity of these small LEDs (light emitting diodes) is set internally so that they light up when the signal passes a certain strength, typically 3 to 8 dB before clipping distortion begins.

Peak (or clip) lights on individual channels often have multiple pickoff points. For example, the peak light may be fed from a point right after the mic preamp, *and* from right after the channel EQ section, *and* even from a point after the channel fader. If you have set the controls too high in any or all of these three stages, the clip light will fire to alert you to the problem.

If the peak lights fire on and off occasionally, that's OK. But if you can read your cue sheet by the glow from the peak LEDs, the system is distorting.

Another LED that you may notice flashing at you from time to time is the *signal presence* indicator. That's all it does—tell you that a signal is present. Its sensitivity is set to acknowledge a predetermined minimum signal strength.

PEAK-READING METERS

Peak-reading meters are another type of signal indicator. These meters are more popular in European equipment, although some US manufacturers provide them in addition to the standard VI meter. While the typical VI meter responds sluggishly, to display an average of the input signal, the ballistics of a peak-reading meter allow it to respond very quickly and therefore track the true peaks of the input signal. Since the true rises and falls of those peaks are sometimes instantaneous, the human eye would have a tough time seeing and interpreting that information. For that reason, the ballistics of the peak-reading meter allow the meter to rise quickly, but force it to fall more slowly, allowing the eyes to see what is happening. The fall of a

peak is unimportant—you want to know how hot the rise is. Although they may take some getting used to, peak-reading meters can be very informative, particularly if you find yourself often pushing the limits of your equipment's capability.

Light (LED) meters, while at times more difficult to read than a swinging needle, can offer the flexibility of displaying either VU ballistics or peak-reading ballistics. If the manufacturer has provided for this, the engineer can, by the touch of a switch, choose which ballistics to display.

HOW TO APPROACH A MIX

As mentioned in Chapter 1, a good way to approach mixing sound is to imagine that you are mixing an album. It doesn't really matter if you're mixing PA or a broadcast feed, and you needn't have experience mixing albums to understand this point. If you spend time mixing at an audio console, certainly you have spent time listening to albums and tapes and CDs of music similar in style to that used in your worship services. Use the tools you have available to shape the sound toward that of a polished recording. (If you've not heard examples of the kind of music found in your services, you should explore the wealth of music out there. It is available today in virtually every style of worship music, and would be time well spent in "training" your ears.)

The mix of your particular worship service should reflect the style of the music, and only through this listening experience can an engineer understand how to combine all the available musical elements into a pleasing whole. He should also pay attention to the "weight" of the mix (how strong and full the low frequencies are), how smooth the midrange frequencies are, and how clean and clear the highs are.

EQUALIZATION AS PART OF THE MIX

As you refine your mix, you may want to use the channel EQ to enhance or clean up the sound of the vocalists and instrumentalists. As you proceed, remember that a little EQ goes a long way. Make slight adjustments and listen for the change. Adding too much EQ can significantly limit the available headroom of the sound system. It can also overstress the drivers working in that particular frequency range.

THE
YAMAHA
GUIDE TO
SOUND SYSTEMS
FOR WORSHIP
PAGE 146

LEARN HOW TO LISTEN

One audio consultant visited three different worship facilities within a few months of each other, each of which had accidentally blown up the high-frequency drivers in their loudspeakers. Each congregation knew that they didn't like the sound they were getting, that a change had taken place, but they couldn't isolate the problem. They didn't like the sound because it was unclear. Of course, the reason for the lack of clarity was that there was nothing above 2 kHz coming out of the speakers.

A good sound man learns much of what he knows by trial and error. Through that process he should make an effort to clearly analyze what he is hearing. Does it sound right? Why not? Stick your ear in it! Sometimes the answer is right under your nose.

THINGS YOU SHOULD NEVER DO

These are the common-sense things that bite every engineer once in a while. They shouldn't.

Never miss mic cues. The engineer has a responsibility to stay alert, to make sure that every mic is up at the appropriate volume and on time, every time, and without feedback. But to keep the mix clean, he wants to turn the mics off when not in use.

Never finish a soundcheck without knowing the limits of gain before feedback. (By the way, it's a good idea to ALWAYS do a soundcheck before a service. More on this in Chapter 14.) Even with proper console gain structure established, a fader pushed up too far on an already feedback-prone microphone will cause the system to go into feedback. The engineer has the responsibility to avoid this. He should learn his limits of fader travel in a variety of console configurations so that feedback isn't likely to occur due to his operation. He should also learn to detect feedback the moment it starts to build. That may seem silly, but we've all sat in a service and heard the system feeding back slightly, while the engineer, clearly oblivious to the problem, makes no move to correct it. One point in his favor—his listening position may not allow him to hear the problem as easily as the congregation can. (See the section on console placement in Chapter 12.)

Never let the mix get out of balance. Many times in the worship service, a song may build to a powerful ending, and then taper off gently. The congregation has been singing along and responds to this change. Now, as the music continues to soften, the song leader or minister may begin to speak. The congregation needs to hear him speaking. The engineer must be alert, to 1) have the speaker's mic up and turned on, and 2) gently squeeze back the volume of the worship team to "make room" for the speaker's voice to be heard without blasting the audience with brute-force volume. Many times the music can even be pulled out of the house system totally; especially if only the keyboard continues to play behind the minister's voice, the spill from the stage monitors can provide a background effect at an appropriate level in the house. As frightening or illogical as this technique may seem to the musicians, this can be a very useful tool. The musicians have no conception of how loud the house system is from their perspective.

Never allow phantom power to reach a microphone from two sources (e.g., from the house console and the monitor console). Either choose one console to supply phantom power (if you're using a microphone splitter, which does its job by means of transformers, choose the console on the non-transformer side of the splitter) or use a splitter that provides its own phantom power.

Never unplug a cable from a phantom-powered mic while the channel fader (or monitor) is up. That 48 V DC jump will be greatly amplified by the mic preamp. Doing this during a service will cause a major distraction. For the same reason, don't disconnect the cable at the console or any mic snake connections, either.

Never be late to arrive. This goes for everyone involved, but especially those in charge. Remember that in order to be on time, you must arrive at least one minute early.

THE
YAMAHA
GUIDE TO
SOUND SYSTEMS
FOR WORSHIP
PAGE 147

DOCUMENTING CONSOLE SETTINGS

It's a good idea to have some sort of documentation of console settings, to ensure that all controls are set where they should be. This is valuable both for the regular operators of the system and for those who must "fill in" when the regular operator is away.

The easiest kind of documentation is a picture of the control panel of the console. Settings can be marked and read easily by way of tick marks made on this picture—perhaps in colored pencil, so that they can be read easily, but also erased if a change is necessary.

Unfortunately, most console manufacturers don't provide such a picture of the entire control panel. What they usually *do* provide, in the operation manual, is a picture of a single input channel "strip," along with any output or master sections.

To produce a representation of the entire console, photocopy the pages necessary for the number of alike strips. If you have a 32-channel console, you'll need 32 copies of the input channel, plus individual copies of each output and master section.

Some console literature shows the controls set a certain way. Opaque these settings with photocopy correction fluid, so that you will not confuse them with the markings that you will make later.

When you have all of the copies you need, cut out the strips and paste them onto a larger piece of paper or illustration board in the correct configuration. When this mockup of the console layout is finished, you can number the channels and add any other finishing touches. For the most polished look, you can use rub-on transfer lettering, available at office supply and art supply stores, for the numbers.

Take the completed diagram to a printer or copying service to have duplicates made. They can be duplicated at a reduced size, if you wish—but be sure they're not too small to be read.

MIXING FOR SPECIFIC SITUATIONS

The following discussions cover the preferred approaches to mixing for different situations, but they are guides, not commandments. Use these ideas as outlines to guide your own creative approach to a solution to your particular needs using the equipment you have to work with.

MIXING FOR THE CONGREGATION

The "house" engineer's job during a worship service combines several objectives. Clearly, one main objective is to help the worship team lead the congregation into worship. During strong, majestic songs, the music must command attention with its full, powerful sound. During quiet, sensitive musical moments, the music can command attention by a soft, clear sound. In each case, if there is a song leader, the congregation must be able to hear that person just ever so slightly above everyone else so that they can follow along.

Think of your mix as a pyramid. At the foundation of the pyramid are the strong, full instruments, particularly instruments capable of producing powerful low frequencies. This would include the organ and the piano, and if used, other rhythm section elements like the drums and the bass guitar. Each of these instruments plays a "leading" role in the sense that their rhythmic patterns drive the music forward. With contemporary music styles, the drums and bass guitar are the very core of this foundation. If a small orchestra is used, the bass viols, celli, low brass, and timpani belong in this foundation as well.

In a layer just above these instruments would be rhythm guitar, trumpets and woodwinds, violas and violins, harp, other percussion instruments, synthesizers, and so on. These elements add body and add some motion to the the harmonic structure of the song.

You might consider the next layer the fun layer, implementing lead guitar lines and light, high-frequency percussion elements like mark trees, triangles, finger cymbals, shakers, and so on. Sparse, rhythmic lead lines on a synthesizer might fit here as well. This layer should not dominate the sound,

THE
YAMAHA
GUIDE TO
SOUND SYSTEMS
FOR WORSHIP
PAGE 148

but should instead be used to add a little sparkle and interest to the mix.

The next layer would include the choir, and just above them the background vocalists if used. The top layer then is the worship leader. You can emphasize the power of strong, majestic music by tucking the level of the song leader back into the mix slightly. You still want to hear him at the top of the pyramid, but pulling his level back will give the impression that he is almost "swamped" by the power of the music. The music seems even more powerful as a result, even though the overall volume has not increased. Be careful though: If you pull him back too far, it will just sound like a bad mix.

At the other extreme, during a quiet piece where the song leader is almost whispering the melody, you must be certain that the audience will be able to follow along.

Whether the song is a powerful and majestic one or a quiet and reserved one, an ideal mix is one in which each instrument and voice is heard clearly, with no one element demanding attention throughout. It's okay for certain elements to call attention to themselves at moments dictated by the music—a trumpet fanfare, for example—but such "surprises" should not get so loud that they are heard to the exclusion of the rest of the mix.

Your responsibility as the house engineer is to both the music director and the congregation. The music director has a vision inside him or her of what the overall sound should be like. There are times when it should be full and powerful, and other times when it should be sparse and quiet. You should not counteract this vision. In fact, you are in a position to bring it to life.

At the same time, there are limits to the dynamic range you can use in a worship service. You must consider the sound from the congregation as part of your mix. On one hand, they are part of the "noise floor"— their coughs and sneezes, murmuring and rustling of papers join forces with the air handlers and other typical room noises. This noise floor is like "tape hiss" in a way, hiding the soft, sensitive sounds that are recorded on the tape but not always heard.

As mentioned in Chapter 1, the congregation should be considered as part of your mix

from a musical standpoint as well. The thrilling sound of corporate worship can be destroyed if the music from the PA system is too loud, while the thrilling sound may never develop if the music from the worship team is too soft. There is a fine line to play here. Most houses of worship play it too safe with overall PA level. They don't want to offend anybody or have to field complaints, so the tendency is to keep the level too soft. It is probably just as offending to the music itself to hear a soloist singing with an accompaniment cassette soundtrack when the music on tape is big and powerful but is played back at a timid, too-soft volume. That poses a contradiction that our brains refuse to accept. Too soft a volume with a big, powerful song leaves our emotions stuck somewhere in the middle. You needn't blow hats off the ladies in the tenth row to achieve an acceptable playback level or overall PA volume. Use common sense at both extremes.

When teaching the congregation a new song, it is helpful to abandon the concept of a slick, smooth album mix slightly and support the congregation's learning experience by increasing the level of the worship leader and the piano (or whatever instrument is the lead instrument in this learning process). As the congregation begins to sing the new song with more confidence, you can, imperceptibly to them, start to tuck the piano and worship leader back down into their respective "places" in the overall mix. Sometimes congregations take two or three attempts to become comfortable with a new song, depending on its complexity, so don't get too anxious to bring things back to normal. Likewise, don't forget to do it.

MIXING FOR THE TAPE MINISTRY

Virtually everything that was just said about mixing for the congregation also applies to many of the other mixes you may need to provide—for the tape and broadcast ministries in particular. The major difference is of course that now you are providing a sound reproduction mix rather than a sound reinforcement mix.

This means, for one, that you will need to mic the congregation so that you have a clean pickup of their voices as well as control over how much of that element to use in the

THE
YAMAHA
GUIDE TO
SOUND SYSTEMS
FOR WORSHIP
PAGE 149

mix at any given moment during the service. The PA engineer is just asking for problems with feedback and muddiness if he tries to reinforce the congregation through the system. (The only reason for miking the congregation in a sound reinforcement application is for the purposes of *electronic architecture*, which is discussed on page 33.)

The mix for the tape ministry is best provided by a separate engineer operating a separate console in a quiet room. He should either have a window that allows him to clearly see the platform area, or at least a TV monitor provided with a camera feed that will accomplish the same purpose.

One creative task that the mixing engineer has the opportunity to pursue here is to "paint a picture" for the end listener. The person who will ultimately sit back and listen to this cassette tape in the car or at home may or may not have actually been in the congregation during the service at which the recording was made. Beyond simply capturing and documenting the event, a creative engineer can employ every tool at his disposal to shape the sound into a believable product that gives the listener the very real sense that he or she participated in the actual service. Admittedly, that is the ideal. Reality may strike, however, and find the typical engineer fortunate to have enough equipment to even get the service on tape, let alone all the bells and whistles that will allow him to carry it on to something more.

What if you don't have a separate console to use for the tape ministry feed? The job can still be done, although it probably won't win any music recording awards; and it will be considerably more difficult to get an acceptable mix. The easy way out is to simply feed the cassette recorder with the same feed that is driving the main house loudspeaker system. Actually, that may provide a reasonable sound IF the auditorium is fairly large. The whole idea discussed earlier about a sound reinforcement mix being decidedly different from a sound reproduction mix starts to diminish in importance as the size of the auditorium increases. At some point, probably at 3,000 seats and up, the auditorium is so large that all instruments on stage will need to be miked. Although acoustic power from the platform still plays a role, it does become a less dominating factor.

This arrangement still wouldn't provide for the problem of miking the audience, although there are creative routing techniques to solve this as well. For example, if the PA console has a matrix mixing section, it would be simple to drive the house system with one matrix output, choosing not to feed the audience mics to that output, while simultaneously driving the tape recorder with a different matrix output, which includes the audience mics.

On a console without a matrix mixing section, a tape recorder feed is often provided by one of the auxiliary busses. You dedicate one of the auxiliary busses to the mix for the tape recorder, and assign someone to watch over that mix and make needed adjustments as the service progresses. If this mix is handled by a person other than the house PA engineer, they had better be good friends and agree on an operating procedure in advance, because they will certainly get in each other's way frequently.

You need to decide which auxiliary bus to use—should it be a pre-fader mix (independent of channel fader movements) or a post-fader mix (subject to the movements of channel faders)? The easiest bus to use is the post-fader send. Once a fairly typical house mix is established, a reasonable mix to feed the tape recorder can be set up on the post-fader auxiliary send. Now, whenever the house engineer makes adjustments in his sound reinforcement mix, the same moves will be reflected in similar proportions in the tape feed. With this arrangement, the assistant may not have to touch anything during the rest of the service.

On the other hand, depending on the size of your auditorium, this may not provide the tape feed with a good balance of the most powerful instruments, like the organ or drums. On occasion, those instruments may not even need to be miked. If they aren't miked at all, the tape feed will be in jeopardy. One solution: If enough inputs are available, the engineer could simply go ahead and mic those instruments, choose not to add them into the house mix, but still have them available in the auxiliary bus mix (or the matrix output, for that matter). By the way, if you want this auxiliary feed to your tape deck to be stereo (if you're that brave), you will need to use two auxiliary busses, one for each side, and set up the "panning" by adjusting the send levels to the two busses accordingly.

THE
YAMAHA
GUIDE TO
SOUND SYSTEMS
FOR WORSHIP
PAGE 150

Choose the solution that works best for your equipment and working arrangements. You can see how having a pre/post switch on each auxiliary send could come in very handy. All of this signal routing may draw panic from the newcomer, but this is one of the fun challenges that a professional engineer revels in every day.

One other side note: Use a compressor/limiter on the pastor's mic, and if possible, on the song leader's mic. The dynamic range of most cassette tapes is not exactly great. You could find yourself with a saturated tape (read "distorted sound") on loud peaks or a barely discernable whisper submerged in tape hiss. Not only that, but most people are going to listen to the sermon while driving in their cars, or on their personal tape players while they're jogging or at the gym. These listeners want to hear a fairly even sound level, and do not want to be blasted any more than they want to strain to hear whispered sentences while they are driving over a bumpy bridge. A properly set compressor/limiter will avert these problems before they get on tape.

MIXING FOR BROADCAST

Mixing the sound for a radio broadcast is much like that for the tape feed just discussed. The one extra word of caution here is that the dynamic range of a radio broadcast is not very wide, so the engineer should all but toss out any thoughts of subtlety and mix the sound so that everything will be heard. This can still be a very musical mix, but he will need to counteract whispers and soft music with upward fader movements to "iron out" the level drops. The signal broadcast over the air will also be subjected to processing by a more complex multi-band compressor, and this will smooth the program even further.

Even during the sermon, you still have a job to do. There is an art to balancing the right amount of audience response with the sermon. The right amount is subject to your own tastes, but take time to listen to similar broadcasts that you enjoy, and take note of how much audience response you hear in that mix. The effect should be one that acknowledges the presence of a congregation, but that does not distract the listener or take away from the message.

Mixing for a TV broadcast or a videotape draws on one more subtle mixing technique.

Here, the audio should "follow the video"; it should accent the picture. For example, if a picture is a close shot of the pianist's hands at the piano, the sound should ever so slightly emphasize the piano. If the picture is a wide shot of the entire room, musicians and congregation included, then the sound should be a full sound of the entire mix, including the congregation as a whole. If the picture is of the men's voices in the choir, then the sound should reflect that picture. These adjustments to the mix should be very subtle changes, and should not distract the listener. The goal is simply to help the sound and the picture work together, not be oblivious to each other's presence.

If the audio console feeding this mix to the videotape recorders has automation capabilities, it may be possible to provide a link between the video switcher and the audio console. The audio engineer can program certain fader settings to correspond to a handful of anticipated camera shots. Then, when the video director calls for "camera one" to be selected on the switcher, the automation on the audio console will automatically jump to that preset audio "scene." Yes, it's expensive, but an engineer has to have something to dream about, right?

Make sure that your sound reinforcement system is free of any technical or operational problems before you tackle an audio-for-video feed. Extraneous hums, buzzes, and pops are bad enough, but PA or stage monitor feedback and late or totally missed mic cues are death to TV.

A lot has been said here about system operation, but what if you have to worry about two systems operating simultaneously? If you find yourself with a need to interface to a remote audio or broadcast truck, things could get interesting very quickly.

Your best plan of defense is to make certain that a transformer-isolated microphone splitter is used. Often the remote truck will come equipped with the splitter. This will place transformers between your equipment and their equipment. Simple "Y-cords" are not adequate. They will pass the audio signal to both systems, but will also pass along any interface problems as well, like hum and buzz and so on. Also be careful where their AC power is pulled from and how it is distributed to the truck.

THE
YAMAHA
GUIDE TO
SOUND SYSTEMS
FOR WORSHIP
PAGE 151

MIXING FOR STAGE MONITORS

The reason for having monitors on stage in the first place is to provide exactly what each person needs to hear in order to perform his or her best. The house system is aimed at the congregation, and a good PA system will deliver very little of the house sound back to the stage area. Likewise, the stage monitors should provide tight control of the sound so that very little of their sound spills out into the seating area.

One of the first mistakes novice musicians and vocalists make is to think that their monitor mix should reflect what the congregation is hearing in the house, as if to "check up on" the sound man's house mix. This is a misuse of the gear.

Give them the mix that they need, determined by mutual agreement during rehearsals and soundchecks. In many musical settings, the background vocalists will generally want to hear quite a bit of piano or organ or acoustic guitar, whatever the lead instrument happens to be, enough of the song leader so that they can keep track of where they are in the song, plenty of themselves so that their harmonies stay in tune and balanced, and sometimes enough bass guitar to define the root of the chord plus kick drum and snare to keep a sense of time. Whew!

By comparison, the song leader may want a lot of piano along with enough rhythm section to fill out the song, a little bit of the background vocalists so things sound "real," and plenty of his or her own vocal.

Back in the rhythm section, the pianist will want lots of the song leader's vocal plus his or her own keyboard, plus kick drum, snare, bass guitar, and probably little else. Keeping the monitor mixes simple has two advantages. One, fewer instruments and voices means you will tax that monitor channel less, which then provides more headroom. Secondly, and probably more important, a sparse monitor mix will provide better clarity for that listener. The performer will be better able to focus on the elements that drive the song for him, and the end result is a better performance from everyone. This, in turn, provides more freedom as the worship team leads the congregation in worship.

In a more traditional worship setting, the choir desperately wants to hear plenty of piano. No offense intended, but probably no choir member has ever complained of hearing too little organ. During the corporate worship times, they also need plenty of the song leader's mic so that they can stay with him. They would like to be able to hear more of themselves, but the laws of physics being what they are, feeding choir mics back through the choir monitors is generally asking for trouble. The mics are placed a fair distance from the sound source, and the choir monitors will certainly spill into where the choir mics are located. Anytime the sound pressure level of that spill at the mic matches the sound level of the source at the mic, a feedback loop will start. Feeding choir voices at high levels to the choir's monitors only exacerbates the problem. Even before feedback occurs, any choir vocal spill from the monitors being picked up by the choir mics will create phase cancellation and result in a hollow, unnatural sound that will be heard distinctly over the house sound system.

The pianist and organist and other players will want to hear each other so they can stay together, and of course the song leader when needed.

One special note about monitors in general, and it applies to mixing for the house sound as well. A cardinal rule in miking technique is to never use two mics when one will do the job. If you are using one mic, set just below the feedback point (for example, a background vocal mic), and you open up a second mic at equal gain, you will have to drop the overall level of the sound system in half (3 dB) to stabilize the system and reduce the threat of feedback. If you double that miking setup to four mics, you will again have to drop the system level by 3 dB for stability. At times during the mix (house or monitors) you may indeed need all those mics operating, but if there are lengthy periods during which certain mics will not be used, turn them off. This simple technique will dramatically clean up your sound, and the congregation won't overhear Cindy asking Sally for a ride home after the service.

You will virtually always want to use a pre-fader auxiliary send for the stage monitor feeds. Consider the console signal flow logic you learned in Chapter 6 and you will better understand this point. For

THE
YAMAHA
GUIDE TO
SOUND SYSTEMS
FOR WORSHIP
PAGE 152

example, let's say that you have a vocal ensemble singing a number, and you are feeding monitors with a post-fader auxiliary send. The monitors are set hot, riding just below feedback. Later in the song, one of the vocalists gets into a low part of her range and is unable to sing as loudly as she had earlier in the song. Being the careful engineer that you are, you push up the fader so that the congregation will continue to get a balanced mix. But that fader move will push their stage monitors right into feedback, which will be picked up by the mics and sent over the PA system, which will send several hundred eyes spinning around to glare at the "incompetent sound man."

Not only that, but generally, musicians and singers do not want their monitor mix to change much; once it is set to their liking, they would rather have it left alone unless they request a change. (By using a post-fader auxiliary bus to feed the monitors, all your house fader moves would be reflected in the monitor mix.) Still, this shouldn't lull you into complacency. Keep a watchful ear over their monitors anyway. Use a small monitor speaker placed behind you, over which you can solo the monitor mixes at will. In lieu of this monitor speaker, and as a last resort, use headphones. You will eventually learn what each person likes to hear, and be able to make corrections to keep it in line. But be sure you communicate with the musicians on this. You might just be using this as another excuse to twiddle the knobs, and maybe you are distracting them as a result. Keep the lines of communication open at all times.

There are certain "tricks" that you can play with the monitor setup if you are equipped to do so. For one, recognize that you have been given a wonderful gift of two ears and a brain that work well together. Your brain can discriminate sounds easily. Using a stereo monitor mix in certain applications can accent this ability. This isn't stereo in the usual sense. Rather, this is really multiple mixes to certain people. For example, you could set up three individual monitors for the keyboardist; one monitor might carry the overall band mix, a second monitor might carry most of the vocals, and a third monitor might carry only his vocal. With these monitors placed around him in strategic locations (arrived at through experimentation), he may find himself with the best possible monitoring arrangement.

Another trick of the trade is to place a signal delay before the stage monitors, and to delay the signal just enough to break a potential feedback loop. This might drive a drummer crazy, so be careful where you use it, but it could be a helpful technique when used in the right application. Be creative—use the tools you have at your disposal.

Mixing for Overflow Areas

This depends on where the overflow area is located. If the overflow area is an expanded seating area that is fully open to the main auditorium, then people sitting in that area will hear a certain amount of spill from the house PA system, and spill of the acoustic power already present in the main room. A tap from the house sound reinforcement mix, feeding speakers located in that area, should serve the need just fine.

One special consideration you should address in this type of overflow area is signal delay. Typically, these adjacent overflow rooms have a relatively low ceiling. The speaker system used to cover this area will either be a distributed ceiling system or a simple two-way speaker (using a woofer and a small-format horn). To make listeners in this area more comfortable, and to provide better intelligibility, an appropriate amount of signal delay should be applied to this system (see pages 80–81 to calculate the amount of delay).

If the overflow room is located in another part of the building instead, like an area normally reserved for meals or social gatherings, then overflow listeners will not benefit from the acoustic power as before, and should receive a sound reproduction mix. Since it is customary to send a live television feed to video monitors or large-screen projectors in such a setting, the normal audio feed to the video control room would work just fine. Another choice would be a tap from the tape ministry feed.

Do not underestimate the importance of this overflow audio feed. Some houses of worship use overflow areas on a regular basis. For many, though, these overflow areas are used only during special seasons—such as Holy Days—when their worship services are bursting at the seams with new faces. Your music director and administration will naturally want to put their best foot forward, and your part in that is to shine with technical excellence.

THE
YAMAHA
GUIDE TO
SOUND SYSTEMS
FOR WORSHIP
PAGE 153

One aside: The speakers in the foyer or narthex, and those lining the outdoor walkways, could be looked at as needing an overflow mix as well. A sound reproduction mix will work the best.

MIXING FOR THE NURSERY AND CRY ROOMS

Nursery workers appreciate being able to hear the service. You can provide them with either a ceiling speaker or a small speaker hung on the wall. Once again, since such a room is closed and away from the main room, the sound reproduction mix will work best. However, if that isn't possible, a house PA mix will serve the need. For their listening comfort, not to mention that of the babies, install a volume control on the wall with which the workers can adjust the loudness of that speaker to their liking.

An alternative solution is to use a small self-powered monitor speaker and run a line-level signal to it. Most such speakers have a level control, and you won't need to add another amplifier to your racks just for this one feed.

MIXING FOR HARD-OF-HEARING SYSTEMS

People using the hard-of-hearing receivers will typically be seated in the main assembly room. Although they may have trouble hearing clearly, they will certainly "feel" the sound of music coming from the platform. For that reason, your house sound reinforcement mix will work fine for this application. On the other hand, if you have another mix bus available, you may want to bring up the relative levels from the pulpit and the song leader for a special feed to the hearing-impaired system.

EXAMPLES OF SYSTEM SETUP

To further illustrate the elements of system operation, consider the following suggested setups and points to consider. Your individual experience may vary, but each of these may be considered typical within the particular situation. These illustrations are presented as guidelines with which you can compare your experience, and can become points to shoot for or confirmation that you are on the right track.

SUNDAY MORNING SERVICE IN A PROTESTANT CHURCH

This type of service typically requires a simple and straightforward setup. The choir will be miked with two or three good cardioid condenser mics. There will probably be a small, relatively inconspicuous mic on a gooseneck at the pulpit. Often the minister wears a wireless lapel mic. If the budget is trim, he can just as easily wear a lapel mic that uses a standard mic cable.

Special music offerings often include a small vocal ensemble, singing with either keyboard accompaniment or a cassette soundtrack. If there are only a few vocalists (five or less), the singers may want to use individual mics. If there are more than five singers, remember the three-to-one rule of miking before you start handing everybody a microphone of his own. Depending on the style of music, you may capture a better sound by simply using one mic on the entire group. Even a trio may sound best with one mic. Using one mic not only eliminates the phase cancellations that more mics may present, but it can also capture the natural vocal blend of the group rather than submit the "group sound" to the interpretation of the sound man.

Some churches provide a special children's time on Sunday mornings, where an adult gathers the kids around him or her on the steps of the platform, and tells them a short Bible story. The storyteller will need a mic so that the congregation can hear the story, too. A wireless lapel mic works best, since 1) there is little time for people to get into position for this, 2) the story teller would like to have both hands free, and 3) kids can trip over mic cables draped over the steps. If a wireless lapel is not available or practical for this type of setting, then either a wireless hand-held mic or a standard cabled mic will do the job.

ROMAN CATHOLIC MASS

Musically, today's Roman Catholic Mass takes one of two forms. The first employs the traditional organ and choir, and requires little or no sound reinforcement. The second, which has grown in popularity since the 1970s, consists of a simple music accompaniment and vocals. One to three acoustic guitars may be used, while piano is rare. The choir is small, often with only three to twelve vocalists. Acoustic guitar

THE
YAMAHA
GUIDE TO
SOUND SYSTEMS
FOR WORSHIP
PAGE 154

can be miked with a good condenser cardioid mic or a smooth dynamic cardioid mic, or use an integral mic, or contact pickup, connected with a direct box. Solos may be sung with a hand-held mic or at the pulpit mic, usually a condenser cardioid mic. In some cases, the priest may have a wireless lapel mic. But usually priests and readers will be picked up by strategically placed mics at the pulpit and at the altar.

MID-WEEK PRAYER SERVICE

This type of service also requires a fairly simple setup. There may be a small musical accompaniment on hand, like a piano or synthesizer, and maybe an acoustic guitar. The song leader will need a mic, and if the song leader is also playing the acoustic guitar or piano, you will need two mic stands with booms to properly position both the vocal mic and the guitar mic. Of course, you will want a boom stand to properly position the piano mic as well.

Often during such a service, the minister or song leader may prefer to be down on the main floor with the people rather than up on the platform far away from them. Hopefully your mic lines and monitor cables will reach far enough, or your installation provided for this in advance by placing extra mic input and monitor output connections in strategically chosen alternate locations.

During open prayer times, the pastor may want a soft, gentle music background tape playing over the system. To ensure that the tape will keep playing over long periods of time, you may want to consider using an auto-reverse cassette deck, which automatically swaps the tape sides when it reaches the end. The only concern here is that some tapes have long quiet periods on one side of the tape, because the songs on the tape did not work out to an equal amount of time on each side. Consider using a programmable CD player instead. By pre-programming several selections and setting the player to repeat mode, you can provide background music of indefinite duration.

Many times a mid-week prayer service or early morning prayer times are so simple technically that just about anybody can be quickly trained to handle it. There may not be any real "mix" to it, other than making sure that the mics work. Many brave church receptionists and secretaries have succeeded at this job with honors.

IMMERSION BAPTISM

From a technical standpoint, this situation should set off a big fat warning signal in your mind. Approach it with caution. The problem is that you will probably need to mic the person who is doing the baptisms, but the guy is standing in water up to his waist, and if a cabled microphone drops into that water, he and whoever is in the pool with him can get a serious electrical shock. This is nothing to play around with.

Many churches put a dynamic mic in a mic clip on a short desk stand and then place the stand on a ledge on the auditorium side of the tank. What if a choir member stretches his arms in a big yawn and knocks that mic into the tank? "Oh, that would never happen." Are you going to assume that? Would you stake your life on it? There's probably no better place to put it, but be absolutely certain that there is no physical way for that mic to reach the water, even if it did get knocked off the stand. Also, educate the person who is doing the baptism services to not even think about grabbing that microphone with his wet hands.

The laugh of technicians a couple years ago was the story of a famous actress who "narrowly escaped electrocution" when she almost fell into a swimming pool wearing a wireless microphone. Right. That nine-volt battery would have really given her quite a buzz. In reality, a wireless mic is probably the safest thing you could use to mic the person who is doing baptisms. Then the only danger would be that the mic could get wet; but a mic is replaceable, unlike a human life.

WEDDING CEREMONIES

Most wedding ceremonies require very basic audio setups. You will want a lapel mic for the minister, wireless if available. You probably won't need to mic the organ, especially if it is a pipe organ or a large electronic one—unless the service is being taped (see the next page). If the room seats more than 100 people, you will probably want to mic the piano. And you may have special music selections performed by guest vocalists and accompanied by acoustic guitar, other instruments, or soundtracks. This, of course, means that the setup may require stage monitors and microphones in unusual positions. For these reasons, it is important that the assigned engineer attend the rehearsal if at all possible.

Some weddings are, of course, larger productions that require creative audio solutions. Like the time the groom/musician wanted to play the melody of the couple's favorite song as his bride walked down the aisle, and hooked up his wireless saxophone microphone so he could serenade her.

A more common occurrence is the wedding that is being videotaped. If at all possible, you should provide a feed from the sound system to the microphone input on the video camera or VCR. In principle, this is the same as any other tape mix. The one technical wrinkle is that it must be a low-(mic-) level signal (unless the VCR has a line-level input), which will necessitate the use of a pad or other appropriate signal transformer at the input to the camera to avoid distorting the audio input.

You should make it a point to be set up, with all equipment checked and ready to go, an hour in advance of the wedding start time. A wedding is the biggest and most exciting "production" that some couples may ever undertake. It is obviously the center of their attention that day. They don't need to be distracted or worried about whether the sound man will be set up on time. Nor do guests arriving early need to see you scurrying around, muttering about how no one cleaned up after the last service.

Telling the minister to turn on the transmitter after he is in position on the platform is not easy. Weddings may not be as common a setting to him as a regular worship service, and it would be safe to assume that most people reading this have had this problem at least once. If he does forget, and you can't get his attention by jumping up and down and waving your hands, try whispering over the stage monitors with your talkback mic, and ask one of the musicians or singers to walk over and remind him to turn the thing on.

CHOIR WITH PIANO OR ORGAN ACCOMPANIMENT

Mixing the stage monitors for a choir and accompanying instruments was discussed earlier in this chapter. Once again, a typical 30- to 45-voice choir is properly miked with two mics, three at the most. A fuller, cleaner, more intelligible, more "choral" choir sound will be obtained when this simple approach is used rather than the more-mics-the-merrier approach often seen.

This simple rule is violated so frequently that the point cannot be overstressed. (See Chapter 5 for more information.)

Often a vocalist will sing a solo with the choir. If the soloist does not sound slightly louder than the choir, then give this person a hand-held mic. Keep this mic turned down or off between the solo passages, only bringing it up when the solos are sung.

The organ need not be miked for sound reinforcement needs—you'll probably spend a lot of time convincing the organist to play softer—but a well-placed microphone will help for the tape ministry or TV feeds. Mic the piano with one or two condenser mics, preferably cardioids, and over the strings.

VOCAL MUSIC WITH PRERECORDED BACKUP

The offertory music in many houses of worship is often a vocal solo, or even the choir, singing with a prerecorded soundtrack. This situation has already been discussed in this chapter, but there is one subtle mixing technique that you might add.

As mentioned earlier, it is important that the sound level used for playback give the listeners a reasonable correlation with the "apparent loudness" of the original soundtrack. Also, many times soundtracks of popular songs have an instrumental solo section, or a long, majestic ending. The singer(s) are often at a loss for ideas of how to carry themselves during these portions. After all, musically, the attention is on the solo. If the band were actually performing there, all eyes would be on the performers. Here no one knows quite what to do, and the longer the section, the more uncomfortable things get. The engineer can help ease these tensions by focusing the congregation's attention on the music. How? Raise the level of the track slightly. As the solo ends, and the vocalist starts to sing again, tuck the track back to where it was earlier. When the last line is sung and the song enters its long, bombastic finale, the engineer can jump the level up slightly to draw attention away from the vocalist and back to the music, and then continue to slowly increase the volume of the soundtrack to emphasize that this indeed is the end of the song. This is basically what the music on the track is doing in the first place; the engineer is just slightly exaggerating the dynamic levels to make the track more "believable."

THE
YAMAHA
GUIDE TO
SOUND SYSTEMS
FOR WORSHIP
PAGE 156

CONTEMPORARY MUSIC PERFORMANCE

So-called contemporary music performances often take advantage of every tool available to today's musician—from traditional acoustic instruments to synthesizers and other electronic instruments, digital effects processors, and so on. The use of this myriad of tools brings with it a degree of complexity that requires extra attention to preventive maintenance. It's not that preventive maintenance is more important here than in other settings, but that the possibilities for something to go wrong are multiplied.

This setting will often include drums (both acoustic and electronic), electric bass guitar, piano, synthesizers and electronic organs, electric and acoustic guitar, percussion instruments, plus background and lead vocalists. When you start adding up the mic inputs needed to close-mic that many instruments and voices, you realize that you're going to need a bigger console than the average house of worship requires.

A *setup list* (or *patch chart*) is valid for any audio setting, but it becomes especially important as the size of the music group grows. Figure 13-5 shows one possibility for the group just mentioned. Even a choir has been included, to keep things interesting.

NOTE: On channel 8, D/I stands for direct inject, and means that an appropriate direct box should be used to feed this instrument directly to the console; in the comments column on that channel, a reminder suggests using the ground lift switch if a buzz from a ground loop is encountered during setup of this instrument. In the comments column for channel 2 (the snare mic), "–10/flat" tells the person setting up the microphone how to set certain switches on the mic—in this case, to use the –10 dB mic pad on the mic itself, and to not use the low-end rolloff. On channel 14 (the left choir mic), "0/70 Hz" indicates that this mic should be set with the

pad in the "off" position (0 dB), and that the low frequency rolloff switch on the mic should be at the 70 Hz position.

Notice that inputs 19, 21, 22, and 24 are fed from devices located near the mixing console, which means that they will not be fed through the snake. Those four open snake lines, plus the two inputs purposely left open, offer six spare lines that can come in very handy for last-minute changes or failed snake lines.

Console channels 13 and 20 are left open to provide physical dividing lines between the rhythm section and vocals and between the vocals and other inputs. While this is not necessary from a technical standpoint, it does reinforce the mental separation in the engineer's thinking during the excitement of the performance. Plus, you will have two strategically located spare channels available if and when the need arises.

Using a setup list like this (usually drawn by hand) can save a lot of time and confusion for everyone involved.

NOTE: A blank setup list is included on page 186.

The engineer is in charge of the setup. If he works out his ideas in advance, he can describe his desires for the initial setup on paper. Copies are distributed to the crew, taped to the snake's stage box, and then the setup can proceed smoothly. If something doesn't look quite right, crew members can seek him out for confirmation, but no one has to keep bothering him with questions that have obvious answers.

Your goal should be to have everything set up, preliminary equipment checks made, and crew members in position when the players walk in. It's not that you are the laborers and the musicians are the bosses—everyone is equal in this task—this is simply how a professional would approach the job. In your pursuit of technical excellence, emulating all that is good from a professional technical standpoint will benefit everyone in the end.

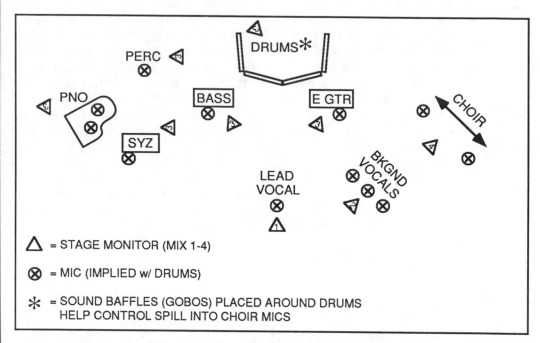

Snake	House	Submix	Microphone	Description	Stand	Comments
1	1	1	cardioid dynamic	Kick	low boom	flat
2	2	1	cardioid condenser	Snare	med. boom	−10/flat
3	3	1	cardioid condenser	Rack #1	med. boom	−10/flat
4	4	1	cardioid condenser	Rack #2	med. boom	−10/flat
5	5	1	cardioid condenser	Floor Tom	med. boom	−10/flat
6	6	1	cardioid condenser	Overhead Kit	tall boom	0/flat
7	7	1	cardioid dynamic	Percussion	—	—
8	8	2	D/I	Bass Guitar	—	lift gnd?
9	9	2	cardioid condenser	Piano Low	med. boom	0/75 Hz rolloff
10	10	2	cardioid condenser	Piano High	med. boom	0/75 Hz rolloff
11	11	2	D/I	Syz #1	—	lift gnd?
12	12	2	cardioid dynamic	Electric Guitar	—	—
13	13	—	(open)	—	—	—
14	14	3	cardioid condenser	Choir Left	fly	0/70 Hz rolloff
15	15	3	cardioid condenser	Choir Right	fly	0/70 Hz rolloff
16	16	4	cardioid dynamic	Debbie	med.	—
17	17	4	cardioid dynamic	Jeff	med.	—
18	18	4	cardioid dynamic	Dale	med.	—
—	19	4	Wireless #1	Lead Vocal	med.	—
20	20	—	(open)	—	—	—
—	21	5	D/I	Cassette Left	—	—
—	22	5	D/I	Cassette Right	—	—
23	23	6	cardioid dynamic	Announce	—	—
—	24	7	Wireless #2	Pastor's Lapel	—	—

Figure 13-5. Stage layout and setup list for a contemporary group.

THE
YAMAHA
GUIDE TO
SOUND SYSTEMS
FOR WORSHIP
PAGE 158

SUNDAY SCHOOL CHRISTMAS PROGRAM

Here's where the engineer really earns his keep. Trying to mic a Sunday school Christmas program is a real challenge. Several factors are working against technical excellence from the start, and if the system is the least bit prone to feedback problems, hair will be lost before it is over.

First off, loudness is not one of a children's choir's strong points. This varies widely with the age of the kids. Generally the smallest ones belt fairly well, the older ones do great in rehearsal but clam up in front of grandma and grandpa, and strangely enough, the teenagers—who ought to be the loudest of the three—are the quietest performers of all, intimidated by all their school friends sitting in the congregation.

All the classic rules of miking technique still apply. You will probably find yourself coming closer with the mics than usual, just to get enough gain before feedback. The sound may get "spotty," but be glad you've got something.

Kids doing dramatic speaking parts are another challenge. Unless you have an abundance of shotgun mics or maybe boundary mics or wireless lapel mics (or the budget to rent them), you are forced to capture the lines with the mics you have on hand—usually hand-held vocal mics. Cardioid (or tighter) patterns will give you the best reach, condensers the best sensitivity. In order for everyone in the audience to hear the kids' spoken lines, it may be best for the tech crew and program producers to swallow their pride and just have the kids walk up to a mic on a stand to deliver their lines. So what if there weren't any mic stands in Jesus' time; maybe you can disguise it to look like a palm tree. There may be no graceful solution other than stuffing the mics in the kids' faces, and to keep reminding them to speak their parts loudly. Try to avoid any unnecessary handling of the mics by the kids, especially the younger ones.

PORTABLE SYSTEM FOR A TRAVELING MUSICAL GROUP

This type of system can range from a simple six-input powered mixer with a couple of mics and speakers to a full-blown concert PA system with racks and racks of outboard processing gear.

The instrumentation of the touring musical group, the style of music involved, and the details of the performance will dictate how complex the portable sound system will need to be. A small vocal ensemble accompanied by an electronic keyboard instrument or an acoustic guitar, or even soundtracks, can be successful with a powered mixer (one that provides a sufficient number of inputs for the group), a couple of small, portable loudspeakers (often set up on speaker stands to project the sound farther into the audience), and a handful of microphones appropriate for the application. A group with fuller instrumentation may require much more equipment. More mics may be needed, which then increases the number of mic inputs needed on the console. A larger group may imply a bigger sound, which will require a more powerful speaker system, not to mention amplifiers to drive it.

Your pursuit of great sound and your penchant for risk taking will determine whether you stock your traveling microphone case with mostly condenser mics or with dynamic mics. Traditionally, dynamic mics are considered more rugged, and condensers more fragile. This is less true with today's crop of mics than in the past, but experience still suggests that you lean more heavily on the dynamics. Use whatever mics you as the engineer prefer to use in miking for sound reinforcement in general, but don't leave the parking lot without a couple of spare, dependable dynamic mics in your kit. For your condensers, forget the batteries. Don't make the trip without a console that can provide phantom power. Separate phantom power supplies are fine, but they require extra cables and extra connections, all of which increase the odds of a connection failure occurring at some time during a performance.

THE
YAMAHA
GUIDE TO
SOUND SYSTEMS
FOR WORSHIP
PAGE 159

BASIC CHECKLIST FOR A PORTABLE SYSTEM

Anytime you find yourself going out with a portable system, make it a point of compiling a checklist before any gear is packed for the trip, and then triple-check it as the gear is packed. It's not a bad idea to check the list again as you pack the equipment away for the return trip. Here are a few suggestions for the equipment to pack for a typical music group's portable system (not including the instruments):

- microphones (with spares)
- console
- house limiter (for speaker protection)
- house EQ
- crossover
- house amplifiers
- house speakers
- house speaker cables
- monitor EQ
- monitor amplifiers
- monitor speakers
- monitor speaker cables
- interconnecting cables (for console to EQ to amp, etc.)
- mic snake
- mic cables
- mic stands (w/ booms)
- mic clips (w/ spares)
- effects devices (if used)
- compressors (if used)
- AC power outlet strips
- AC extension cords
- gaff or duct tape
- white labeling tape
- felt-tip markers
- flashlights
- batteries for flashlights
- volt-ohm meter
- batteries for meter
- cable checker
- test tone generator (portable, for troubleshooting)
- soldering station
- solder
- small vise (for cable repairs, etc.)
- tool kit (wire strippers, small screwdrivers, etc.)
- spare XLR connectors (male and female, in-line)
- spare ¼" phone plug connectors
- work lights
- console light(s) (with colored gels)
- spare fuses for ALL equipment (including speaker fuses)
- (include assortment of fuses for musical instruments, if possible)
- spare high-frequency drivers, if possible
- cassette deck (for soundtracks and recording)
- work gloves for the setup crew
- spare clothes (for after you get drenched in a rain shower)
- tarps and plastic sheeting to protect equipment from environment
- towels to dry things off after a shower, or an overnight stay outdoors
- production intercom system (if the setting dictates it)
- walkie talkies (again, if the setting dictates it)

These are the basics. Better plan to take something bigger than the family station wagon.

SHARING THE STAGE

Another factor to consider is whether or not other musical or dramatic performing groups will require the use of the system along with your music group. Decisions must be made early on about how to handle such a situation. With two or more large music groups involved, all trying to use the same sound system, problems will surface that need to be addressed. Audiences don't have a great deal of patience when set changes take a lot of time. Sharing of musical equipment like drums, guitar amps, and sometimes keyboards will simplify the sharing exercise, not to mention shorten the set changes. It will also greatly simplify connecting the right equipment to the right inputs on one shared console.

No one expects any equipment to get stolen during such an event, but pieces of equipment do look alike, and many people have the same models and brands of equipment. Confusion about which equipment belongs to whom is bound to arise. The most efficient safeguard in this case is to positively identify all of the equipment that belongs to your group— mics, cables, speakers, equipment racks, and so on—so that there is no question about whose it is. The equipment can be engraved, adhesive stickers can be ordered with the name and logo of the house of worship printed on them, or inventory stickers with an identification number typed on the label can even be used. Even colored tape will work, until another group uses the same color of tape. Cables can be marked with shrink tubing that has the name of the congregation printed on it.

THE
YAMAHA
GUIDE TO
SOUND SYSTEMS
FOR WORSHIP
PAGE 160

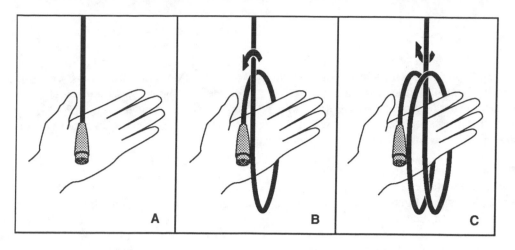

Figure 13-6. Over/under cable wrapping technique.

A CABLE WRAPPING TUTORIAL

By the way, do you wrap your mic cables over your arm, around your elbow and hand, and then twirl the last few feet of what's left of the shriveled-up mess that once was a decent, well-behaved mic cable? Or worse, do you just throw your cables all together into a box, dreading the next time you'll have to set up? There is a much more efficient and friendly method of wrapping mic cables, speaker cables, even power extension cables, that will save you a great deal of time during setup. This applies to any and all audio settings, portable or permanent, but since time is often a precious commodity for traveling groups, this technique will be doubly useful there. If you employ this technique properly, you can throw out a 100-foot mic cable and not even bother to look back to confirm that it uncoiled without tangling—it will always work.

For lack of a better name, call it the *over/under technique*. To wrap the cable for storage, first stretch the cable straight out on the floor and then pick up one end. Since most people throw the cable out from the mic stand location, choose the female XLR connector. Hold the connector in the palm of your left hand (if you are right-handed), with the sockets facing you (Figure 13-6A). The length of the cable trails off the far side of your left hand and away from you. With your right hand, reach about two feet down the cable, grab the cable and lay it in the palm of your left hand, adding a half twist to the left in the process (Figure 13-6B). Reach down the cable again with your right hand, but this time take the cable in your palm, reaching underneath and grabbing it from the left side (as you're looking at it),

and lift it up so that both of your hands are side by side, palms facing up (giving your right hand, and the cable, a half twist to the *right* in the process), and then lay the cable in your left hand (Figure 13-6C). Repeat the entire over-and-under process until you reach the end of the cable. Try to keep the loops roughly even in length.

There are a couple of extra points to consider here. The half twist for each loop is important. You must alternate the way you grab the cable each time, and you must also keep the two ends separated on their respective sides of the finished coil. If you fail to do any of these things, you run the risk of creating a knot when you toss the cable out. Use any method that is convenient to you to tie the cable so that it stays coiled. Velcro™ cable ties, leather shoe strings, duct tape (messy), masking tape (even messier), or twist ties will do the job.

If your cables have not been coiled loosely like this, and especially if they have been kinked and knotted from use, it may take time for them to behave themselves again.

When you go to set up, undo the tie and hold the coil in your right hand. Grab the female XLR with your left hand and then toss the coil with a smooth swing of your right arm. Then smile real big when you realize just how much time this is going to save you during setup from now on.

THE
YAMAHA
GUIDE TO
SOUND SYSTEMS
FOR WORSHIP
PAGE 161

TENT MINISTRY

A special problem of portable systems is finding proper AC with which to power the system. Tent ministries run into this problem often because they have this habit of setting up in remote locations where there is no convenient source of AC power.

This forces them to seek out gasoline-powered generators to supply power for the tent lights, stage lights if used, and for the PA system and electronic musical instruments. You will need to determine how big a generator to rent, how many you will need, and learn some precautions on how to connect them.

Generators, although physically noisy, are fairly reliable sources of power. All you have to do is get them running and then keep them running. For the uninitiated, this can be more "interesting" than it seems. It would behoove you to hire an experienced generator operator to stay on site for the first day or so of your experience, and to properly train someone in your group in the idiosyncrasies of generators.

Make sure that you establish a solid ground connection by driving a rod into the ground near where the generator will be. This will provide the third-pin ground for the AC cables. Without it, you may find yourself with an awful buzz in the equipment that cannot be resolved any other way.

Also make sure that you have plenty of fuel safely stored nearby. You will need to estimate the rate of fuel flow for each of the generators you will be using, and plan your supplies accordingly.

It is preferable that you provide one generator that will handle all audio and musical instrument needs, and that nothing other than audio devices uses that generator feed for power. You can determine the amperage needed by simply adding up all the fuse values for every piece of audio and musical equipment that will be in use. That total will be the total current drain possible for all that gear, and would occur only with everyone playing full out and with the PA system running wide open. For night programs, provide a second generator to power the tent lights, and stage lights if used. To determine how powerful a generator to choose for the lights, add up the wattage of all the lights that will be

used. Divide this by the voltage (e.g., 115 V) to calculate the size generator to ask for (This equation yields the number of *volt-amperes* [VA—also known as watts] needed; divide this figure by 1,000 to yield the number of *kilovolt-amperes* [KVA], a more common measurement for large generators.).

OUTDOOR EASTER SUNRISE SERVICE

From a technical standpoint, an outdoor Easter sunrise service isn't any different than any of the remote situations just described. However, another important consideration for any outdoor event is to make sure that your staff has secured an outdoor amplification permit. There may be people in the neighborhood who will take issue with you over being awakened at sunrise on Easter morning, and you might find several police cars rushing up to pull the plug on your service. This permit, required in many communities, is your only legal protection in such a situation. Furthermore, even with a permit in hand, there are communities that will monitor how loud your event is at a measured distance away. If you exceed community standards, the authorities will warn you of the problem. If you continue to exceed those standards, they can and will pull the plug.

If at all possible, consider setting up the system the day before. Sunrise comes awfully early for many of us, and tech crews are more used to working until late at night than getting up early in the morning. To protect the gear overnight from dew, cover the speaker stacks and all other equipment with tarps or plastic sheeting. (The protective covers should stay close by in case of inclement weather.) Once the system is checked thoroughly, put the mics away overnight. In the morning, an hour or so before the service will start, reset the mics and reconfirm proper system operation. Ask for volunteers or hire security guards to protect the equipment from walking away overnight. For an extended stay by a tent ministry, you will want to continue that security arrangement throughout your stay.

THE
YAMAHA
GUIDE TO
SOUND SYSTEMS
FOR WORSHIP
PAGE 162

ATTENDED VS. UNATTENDED SOUND SYSTEMS

Many houses of worship have such simple sound reinforcement requirements that they have decided that a mixing engineer is not needed in their situation. The sound man is often also the janitor, a person who has been trained to set up the equipment in a certain way, to adjust the volume knobs to a certain position, and to come running if he hears a problem.

In many cases, this operation works fine year after year. The obvious concern is the ever-present danger of feedback. If the sound system has a tremendous degree of stability in that regard, if there are no system failures, and if it serves the needs of the staff, then the unattended system is a reasonable solution.

A better and more realistic alternative to the unattended sound system is, in effect, an automatic system. An automatic mixer won't prevent the possibility of feedback occurring, but it can effectively guard your sound system against it. The automatic mixer operates each connected microphone at equal gain. A "sensitivity" adjustment is provided for each channel. This sensitivity setting determines how loud a sound source it "hears" must be in order for the channel to open up. If these controls are properly adjusted, each mic will in effect be turned off until someone speaks or sings into it. Remember the discussion of NOM (number of open mics) in Chapter 5? Sophisticated automatic mic mixers have the ability to reduce overall gain as more microphones are "gated on." Since only the mics in use at any given moment are turned on, the possibility for feedback is greatly diminished. The shortcoming of this system is that it doesn't provide much "mixing" capability. The mics are either on or off, and all are adjusted to an equal volume.

Unattended sound systems obviously offer less flexibility than attended systems. A mixing engineer can provide creative, musical choices in the dynamic process of mixing the music for a worship service. An unattended system would not serve the needs of a videotape feed very well either, for the reasons discussed earlier in this chapter. But many houses of worship choose this approach, and if properly installed and operated, such a system will continue to work until the needs of their program outgrow its limitations.

THE
YAMAHA
GUIDE TO
SOUND SYSTEMS
FOR WORSHIP
PAGE 163

CHAPTER 14.
WHAT TO DO WHEN THINGS GO WRONG

One of the most valuable skills the operator of a sound system can possess is the ability to isolate and correct problems that occur (they *will* occur). Effective troubleshooting combines consistent, logical thought with experience and a dash of intuition—in precisely that order of importance.

The lessons of experience cannot be adequately conveyed in a book such as this, nor can any number of words bestow an intuitive grasp of electronics. But the logical basis of troubleshooting can be described. The principles given here can be expanded to cover a variety of problems.

KNOW THY SYSTEM

Before you can start working on system problems, you must know how the system functions. This applies to both the person in charge of the system and those responsible for running it from week to week. You must know how things are connected, from microphones through loudspeakers. You must understand the signal flow of your mixer or console. (See Chapters 4 and 6 for information on making sense out of block diagrams.) This knowledge will also benefit the "Wilburs" among you, for it will serve to temper your enthusiasm to change things that you don't understand.

In the event of trouble during a service, remember these two words: Remain Calm. It is possible that very few people will even be aware that there is a problem, so you don't want to call undue attention to the situation by getting all excited. You also don't want to disrupt the mood of worship, if you can help it.

For the ministers reading this: Standing at the pulpit and making public comments about problems with the sound system won't make the problems go away any faster. It serves only to frustrate and humiliate the system operator. The worship service is a team effort; don't go around shooting your own wounded.

WHAT'S THE PROBLEM?

Before beginning to remedy a problem, it is necessary to analyze and understand clearly what the problem is. All too often a simple problem is made complex by attempts to make repairs before there is any clear understanding of what needs to be repaired.

EXAMINE THE CLUES

In the best tradition of detective fiction, you should first take careful inventory of the available clues. Running through the following mental checklist should help you get a better grasp of the problem.

*   What are the primary symptoms of the problem?

*   Is the problem global, or is it isolated to one small part of the system? What parts of the sound system are performing properly? What parts of the system are malfunctioning?

*   Is the problem intermittent? If so, what conditions are present when the symptoms are manifest?

*   Has anything about the system been changed since the last time it is known to have functioned properly?

Gathering the basic clues may be sufficient to guide you to the cause of the problem. If so, congratulations; if not, it's time to move on to the investigation.

INVESTIGATION

Consider the clues that you have already gathered and start to narrow the problem down. Is any part of the sound system common to all the symptoms? What parts of the system can be eliminated as the culprit? If the minister's voice can't be heard over the main speaker system but comes through loud and clear when you use headphones to monitor the tape recorder, the pulpit microphone can probably be eliminated as a suspect.

THE
YAMAHA
GUIDE TO
SOUND SYSTEMS
FOR WORSHIP
PAGE 164

ABSENCE OF SIGNAL

Well, it looks like it's time to roll up your sleeves and do some real troubleshooting. Start by checking the basics.

- Simple as it may seem, check to be sure that every component is plugged in and turned on. Check battery-operated equipment (such as wireless microphone transmitters) to make sure that the batteries are fresh and properly installed. Seasoned audio professionals install fresh batteries in wireless microphone transmitters before every performance.

- Before assuming component failure, carefully examine all equipment settings. Check input gain and pads, channel faders, group faders, and master faders. Make certain that the offending channel is properly assigned and that the channel is not muted or that another is not soloed. Few things can provide a better lesson in humility than spending 30 minutes repatching, substituting equipment, and tracing cables, only to discover that the cause of the problem was failure to assign a channel to a group.

- Check that the signal path is complete. Are any connections missing?

- If you make changes during troubleshooting, make them one at a time and restore the last change before making the next. No sense adding another problem to the one that already exists.

If everything looks correct but the problem remains, it's time to begin tracing the signal.

Figure 14-1 is a flow chart illustrating a logical approach to system troubleshooting when distortion or absence of signal is the problem. As a signal source you can use a small, battery-operated audio oscillator or the output from a tape deck or CD player. The "tracer" can be a small powered loudspeaker or a battery-operated headphone amplifier and headphones. To simply determine if signal is present or absent at various points in the signal flow of the system, use the indicators provided on the equipment. Mixing consoles have VI meters that can tell you at a glance if the signal has made it to the console output. The Cue, or PFL (pre-Fade Listen), system of a console should also be used to determine if the signal is getting at least as far as the mixing console. Many power amplifiers have "signal present" LED indicators that can tell you if the signal is getting to the power amplifier input.

By proceeding in this logical manner, you can check each component, connection, and cable in the system, and eventually isolate the offending component.

UNDESIRED SIGNALS

Undesired signals include hum, RFI (radio-frequency interference), or distortion superimposed upon the desired signal. Once again, it is necessary to isolate the problem before any steps can be taken to solve it. A few simple procedures can help you zero in on the problem. For example, you may begin by turning down the input level control of the power amplifier. If the problem remains, then the amplifier is probably responsible. If the problem disappears, then it is originating farther upstream.

The appropriate starting point for tracing depends in part on the character of the interference. If you are sure that the loudspeaker cables could not possibly be at fault, start with the power amplifier.

Unplug the cable to the amplifier input. (You may want to plug in a portable cassette player as an alternate signal source.) If the problem remains, it is certainly the amplifier. If it goes away, then it is originating farther upstream. Proceed backward through the signal path until you have isolated the component (or cable) that is at fault; then replace or bypass it.

If the undesired signal is isolated to one input, start with the console. Connect the source to a different channel. If the noise is still there, switch back to the original channel and move on to the next item. If you are using a patch bay, change the patch cable. Jiggle the patch plugs to see if dirt or corrosion in the jacks is causing the noise. If everything is okay here, try a different line from the snake. If this still doesn't rid you of the noise, change the position of the mic cable. Does the unwanted signal change in intensity? Change the mic cable itself. Any

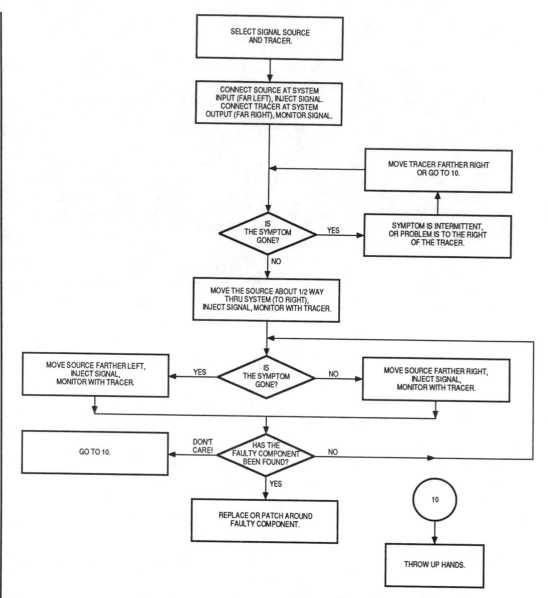

Figure 14-1. Troubleshooting distortion or absence of signal. Assumes that the block diagram flow is from left to right. Method is to use a signal generator and tracer (a tape deck and powered loudspeaker may suffice) to locate the faulty component. From *Handbook for Sound Engineers*, ed. Glen Ballou.

improvement? As a last resort, try using a different microphone.

Following are some common unwanted signals and their probable causes:

*   **Hum.** Hum is most often caused by ground loops or faulty ground connections. See the discussion of grounding in Chapter 12. Watch out in particular for inadvertent shorts between grounds such as might be caused by setting one chassis atop another or allowing connector shells to touch. (There is nothing wrong with intentionally grounding all chassis together through the rack or with a bus bar, provided your system grounding scheme allows for this.) Never assume

that bolting a unit into the rack grounds it; paint, for example, may electrically isolate it from the rack.

Hum can also be induced by a component nearby. Power amplifiers, for example, sometimes radiate a significant hum field from their power transformers. If a sensitive low-level component is racked just above such an amplifier, it can pick up and amplify the hum. This can also occur when microphone lines run too close to power cables. Physically separating the components or cables is the best solution. If you can't separate cables, have them cross one another at right angles rather than near-parallel angles.

THE
YAMAHA
GUIDE TO
SOUND SYSTEMS
FOR WORSHIP
PAGE 166

- **Buzz.** Buzz generally refers to high-frequency harmonics of the power line frequency.

  If buzz emanates from the high-frequency drivers of a biamplified loudspeaker system but no corresponding hum is detected from the woofers, the high-frequency amplifier and the cables connecting to the crossover are suspect. A ground loop may exist, or the cable shield may be ungrounded.

  Buzz may also be induced in mic cables by SCR (silicon-controlled rectifier) light dimmer circuits. Experiment with alternate positions and orientations of the mic cables. If you trace the buzz to a line-level connection, it may be caused by electrostatic coupling. Either insert an appropriate signal transformer with Faraday shielding or try a different grounding scheme. Some cables are better at rejecting this noise than others.

- **Hiss.** Hiss is most often caused by a poor gain structure, which causes the self-generated noise of components early in the signal path to be amplified to unacceptable levels.

  Review the procedure for setting the gain structure, found on pages 139–142. Examine the gain settings of every component in the chain. Is each working equally hard?

  The most frequent cause of hiss is excessive gain in the power amplifiers. Is a 0 VU signal required from the console to achieve full power? If not, the console isn't working hard enough; it's operating too close to its noise floor, and the power amps are magnifying this noise unduly. Reduce the gain of the power amplifiers, and increase the appropriate settings on the console. If the masters and channel faders of the console must be at maximum level to get a barely audible signal, reduce the input channel attenuation (pad) or turn up the input gain trim and bring the faders down somewhat.

  Hiss may also be caused by oscillation or other malfunctions in one or more components in the chain. The offending component can be identified by signal tracing, then checked apart from the signal path. If the offending component functions properly when disconnected from the signal path, the input or output connections may be at fault. Check for partial shorts in cables and for excessive output loading. If the equipment features a balanced output and is driving an unbalanced input, make sure that the low-output driver (e.g., microphone) is not shorted to ground at either end of the connecting cable. Unfortunately, some equipment does not have well-designed output driver circuitry, and nothing more than a long output cable may be needed to force the output circuit into instability or oscillation.

- **Static and Crackling.** Static and crackling are usually due to intermittent signal or shield connections. Shorts in cables, and microphonic noise due to the shield shifting in relation to the signal lead(s), can also cause such noises, particularly when a cable is moved. By signal tracing, the offending cable(s) usually can be isolated and replaced.

  On occasion, a dirty control may be at fault. Exercising the control can provide a temporary fix, but the part should be cleaned or replaced by a technician as soon as practical.

  Static bursts can also be caused by RF interference. Good grounding practice and, possibly, judicious use of transformers will normally solve the problem.

Figure 14-2 demonstrates a logical approach to tracing a problem of hum or noise.

DISTORTION

A weed can be described as a plant that's in the wrong place. Similarly, distortion can be defined as any unintended difference between the input signal and the output signal. A signal from a microphone that has been equalized, compressed, and has had reverberation added to it certainly differs from the original signal, but since the changes to the signal are presumably intentional, those changes would not be considered distortion.

THE
YAMAHA
GUIDE TO
SOUND SYSTEMS
FOR WORSHIP
PAGE 167

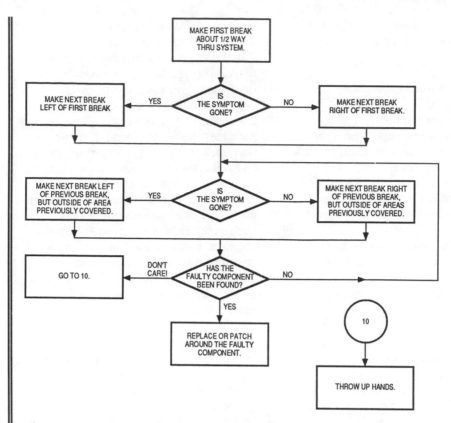

Figure 14-2. Troubleshooting hum, noise, or oscillation. Assumes that the block diagram flow is from left to right. Method is to break the system (disconnect) at indicated points until the faulty component is located. From *Handbook for Sound Engineers*, ed. Glen Ballou.

dBV input from a +4 dBu output without an intervening pad. Within the console itself, are the input clip lights on before the output VI meters approach zero? If so, this suggests the need to reduce the input gain trim or introduce some input attenuation padding, and to then turn up the output level.

Distortion can also be caused by a failure of a component. By testing or substitution, the failed component can be identified and repaired or replaced.

Since no device made by man is perfect, all audio equipment adds some distortion to the signal. This distortion is typically expressed as "%THD" (Total Harmonic Distortion). For further discussion of this specification, see page 86. Contemporary professional audio equipment produces extremely low levels of distortion when it is functioning properly and operated correctly. Problems with these types of low-level distortion may be objectionable, but solving them should have been the job of the engineer who designed or specified the equipment, and is beyond the scope of this book. Of greater concern to you will be dealing with those problems that are caused by improper settings or component failure.

In the realm of improper settings and operation, distortion is often caused by overloading of a stage (too high a signal level) somewhere in the signal path. Examine the gain structure of the system carefully. Are the clip lights on the console or outboard signal processors lit steadily long before the system reaches full power? If so, some gain adjustments are in order. Be sure that you're not trying to drive a –10

HOW VARIOUS SOUND SYSTEM COMPONENTS FAIL

An understanding of how and why system components fail is important. If you have a thorough grasp of this topic, you will be better equipped to prevent, recognize, and work around problems. Following is a list of sound system components, typical kinds of failure, and some tips on avoiding or working around these failures.

ELECTRONIC DEVICES

FAULTY CIRCUIT COMPONENTS AND ASSEMBLY

On occasion a faulty component, or "cold" solder joint, or badly seated connector will find its way into an electronic device. These defects will typically make their presence known early in the life of an amplifier, mixer, or signal processor. Reputable manufacturers will cover such failures under warranty and at no charge to the end user.

Unless you are a skilled technician with experience in audio equipment repair and access to service manuals and test equipment, it is highly unadvisable for you to make any attempts to repair electronic circuitry.

You can be of great help to the servicer by providing an accurate and complete written description of the symptoms, the conditions at the time of failure, and how the failed equipment is used in the system. Telling the technician that "it quit working" is not especially helpful. Contrast that with the following: "Fifteen minutes after the system was turned on I heard a loud buzz through the speaker system, then the amplifier protect light went on. I turned the amp off, and when it was turned on again 30 minutes later, it worked." The latter could provide a valuable clue that will assure that your amplifier is fixed the first time.

MECHANICAL PROBLEMS

Many equipment problems stem from simple mechanical causes rather than failure of any electronic components. Following are examples of potential mechanical problems and some suggested remedial actions:

- **Loose screws or nuts on connectors** can break a ground path and cause absence of signal, intermittent signal, or hum. Simply tightening the screw or nut (being careful not to over-tighten) will often restore normal operation.

- **Improperly seated connectors on circuit boards** can be at the root of many problems with varying symptoms. An input channel on a modular mixing console may be fixed by reseating (with the console power turned off and the power cable disconnected).

AGING

Modern solid-state circuitry is remarkably long-lived, but age can still take a toll on equipment. Mechanical parts (such as fans, meters, connectors, switches, and level controls) may fail due to use. Capacitors, in particular, will deteriorate over time— although materials technology is improving all the time. As above, repair should be referred to a technician, along with a comprehensive description of the problem.

Controls such as faders, switches, or rotary "pots" (potentiometers) may accumulate dust or other small particles that will cause a "scratching" noise when they are moved. Often it is possible to clear the debris from the control by "exercising" it (moving the control over its full range of motion a dozen or more times).

EXCESSIVE HEAT

All electronic equipment should be protected from extremes of heat. Make certain that ventilation openings are not blocked on mixing consoles, and that racks provide a path for the entry of cool air and the exit of hot air.

Power amplifiers typically generate large amounts of heat in normal operation, and are therefore the most likely component of a sound system to succumb to heat. Professional amplifiers have sensing circuitry that will protect the amp if internal temperatures at certain points (typically the power supply transformer and the output device heat sinks) exceed a predetermined level. When this happens, the amplifier will usually protect itself by shutting down; an LED, labeled THERMAL, or PROTECT, will light. There are several possible causes for a thermal shutdown:

- **Too much load on the amplifier.** If an amplifier is driving a speaker load with an impedance below the minimum rated impedance of the amplifier, excessive heat will be generated. For example: An amplifier specification states that it is for use with no less than a 4-ohm speaker load. Three 8-ohm speakers are connected, in parallel, to the amplifier. Using the equation for calculating the impedance of a parallel load, given on page 89 of this book, you can see that the amplifier is looking at a load of 2.67 ohms—well below its rated capacity. Disconnecting one of the loudspeakers should solve the problem.

So-called 70-volt distributed systems (also known as "constant-voltage" systems) can present special problems for an amplifier. These systems may have a nominal impedance that is well within the capacity of the amplifier. At the same time, the impedance of some frequencies (typically in the bass region) will be very low—sometimes less than 1 ohm. A well-designed constant-voltage system will include high-pass filtering to prevent the amplifier from having to operate into these frequency-dependent low impedances. By using a device called an *impedance bridge*, an audio contractor can check the impedance of a constant-voltage system.

- **Inadequate ventilation.** In order for an amplifier to dissipate heat, it is necessary for the amplifier rack to have adequate ventilation. See that there is adequate air flow around the amplifier.

  Some amplifiers use internal fans to ensure adequate cooling. If the amplifier is running hot, you should be able to hear the fan run (some fans are quieter than others). If you can't, refer the amplifier to a trusted technician. Amplifiers using internal fans will typically include air filters to prevent dust from accumulating inside the amp. Check the operating manual for the amplifier for instructions on cleaning the filter.

LOUDSPEAKERS

A transducer is a device that converts one type of energy (electrical) into another type of energy (acoustical). Loudspeakers (and most other transducers) combine elements of electrical and mechanical technology with more than a little art. The basic principles of loudspeaker design are well known, and true breakthroughs in technology are rare. Most improvements can be attributed to incremental advances in manufacturing, measurement techniques, and materials. An understanding of how and why loudspeakers fail will help you prevent failures.

AGING

The materials used in a transducer are subject to the effects of aging. The surround of a speaker (the flexible material at the circumference of the cone) may become brittle with age, lose its resilience, and eventually shatter. Age, heat, and other environmental factors can break down the adhesives that hold the voice coil, the former, and the cone or diaphragm together. Refer to Figure 9-4, on page 94, for an illustration of a low-frequency driver.

A cone-type speaker can be returned to "like-new" condition or better by reconing. Reconing involves the removal and replacement of the cone and voice coil

assembly. If properly done, it will result in a speaker that is every bit the equal of a new one. The process isn't especially mysterious, but it does require training and the access to the appropriate reconing kits and other materials. High-quality speakers may be worth reconing—check with your favorite pro audio dealer or the manufacturer. Most low-cost speakers are throw-aways and cannot be reconed economically.

High-frequency compression drivers can usually be restored to like-new condition by replacement of the diaphragm assembly. Anyone with a steady hand and good mechanical skills can replace a compression driver diaphragm—but many compression drivers require centering of the diaphragm, a process that requires a sweepable test oscillator and some training and experience. Once again it is best for the novice not to tackle this job.

EXCESSIVE EXCURSION

Excessive excursion occurs when the input signal is sufficient to drive the cone or diaphragm farther than it was designed to travel. Sometimes the voice coil will actually be driven out of the gap. Other times the surround or the spider will be damaged in such a way that the voice coil is no longer centered in the gap. In the case of compression drivers, the diaphragm may be shattered. Possible causes for this type of failure include:

- **Unexpected and extreme transients.** An accident such as a dropped microphone can cause this type of failure. It is also possible that a synthesizer patch or bass guitar with extraordinary low-frequency content can be at fault.

  An improper system turn-on or turn-off sequence can also damage components—especially if the system is bi- or triamplified. If the amplifiers are switched on before the rest of the system, any "thumps" or "turn-on transients" will be sent to the speakers. If the amplifiers are the last things to be switched off after the system is used, any thumps or other signals that the equipment produces when it is switched off may damage the transducers. *Always remember that the power amplifiers should be switched on LAST and switched off FIRST.*

THE
YAMAHA
GUIDE TO
SOUND SYSTEMS
FOR WORSHIP
PAGE 170

- **Crossover maladjustments or failure.** The failure, improper connection, or improper setting of a crossover can cause a high-frequency transducer to fail. Compression drivers and tweeters are designed to reproduce the high-frequency portions of the audio spectrum. In order to respond to very fast transients, these devices must be extremely low in mass. Low mass dictates that the devices are necessarily less robust than those used to reproduce low frequencies. If a crossover is set improperly, it is possible that frequencies below those for which the driver is intended will reach the diaphragm and cause it to shatter.

A common cause of compression driver failure in bi- and triamplified systems is accidentally reversing the high-frequency and low-frequency connections from the power amplifier(s). Proper connector selection and labeling can reduce the chances of this happening. If you are in doubt, it is a good practice to bring up the levels of the high-frequency amplifiers first, and ascertain that the high-frequency signal is coming from the high-frequency drivers.

INADEQUATE AMPLIFIER POWER

Inadequate amplifier power can cause loudspeakers to fail. While this statement is counter-intuitive, it is probably true that more speakers have failed because of inadequate amplifier power than because of excessive amplifier power.

An amplifier that is too small for the job is also more likely to be overdriven—that is, the signal from the mixer will be increased past the point at which the amplifier is producing maximum output power. When the amplifier is overdriven, clipping occurs (see page 88). Clipping generates additional harmonics that can stress a driver and cause thermal failure. In addition, the plateaus of the clipped waveform represent relatively long periods of time during which the cone or diaphragm is being held at the extreme of its travel, reducing heat dissipation and creating mechanical stress. It is only a slight exaggeration to say that any amplifier can destroy any speaker.

CABLES AND CONNECTORS

Cabling and connections should always be considered prime suspects in any troubleshooting investigation, for several reasons. First, since even a simple system can include a dozen or more cables, the odds are in favor of a cable problem. Second, cables are subject to abuse, stress, and improper assembly. Finally (and most importantly), a cable failure is something that you can certainly do something about.

FINDING THE FAULTY CABLE

Refer to the instructions on troubleshooting earlier in this chapter to narrow down the possibilities when looking for a faulty cable. Once you have done so, you can substitute a cable known to be good for the one suspected to be faulty. Substitution of a component known to be good for one suspected to be faulty is a time-honored troubleshooting practice that is especially effective for finding bad cables—it's a great deal less expensive to have a few spare cables on hand than to have a spare mixing console or amplifier. As mentioned earlier, once a particular cable has been exonerated as the culprit, restore the connection before moving on to the next cable. Once a faulty cable has been found, it should be marked clearly (using tape) and set aside or repaired immediately.

WHY DO CABLES AND CONNECTORS FAIL?

Improper soldering or assembly is a common problem, especially when the cables were made by those who lack experience and training in the art of soldering. Most such problems can be identified easily by visual inspection. Here's what to look for:

- **Cold solder joints.** A good solder connection is made by first heating the contact point and the wire, then applying the solder to the work—not to the tip of the iron. This technique causes the solder to flow evenly over the contact and into the strands of wire. Examine the suspect joint; if it does not show evidence of even flowing, or if the surface of the joint looks dull and gritty, get out your soldering iron and resolder the connection.

THE
YAMAHA
GUIDE TO
SOUND SYSTEMS
FOR WORSHIP
PAGE 171

- **Solder bridges or stray strands of wire.** Occasionally a strand of wire or a solder bridge can short two conductors together. A stray strand of wire can be hard to see, but it will certainly interrupt the flow of signal in your system. Removal of the bridge or strand should restore normal operation.

- **Loose screws.** Some connectors, such as the dual banana connectors commonly used on power amplifier outputs, use a set screw to secure the wire. If this set screw is not tight enough, the electrical contact may be interrupted. Keep a small screwdriver handy to tighten these set screws.

  Some manufacturers offer phone plugs that secure the wire with screws, to allow assembly by those who do not solder. These connectors have no place in a professional audio system.

- **Damaged insulation.** The contacts of many connectors are molded into, and separated by, a plastic insulator. This insulation may fail due to excessive heat during soldering, or because of physical damage, thus allowing conductors to short together. If this appears to be the cause of your problem, discard and replace the connector. Generally, high-quality connectors use materials that are resistant to heat and physical damage. The money that cheap connectors save is rarely worth the aggravation they cause.

Mechanical damage to the cable is also a cause of failure. Cables may "short out" internally or develop "open" conductors (the commonly misused term "short" means that a path for current flow exists that is not intended; the term "open" means that an intended path for current has been broken). Some cable damage (such as when a cable has been cut) can be seen. But many times a faulty cable will have no visible flaws.

Some type of device for testing cables should be in the toolbox of every audio professional. One such device is a simple battery-powered cable tester that uses LEDs to indicate that all conductors in a cable are functioning and that no short or open conductors are present. Cable testers are inexpensive and are available from many sources. A second method of testing requires the use of a small battery-powered oscillator to inject a signal into one end of a cable while the other end is being monitored.

Cables may cause problems for one or more of the following reasons:

- **Improper coiling.** Chapter 13 includes a discussion of the proper technique for coiling audio cables. This method not only makes the cables easy to handle, it can also prevent cable failure. The relative positions of the conductors, insulation, and shielding within a cable are a critical part of the design. When a cable is coiled improperly, (wound around the arm, for example), the conductors and the shield can twist within the outer insulation. It is even possible that the insulation of the internal conductors will be damaged, allowing them to short to each other or to the shield. Even if no such shorting takes place, displacement of the conductors within a cable can alter the distributed capacitance of the cable, causing noise, handling noise ("microphonic cable"), or loss of audio quality. A cable that has been abused will eventually avenge itself—probably at the most inopportune moment.

- **Using the wrong cable for the job.** Many types of wire are available, and each is intended for certain functions. Occasionally, wire that was designed for one function is inappropriately employed for another function. Figure 14-3 is a table of various common cable types and applications. If the system you are charged with operating is using the wrong cables for the job, replacement at the earliest opportunity is recommended.

WIRELESS MICROPHONES

Wireless microphones involve a whole class of problems all their own, from various kinds of interference and distortion to signal dropouts. These are dealt with at the end of Chapter 5.

THE
YAMAHA
GUIDE TO
SOUND SYSTEMS
FOR WORSHIP
PAGE 172

Cable Type	Application
1-conductor, braided shield	musical instruments and unbalanced line-level signal
2-conductor, braided shield	microphone and balanced line-level signal
"coil cords"	electric guitar—when absolutely necessary
1- and 2-conductor, foil shield	internal rack wiring and permanent wiring not subject to handling
multiple shielded pairs	"snakes," various rack and permanently installed microphone and line-level applications
18–20-gauge unshielded pair	doorbells
16-gauge unshielded pair	short runs (less than 50 ft/15 m) from low-powered amplifiers to 8- or 16-ohm speakers
14-gauge unshielded pair	longer runs (100 ft/30 m) from moderate-powered amplifiers to 8- or 16-ohm speakers
12-gauge unshielded pair	long runs from high-powered amplifiers to most speakers
10-gauge unshielded pair	long runs from high-powered amplifiers to subwoofers
2-gauge unshielded pair	jumper cables, arc-welding

Figure 14-3. Cables and applications.

MISCELLANEOUS PROBLEMS

Sometimes a problem isn't as simple as no signal or an undesired signal. Sometimes the sound "just isn't right." What do you do?

First of all, really *listen* to the sound. This is another justification for placing the console in the position of a typical listener. During the times when you run your system checks (see page 181), it is a good idea to walk around the room and listen to your system. Learn to listen closely, to analyze what you hear, so that you can determine what about it is wrong. This will point you in the right direction to track down the cause of the problem.

Bank tellers are trained to identify counterfeit money not by examining phony bills, but by becoming familiar with the genuine article in every detail. In the same way, you should become so accustomed to the best sound that your system is capable of producing that you will recognize when the slightest detail is awry.

Also listen to the comments you receive from members of the congregation; don't become defensive and dismiss them by saying, "They don't know what they're talking about." At the same time, you may have to interpret their comments, because although they may indeed know when something is wrong with the sound, they may not know how to accurately describe the symptoms they hear, much less diagnose the problem.

Finally, problems with the sound may be due to the limitations of the system itself. This tends to be the first place to which under-educated system operators point when ascribing blame (the people in the pews tend to blame the operators!). And the capabilities of the system *should* be the first consideration when it is being planned, designed, and installed. But assuming that you did your homework when you purchased the system, you should only consider blaming problems on it after you have eliminated the possibilities of malfunctioning equipment, faulty connections, and operator error.

THE
YAMAHA
GUIDE TO
SOUND SYSTEMS
FOR WORSHIP
PAGE 173

Figure 14-4. Standard MIDI cable.

MIDI

MIDI (Musical Instrument Digital Interface) represents a realm of knowledge that would take another book this size to cover (see "For Further Reading," in the Appendices). And although an understanding of MIDI is not essential in the purchase of a sound system, it is often helpful in the operation of one nowadays, with the increasing prominence of electronic musical instruments in worship. This is especially true when it comes to troubleshooting.

MIDI is two things: 1) a hardware standard by which devices can be connected, and 2) a communications protocol that allows information to be transmitted and received via that connection. This combination can be put to a number of uses, including:

• Playing a musical instrument (called the "slave") remotely from another instrument (the "master").

• Recording and playing back musical performances using MIDI sequence recorders (sequencers). This offers advantages over tape recording that include the ability to change tempo without changing pitch, and to use different sounds on playback than were used in recording.

• Transferring sound settings or sampled waveforms between like instruments, or between an instrument and a computer or storage device.

• Controlling the settings of signal processors remotely during live performance, or during playback of a sequence.

• Automating the fader movements and other settings of a mixing console by use of a MIDI sequencer.

• Automating a lighting controller by use of a MIDI sequencer.

The MIDI specification is incorporated not only into most modern electronic musical instruments, but also into an increasing number of other kinds of equipment (signal processors, etc.). It offers the possibility of combining equipment from different manufacturers into a cohesive system.

MIDI HARDWARE

The MIDI hardware specification calls for the use of cables with male 5-pin DIN (Deutsche Industrie Normen) connectors at each end, as shown in Figure 14-4. Pins 4 and 5 are connected to a twisted pair of signal wires; pin 2 is connected to the cable shield.

MIDI equipment uses panel-mount female connectors. Three kinds of MIDI connectors, or "ports," are possible (see Figure 14-5):

• **IN** receives MIDI information from other equipment.

• **OUT** sends MIDI information to other equipment.

• **THRU** provides a duplicate of the information received by IN, to be passed along to other equipment.

Not all MIDI equipment has all three ports. Some devices, such as sequencers, may have more than one of a given type of port.

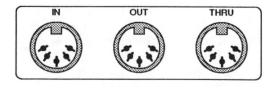

Figure 14-5. MIDI ports.

THE
YAMAHA
GUIDE TO
SOUND SYSTEMS
FOR WORSHIP
PAGE 174

Within MIDI devices, electrical isolation is obtained through the use of *optoisolators,* which transfer signals by light. In addition, pin 2 (shield) is connected to ground only on the OUT and THRU ports (not the IN), creating a telescoping shield and eliminating the possibility that the MIDI cable might cause ground loops.

Most popular personal computers can be fitted with MIDI ports by way of a *MIDI interface* (that's right: a "Musical Instrument Digital Interface interface"); a few models are made with ports built-in. The use that a computer makes of these ports depends on the software (programs) it runs.

MIDI MESSAGES

MIDI information, or data, takes the form of *messages*—groups of numbers (hence "*digital* interface") whose meanings and syntax are defined by the MIDI specification.

The classification of MIDI messages is shown in Figure 14-6. This classification bears out what the name "Musical Instrument Digital Interface" declares: MIDI was designed with musical instruments in mind. Nevertheless, it has shown itself to be remarkably adaptable to other applications—especially through the use of Control Change and Program Change messages.

Channel Messages	System Messages
Transmitted on a given MIDI channel. There are 16 channels available, and a piece of equipment has to be "tuned" to receive the proper channel in order to respond to these messages. (The exception is an instrument receiving in Omni mode, which can respond to all channels.)	Transmitted to all equipment that is connected in a MIDI system.
Channel Voice Messages Performance messages, including Note On, Note Off, After Touch (Pressure), Pitch Bend, Control Change (continuous and on/off functions), and Program Change (patch select).	**System Common Messages** Common messages, including Tune Request (so that analog synthesizers tune their oscillators), Song Position Pointer (so sequencers or drum machines locate the same place in a song), and Song Select (to select a song from those in memory).
Channel Mode Messages Commands to change mode, including whether Omni is on or off, and whether response is monophonic (one note at a time) or polyphonic (more than one note at a time). Also includes messages for Local Control (e.g., whether a synthesizer produces sound when played from its own keyboard) and All Notes Off (to silence notes).	**System Real Time Messages** Messages governing the operation of sequencers and drum machines, including Timing Clock, Start, Stop, and Continue.
	System Exclusive Messages Messages that are exclusive to one brand or model of equipment, to communicate data such as internal settings or contents of memory.

Figure 14-6. MIDI messages.

THE
YAMAHA
GUIDE TO
SOUND SYSTEMS
FOR WORSHIP
PAGE 175

MIDI RULES

The "MIDI rules" given here are not found in the MIDI 1.0 Specification. Rather, they are the fruit of practical experience.

RULE 1: MIDI CANNOT MAKE A DEVICE DO ANYTHING THAT IT WAS NOT DESIGNED TO DO.

All too many MIDI problems stem from ignorance of this rule. For example:

- Playing back multiple parts from a sequencer into a monotimbral (one sound at a time) synthesizer will not make the different parts play with different sounds.

- Connecting a digital piano that doesn't implement pitch bend to a synthesizer with a pitch bender will *not* enable you to bend the pitch of the piano.

On the other hand, some functions may be accessible *only* via MIDI. A typical example is the budget synthesizer that doesn't respond to key velocity (the speed with which the keys are pressed) from its own keyboard, but can respond to it over MIDI.

RULE 2: MIDI TRANSMITS DATA, NOT SOUND.

Even people who understand MIDI are likely to slip up on this one occasionally. For example:

- A MIDI guitar connected to a MIDI guitar amplifier will not be heard by virtue of the MIDI connections; audio connections are still necessary.

- A part recorded into a sequencer will not necessarily play back using the same sound; it is the performance that is recorded, not the sound itself. The desired sound must be selected on the playback instrument, either manually or via a Program Change message recorded in the sequence.

RULE 3: DIFFERENT DEVICES IMPLEMENT MIDI DIFFERENTLY.

Although the MIDI specification is adhered to by many manufacturers, nevertheless not all MIDI equipment needs to accomplish the same things. For example:

- A synthesizer may not use any of the System Real Time commands.

- A controller keyboard that has no sound-producing circuitry of its own may have a MIDI OUT port, but no IN port; consequently, it will transmit MIDI messages, but not receive them.

Every MIDI device is supposed to have a *MIDI Implementation Chart* to show what aspects of the MIDI specification that device makes use of. The "imp chart" is a standard form that allows the implementations of different MIDI devices to be compared.

RULE 4: EVEN IF A DEVICE IMPLEMENTS A MIDI MESSAGE, IT MAY HAVE TO BE PROGRAMMED TO TRANSMIT IT, RECEIVE IT, OR RESPOND TO IT.

MIDI equipment is computer equipment. And MIDI devices sometimes require programming. Fortunately, this usually means merely pressing a few buttons and setting a few controls. For example:

- A given sound program on a velocity-sensitive synthesizer may not respond to velocity. Such response has to be programmed into the sound (the synthesist can control whether higher velocities make the sound louder, softer, brighter, higher in pitch, etc.).

- Changing programs on a master device may or may not result in a program change on the slave. The master may be able to turn off transmission of Program Change messages, and the slave may likewise be able to turn off reception of the same.

MIDI PROBLEMS

There is no substitute for a thorough understanding of the layout of a system when tracking down MIDI problems. Most common problems yield to the same logical signal tracing and systematic elimination of possibilities that apply to audio troubleshooting. With that said, the great majority of such problems are fairly easy to troubleshoot; they suggest their cause and the required solution by their very nature. A table of these follows.

THE
YAMAHA
GUIDE TO
SOUND SYSTEMS
FOR WORSHIP
PAGE 176

Symptom	Cause	Solution
The instrument makes no sound.	Faulty or missing audio connections, or a level control turned down.	Check the audio connections and console settings. Check to make sure that the volume on the unit is turned up, and that a sound-generating program (patch) is selected.
The slave makes no sound.	Faulty or missing MIDI connections.	Connect a MIDI cable that you know to be good.
	Misconnected MIDI cable.	Connect OUT to IN or THRU to IN. Master units send commands from OUT, not THRU; slaves pass data on via THRU, not OUT. If there is a sequencer connected between the master and the slave, set its "echo back" ("soft thru") on, so that the OUT port acts as both an OUT and a THRU.
	Unit turned off upstream.	Turn on all units in a "daisy chain" configuration (OUT to IN to THRU to IN to THRU to IN...) in order for data to flow to all units.
	Incorrect channel assignment.	Set the slave to receive on the same channel that the master is transmitting on.
The master makes no sound.	Local Control is off.	Set Local Control to on. Or, if connected to a sequencer, turn on the "soft thru" in the sequencer and connect the sequencer OUT back to the master IN.
One or more notes continues to sustain when it shouldn't.	The MIDI cable became disconnected before a Note Off message was received.	Turn off the instrument with the stuck note(s), wait a few seconds, then turn it back on. This will reset the unit and silence any hanging notes. As an alternative, some sequencers and other devices feature a "MIDI panic button," which, when pressed, is designed to silence stuck notes.
	The MIDI transmit channel was changed before a Note Off message was received.	
	With sequencer playback: A Note Off message was erased during editing or re-recording into the sequencer.	
	With sequencer playback: Playback was stopped before a Note Off message was sent.	

THE
YAMAHA
GUIDE TO
SOUND SYSTEMS
FOR WORSHIP
PAGE 177

Symptom	Cause	Solution
Slave produces additional notes it is not supposed to.	Omni is on.	Turn Omni off in the slave instruments when they are supposed to play only one channel of multichannel music.
	All parts are being played on one channel.	Play different parts on different channels. When sequencing, record different parts on different channels.
Slave produces strange, non-tonal note patterns.	The drum machine (or drum track of the sequencer) is playing the slave.	Turn Omni off or change receive channel on the slave. Set the drum machine so that it does not transmit notes.
Slave responds to some messages, but not to others.	Slave does not implement some messages.	Do without the messages that the slave doesn't implement, or use a different instrument.
	Transmission or reception of some messages is disabled.	Enable transmission and reception of all desired messages.
Fewer notes of polyphony are available on the master than normal. Tone color of sound is different than normal, with a sound like flanging.	MIDI echo. The messages being sent OUT of the master are finding their way back to the IN, probably by way of the THRU of a connected instrument.	Turn local control off for the master. If this option is not available, eliminate the return path for the MIDI data. (If the master is connected to a sequencer, the return path may be via the OUT of the sequencer, if the "soft thru" function is on.)
Sequencer playback produces cacophony. Many more notes are being played than you expected.	MIDI feedback. The messages being sent OUT of the sequencer are finding their way back to the IN, and being sent out again and again by the soft thru function.	Eliminate one of the return paths for the MIDI data. If using a playback instrument, disconnect the THRU from the sequencer IN. If transferring data between two sequencers, turn off the "soft thru" function on at least one of them.
The sequencer or playback instrument locks up shortly after you begin sequencer playback. Some notes may be stuck on.		
The playback instrument displays an error message such as "MIDI Buffer Full."		
In transferring a sequence from one sequencer to another, lockup or errors occur.		

THE
YAMAHA
GUIDE TO
SOUND SYSTEMS
FOR WORSHIP
PAGE 178

Symptom	Cause	Solution
Drum machine and sequencer do not play in sync.	Both are using their internal clocks.	Set one to external (MIDI) clock, and connect it so that it is the slave of the unit that is set to internal clock.
Sequencer or drum machine does not run.	Unit is set to external (MIDI) clock, but no master unit is connected to it, or master unit has not been started.	Connect master unit to slave, and start and stop using the controls on the master unit. Or set the nonfunctioning unit to internal clock.
Slaves respond sluggishly.	Slow response of instrument to incoming MIDI data.	Complain to the manufacturer. Use a different instrument. If a delay in response to sequencer playback is consistent, and the sequencer allows tracks to be shifted in time, shift the track in question ahead by enough time to compensate for the delay.
Slaves in a "daisy chain" respond sluggishly or inaccurately.	Distortion of MIDI data as they are passed from successive INs to THRUs.	Use a MIDI THRU box to connect multiple slaves to a sequencer or other master controller. As a quick fix, you might try changing the order of the slaves, placing the most temperamental instruments nearest the start of the chain.
Slaves respond sluggishly to sequencer.	MIDI choke; too much MIDI data is being transmitted for accurate timing to be maintained.	Filter out unnecessary types of messages (such as after touch, pitch bend, or continuous controllers).
		Thin out continuous data, if the sequencer offers this option.
		Use separate MIDI OUT ports for different groups of parts, if the sequencer has them.
		Synchronize playback of two sequencers, each playing some of the parts.

Symptom	Cause	Solution
Sequencer memory runs out sooner than expected.	Too much data being recorded.	Filter out unnecessary data, (such as after touch, pitch bend, or velocity) on reception, or disable transmission of it by instruments.
		Thin out continuous data, if the sequencer can do this.
The sound program used when recording a sequencer track is not the same one that sounds on playback.	Program change message was not recorded as part of sequence.	Record the correct program change message at the beginning of the sequencer track, so that the program will be selected automatically when the sequence is played back.
A bass line was recorded into the sequencer using a bass program, and a rhythm part using a piano program, but they both play back using the piano program.	The instrument is not multitimbral; it will only produce one sound program at a time.	Use additional instruments to produce additional parts, or substitute a multitimbral instrument.
	The parts are recorded on the same MIDI channel.	Record different parts on different MIDI channels.
Sending a Program Change message calls up a different program than expected.	Program numbering is misleading on master, slave, or both.	MIDI Program Change messages correspond to the *number* of the program. Figure out what MIDI program number is called up by what panel number. For example, MIDI program number 0 may be labeled 00, 1, or 11 on different equipment.
	Program changes are *remapped* on the master, the slave, or both. For example, when you select program 1 on the master, it might be set to transmit 5 instead. And the slave, upon receiving 5, might be set to select 19 instead!	Set the program map tables so that pressing the desired button calls up the desired program.
Sending a Program Change message causes the volume to jump.	The output level of the new sound program is not comparable to that of the previous one.	Program the desired output level or MIDI Volume setting into the slave as required. As a quick fix, use the volume control on the master to change the volume level *after* sending the Program Change message.
	Some slaves, in response to Program Change messages, alter the MIDI Volume setting (Controller 7), too.	

THE
YAMAHA
GUIDE TO
SOUND SYSTEMS
FOR WORSHIP
PAGE 180

Symptom	Cause	Solution
A controller produces a different effect than intended, or no effect at all.	The physical controllers on the master are not set to the MIDI controller numbers expected by the slave.	Change the controller assignment settings on the master, the slave, or both.
Instruments go out of tune when pitch bend is used.	Pitch bend range is set differently for the instruments.	Set the pitch bend range to the same value for all instruments concerned.
The pitch of an instrument has supposedly been transposed, but it still plays back sequenced music at the original pitch.	The transposition affects the pitch played from the instrument's own keyboard, and the MIDI messages the instrument transmits, but not the response to MIDI messages it receives.	Transpose the instrument before recording from it. If recording is already complete, transpose the sequence, if possible.
Some notes played by the sequencer are chopped short.	The total number of notes playing at a given time exceeds the available polyphony of the instrument(s) being used.	Reduce the number of notes playing at one time.
		Use sound programs or instruments that offer greater polyphony.
	The master controller generates All Notes Off messages, which are being recorded and played back.	Filter out the recording of the All Notes Off messages, if possible.
		Set the playback instrument(s) to ignore All Notes Off messages, if possible.

AN OUNCE OF PREVENTION

Rather than merely solving problems as they occur, try to prevent them from occurring in the first place. This goes as far back as the initial decision to purchase a sound system. Assess your needs accurately. Choose the system designer or contractor carefully. You are responsible for using the funds at your disposal in the best possible way. Consider hiring an impartial consultant to review a proposed system design. Insist on having good documentation, and use it.

SOUNDCHECKS AND SYSTEM CHECKS

Before each worship service or event takes place, make sure everything is patched (connected) correctly. Turn the sound system on, run taped music through the system to ensure that it is functioning properly. Next have someone talk at the pulpit microphone. Establish that the system is fully operational.

Set up a schedule of soundchecks with the musicians and other members of the worship team before your program starts. Check everyone's mic(s) in turn. Make sure everything is in place, connected, and working properly. Set levels and EQ, including the monitor systems. Plan these soundchecks so that they end no later than half an hour before the service or program. In a large congregation, you may need to end sooner, to allow people enough time to arrive and be seated.

As you make up your schedule for soundchecks, you will see a block of time developing. You can back up from that block of time for your system check. Then you will know what time of day you will need to arrive at your facility. If you regularly perform these basic checks of the system, you will find that your services and programs will tend to run more smoothly, with fewer sound problems, than they would otherwise. At the very least, you will find the problems before the service or program begins.

THE
YAMAHA
GUIDE TO
SOUND SYSTEMS
FOR WORSHIP
PAGE 181

APPENDICES

FOR FURTHER READING

Badmaieff, Alexis and Davis, Don. *How to Build Speaker Enclosures*. Indianapolis: Howard W. Sams & Co., 1966.

Ballou, Glen, ed. *Handbook for Sound Engineers: The New Audio Cyclopedia*. Indianapolis: Howard W. Sams & Co., 1987.

Bartlett, Bruce. *Introduction to Professional Recording Techniques*. Indianapolis: Howard W. Sams & Co., 1987.

Davis, Don and Carolyn. *Sound System Engineering*, 2nd ed. Indianapolis: Howard W. Sams & Co., 1987.

Davis, Gary and Jones, Ralph. *Yamaha Sound Reinforcement Handbook*, 2nd ed. Milwaukee, WI: Hal Leonard, 1989.

Eargle, John. *Handbook of Sound System Design*. Plainview, NY: Elar, 1989.

————. *The Microphone Handbook*. Plainview, NY: Elar, 1982.

Egan, M. David. *Architectural Acoustics*. New York: McGraw-Hill, 1988.

Everest, F. Alton. *Successful Sound System Operation*. Blue Ridge Summit, PA: TAB Books, 1985.

————. *The Master Handbook of Acoustics*. Blue Ridge Summit, PA: TAB Books, 1983.

Huber, David Miles. *Audio Production Techniques for Video*. Indianapolis: Howard W. Sams & Co., 1987.

————. *Microphone Manual: Design and Application*. Indianapolis: Howard W. Sams & Co., 1988.

Lubman, David and Wetherill, Ewart, eds. *Acoustics of Worship Spaces*. New York: The American Institute of Physics, 1983.

Rona, Jeff. *MIDI: The Ins, Outs & Thrus*. Milwaukee, WI: Hal Leonard, 1987.

Rossnagel, W.E. *Handbook of Rigging*. New York: McGraw-Hill, 1964.

Runstein, Robert E. and Huber, David Miles. *Modern Recording Techniques*, 2nd ed. Indianapolis: Howard W. Sams & Co., 1986

Taipale, Curt. *How to Start, Train & Operate an Audio Ministry*. St. Charles, MO: Taipale Media Systems, Inc., 1989.

Woram, John M. *Sound Recording Handbook*. Indianapolis: Howard W. Sams & Co., 1989.

ASSOCIATIONS AND CONVENTIONS

Audio Engineering Society (AES)
60 East 42nd Street
New York, NY 10165
(212) 661-8528
annual spring and fall conventions

National Association of Broadcasters (NAB)
1771 "N" Street NW
Washington, DC 20036
(202) 429-5300
annual spring convention

National Religious Broadcasters (NRB)
P.O. Box 1926
Morristown, NJ 07962-1926
(201) 428-5400
annual winter convention in Washington, D.C.

National Association of Music Merchants (NAMM)
5140 Avenida Encinas
Carlsbad, CA 92008
(619) 438-8001
annual Winter Market in Anaheim, CA, in January, and Expo in Chicago (alternating with other cities every third year) in June

National Sound & Communications Association (NSCA)
10400 Roberts Road
Palos Hill, IL 60465
(800) 446-6722
annual spring Contractor's Conference & Expo

THE
YAMAHA
GUIDE TO
SOUND SYSTEMS
FOR WORSHIP
PAGE 182

Aarmor Case
2100 Lapo Rd.
Lake Odessa, MI 48849
(800) 722-5763, (616) 374-5431
equipment cases, racks

Acoustic Sciences Corp. (ASC)
385 Lawrence
Eugene, OR 97401
(503) 343-9727
acoustical control devices

Acoustone Grille Cloth
80 Wythe Ave.
Brooklyn, NY 11211
(718) 782-5560
speaker grille cloth

ADC/Magnetic Controls
4900 W. 78th St.
Minneapolis, MN 55435
patch bays

Aiphone
P.O. Box 90075
Belleville, WA 98009
(206) 455-0510
intercoms

Alpha Audio Acoustics
2049 W. Broad St.
Richmond, VA 23220
(804) 358-3852
acoustical treatments

Anvil Cases
4128 Temple City Blvd.
Rosemead, CA 91770
(818) 575-8614
equipment cases

Atlas/Soundolier
1895 Intertech Drive
Fenton, MO 63025
(800) 876-7337, (314) 349-3110
intercoms, stands, racks, cabinetry

Audio Accessories, Inc.
Mill St.
Marlow, NH 03456
(603) 446-3335
patch bays

Audra International
P.O. Box 38
Silverado, CA 92676
(714) 640-2207
signal transformers, mic splitters

AVL Systems
5540 S.W. 6th Place
Ocala, FL 32674
(904) 854-1170
acoustical treatments

Belden Wire & Cable
P.O. Box 1980
Richmond, IN 47375
(317) 983-5200
cable

Cabletronix
366 Washington St.
Newburgh, NY 12550
(800) 431-WIRE, (914) 565-7570
cable

CAE Inc./Littlite
10087 Industrial Dr.
Hamburg, MI 48139
(313) 231-9373
equipment lighting

Cal Switch
13717 S. Normandie Ave.
Gardena, CA 90249
(800) 225-7924
cable, connectors, patch bays

Calzone Case Co.
225 Black Rock Ave.
Bridgeport, CT 06605
(800) 243-5152, (203) 367-5766
equipment cases, covers, racks

Canare Cable, Inc.
511 5th St., Unit G
San Fernando, CA 91340
(818) 356-0479
cable

Cavallaro Case Covers
20 Vernon St.
Sommerville, MA 02145
(617) 628-6731
covers

Clear-Com Intercom Systems
945 Camelia Street
Berkeley, CA 94710
(415) 527-6666
intercoms

Connectronics
652 Glenbrook Rd.
Stamford, CT 06906
(800) 322-2537, (203) 324-2889
cable, patch bays

Conquest Sound, Inc.
RR #2, Box 1AB
Monee, IL 60449
(800) 323-7671
cable, connectors, direct boxes

Covertron
2208 W. Vernon Ave.
Los Angeles, CA 90008
(800) 257-8727, (818) 988-1334
equipment cases, covers

Dago Cases
6945 Indiana Ct., #600
Golden, CO 80403
(800) 342-3246
equipment cases

Flight Form Cases
5950 192nd St. NE
Arlington, WA 98223
(206) 435-6688
equipment cases

THE
YAMAHA
GUIDE TO
SOUND SYSTEMS
FOR WORSHIP
PAGE 183

Gotcha Covered Dustcovers
22N159 Pepper Rd.
Barrington, IL 60010
(312) 382-3210
covers

H.M. Electronics, Inc. (HME)
6675 Mesa Ridge Road
San Diego, CA 92121
(619) 535-6060
intercoms, wireless microphones

Hosa Technology
13042 Moore St.
Cerritos, CA 90701
(800) 255-7527, (213) 926-0808
cable

Hybrid Cases/FM Tubecraft
1121-20 Lincoln Ave.
Holbrook, NY 11741
(800) 645-1707, (516) 563-1181
equipment cases, covers, racks

Invisible Products
159 Commercial St.
Lynn, MA 01905-2909
(617) 592-5992
stands

Island Cases 1121-I Lincoln Ave.
Holbrook, NY 11741
(800) 343-1433, (516) 563-0633
equipment cases

Jan-Al Cases
4452 E. Washington Blvd.
Los Angeles, CA 90023
(213) 669-0550
equipment cases, racks, cabinets

Jensen Transformers
10735 Burbank Blvd.
North Hollywood, CA 91601
(213) 876-0059
signal transformers

Juice Goose
7320 Ashcroft, #302
Houston, TX 77081
(713) 772-1404
power supplies and conditioners

Mag-Tags, Inc.
2531 W. Tharpe St.
Tallahassee, FL 32303
(800) 677-TAGS, (904) 386-5611
magnetic labeling

Mellotone/Div. Wendell Fabrics Corp.
108 E. Church St.
Blacksburg, SC 29702
(803) 839-6341
acoustical treatments

Monster Cable Products
101 Townsend St.
San Francisco, CA 94107
(415) 777-1355

Neutrik USA
1600 Malone Street
Millville, NJ 08332
(609) 327-3113
connectors

Omnirax by Sausalito Craftworks
P.O. Box 1792
Sausalito, CA 94966
(800) 332-3393, (415) 332-3392
equipment racks

The Original Drum Screen, Inc.
2565 28th St. SW, #7
Grand Rapids, MI 49509
(800) 992-2434, (616) 534-8787
acoustical treatments

Penny & Giles, Inc.
2716 Ocean Park Blvd., #1005
Santa Monica, CA 90405
(213) 393-0014
patch bays

Phonic Ear, Inc.
250 Camino Alto
Mill Valley, CA 94941
(800) 227-0735, (415) 383-4000
intercoms, hearing-assistance systems

Pro-Co Sound Company
135 E. Kalamazoo Ave.
Kalamazoo, MI 49007
(616) 388-9675
cable, patch bays, direct boxes, signal
transformers

Pro Sound (see Cal Switch)

Pro Tec International
165 E. Liberty Ave.
Anaheim, CA 92801
(800) 325-3455, (714) 441-0117
equipment cases, covers

Rapco International, Inc.
Rt. 1, Box 50
Jackson, MO 63755
(800) 325-0266
cable, patch bays

Rok-Steady Support Systems
P.O. Box 14250
Greensboro, NC 27405
(919) 272-5123
stands

Rolls Corp.
7023 S. 400 West
Salt Lake City, UT 84047
(801) 562-5628
direct boxes, audio interfaces

RPG Diffuser Systems, Inc.
12006 Wimbleton St.
Largo, MD 20772
(301) 249-5647
acoustical treatments

RTS Systems, Inc.
1100 West Chestnut St.
Burbank, CA 91506
(818) 566-6700
intercoms

Russco Electronics Mfg., Inc.
5690 E. Shields Ave.
Fresno, CA 93727
(209) 291-5591
audio interfaces

THE
YAMAHA
GUIDE TO
SOUND SYSTEMS
FOR WORSHIP
PAGE 184

Schell Electronics
120 N. Lincoln
Chanute, KS 66720
(316) 431-2350
wireless mics, hearing-assistance systems

Sescom, Inc.
2100 Ward Drive
Henderson, NV 89105
(702) 565-3400
signal transformers

Signal Cable
2500 Commonwealth Ave.
North Chicago. IL 60064
(312) 689-9090
cable

Solid Support Industries
2453 Chico St.
South El Monte, CA 91733
(800) 782-6377, (818) 579-6063
stands

Sonex (see Alpha Audio Acoustics)

Sound Absorbent Materials Co., Inc.
P.O. Box 837
Westwood, NJ 07675
(201) 742-7078
acoustical treatments

Square D Company/Power Protection Systems
9192 Topaz Way
San Diego, CA 92123
(619) 279-0111
power conditioning

Standard Wire & Cable
2345 Alaska Ave.
El Segundo, CA 90245
cable

Standtastic
1325 Meridian St.
Anderson, MI 46016
(800) 876-6923, (317) 642-5205
stands

Star Case Mfg. Co. Inc.
648 Superior
Munster, IN 46321
(219) 922-4440
equipment cases, covers

Stewart Electronics Corp.
P.O. Box 60317
Sacramento, CA 95860
(916) 635-3011
preamplifiers, direct boxes

Switchcraft, Inc.
5555 N. Elston Ave.
Chicago, IL 60630
(312) 792-2700
signal xfmrs, cable, connectors, patch bays

Tappan Wire & Cable
256 Oak Tree Rd.
Tappan, NY 10983
(800) 247-9099, (914) 359-9300
cable

Telex Communications, Inc.
9600 Aldrich Avenue South
Minneapolis, MN 55420
(612) 887-5578
intercoms, wireless mics, cassette duplicators

Toleeto Products
170 Mace St., D-10
Chula Vista, CA 92011
(619) 426-3725
cable ties

Ultimate Support Systems
P.O. Box 470
Ft. Collins, CO 80522-4700
(303) 493-4488
stands

Viking Cases
10480 Oak St. NE
St. Petersburg, FL 33716
(813) 577-1216
equipment cases

West Penn
2833 W. Chestnut St.
Washington, PA 15301
(412) 222-7060
cable

Whirlwind
100 Boxart St.
Rochester, NY 14612
(716) 663-8820
cable, direct boxes, phantom power

Williams Sound Corp.
5929 Baker Road
Minnetonka, MN 55345-5997
(800) 328-6190, (612) 931-0291
hearing-assistance systems, intercoms, wireless microphones, language-interpretation systems

Wireworks
380 Hillside Ave.
Hillside, NJ 07205
(800) 624-0061
cable

THE
YAMAHA
GUIDE TO
SOUND SYSTEMS
FOR WORSHIP
PAGE 185

MICROPHONE PATCH CHART (SETUP LIST)

STAGE LAYOUT:

Snake	House	Submix	Microphone	Description	Stand	Comments

INDEX

THE
YAMAHA
GUIDE TO
SOUND SYSTEMS
FOR WORSHIP
PAGE 187

THE
YAMAHA
GUIDE TO
SOUND SYSTEMS
FOR WORSHIP
PAGE 188

THE
YAMAHA
GUIDE TO
SOUND SYSTEMS
FOR WORSHIP
PAGE 189

THE
YAMAHA
GUIDE TO
SOUND SYSTEMS
FOR WORSHIP
PAGE 190